Critical Muslim 13

Race

T0333227

Editor: Ziauddin Sardar

Deputy Editors: Hassan Mahamdallie, Ehsan Masood, Shanon Shah

Senior Editors: Aamer Hussein, Ebrahim Moosa, Samia Rahman

Publisher: Michael Dwyer

Managing Editor (Hurst Publishers): Daisy Leitch

Cover Design: Fatima Jamadar

Associate Editors: Alev Adil, Nazry Bahrawi, Merryl Wyn Davies, Abdulwahhab El-Affendi, Merilyn Hacker, Nader Hashemi, Jeremy Henzell-Thomas, Vinay Lal, Iftikhar Malik, Boyd Tonkin

International Advisory Board: Karen Armstrong, William Dalrymple, Farid Esack, Anwar Ibrahim, Robert Irwin, Bruce Lawrence, Ashis Nandy, Ruth Padel, Bhikhu Parekh, Barnaby Rogerson, Malise Ruthven

Critical Muslim is published quarterly by C. Hurst & Co. (Publishers) Ltd. on behalf of and in conjunction with Critical Muslim Ltd. and the Muslim Institute, London.

All correspondence to Muslim Institute, CAN Mezzanine, 49-51 East Road, London N1 6AH, United Kingdom

e-mail for editorial: editorial@criticalmuslim.com

The editors do not necessarily agree with the opinions expressed by the contributors. We reserve the right to make such editorial changes as may be necessary to make submissions to Critical Muslim suitable for publication.

C. Hurst & Co. (Publishers) Ltd., 41 Great Russell Street, London WC1B 3PL

ISBN: 978-1-84904-489-9 ISSN: 2048-8475

To subscribe or place an order by credit/debit card or cheque (pound sterling only) please contact Kathleen May at the Hurst address above or e-mail kathleen@hurstpub.co.uk

Tel: 020 7255 2201

A one year subscription, inclusive of postage (four issues), costs £50 (UK), £65 (Europe) and £75 (rest of the world).

The right of Ziauddin Sardar and the Contributors to be identified as the authors of this publication is asserted by them in accordance with the Copyright, Designs and Patents Act, 1988.

A Cataloguing-in-Publication data record for this book is available from the British Library.

HALAL FOOD FOUNDATION

Halal Is Much More Than Food

The Halal Food Foundation (HFF) is a registered charity that aims to make the concept of halal more accessible and mainstream. We want people to know that halal does not just pertain to food – halal is a lifestyle.

The Foundation pursues its goals through downloadable resources, events, social networking, school visits, pursuing and funding scientific research on issues of food and health, and its monthly newsletter. We work for the community and aim at the gradual formation of a consumer association. We aim to educate and inform; and are fast becoming the first port of call on queries about halal issues. We do not talk at people, we listen to them.

If you have any queries, comments, ideas, or would just like to voice your opinion - please get in contact with us.

Halal Food Foundation

109 Fulham Palace Road,
Hammersmith, London, W6 8JA
Charity number: 1139457
Website: www.halalfoodfoundation.co.uk
E-mail: info@halalfoodfoundation.co.uk

 @HFF_UK

 Halal Food Foundation

The Barbary Figs

by

Rashid Boudjedra

Translated by
André Naffis-Sahely

Buy a copy of Rashid Boudjedra's *The Barbary Figs* at
www.hauspublishing.com or by calling +44(0)20 7838 9055
and a recieve a copy of Khaled al-Berry's memoir
Life is More Beautiful than Paradise free.

RASHID AND OMAR are cousins who find themselves side by side on a flight from Algiers to Constantine. During the hour-long journey, the pair will exhume their past, their boyhood in French Algeria during the 1940s and their teenage years fighting in the bush during the revolution. Rashid, the narrator, has always resented Omar, who despite all his worldly successes, has been on the run from the ghosts of his past, ghosts that Rashid has set himself the task of exorcising. Rashid peppers his account with chilling episodes from Algerian history, from the savageries of the French invasion in the 1830s, to the repressive regime that is in place today.

RASHID BOUDJEDRA has routinely been called one of North Africa's leading writers since his debut, *La Répudiation*, was published in 1969, earning the author the first of many fatwas. While he wrote his first six novels in French, Boudjedra switched to Arabic in 1982 and wrote another six novels in the language before returning to French in 1994. *The Barbary Figs* was awarded the Prix du Roman Arabe 2010.

CM13

January–March 2015

CONTENTS

RACE

REVIEWS

ET CETERA

Subscribe to Critical Muslim

Now in its third year, *Critical Muslim* is the only publication of its kind, giving voice to the diversity and plurality of Muslim reporting, creative writing, poetry and scholarship.

Subscribe now to receive each issue of Critical Muslim direct to your door and save money on the cover price of each issue.

Subscriptions are available at the following prices, inclusive of postage. Subscribe for two years and save 10%!

	ONE YEAR (4 Issues)	TWO YEARS (8 Issues)
UK	£50	£90
Europe	£65	£117
Rest of World	£75	£135

TO SUBSCRIBE:

CRITICALMUSLIM.HURSTPUBLISHERS.COM

41 GREAT RUSSELL ST, LONDON WC1B 3PL
WWW.HURSTPUBLISHERS.COM
WWW.FBOOK.COM/HURSTPUBLISHERS
020 7255 2201

RACE

INTRODUCTION
THE COLOUR LINE

Hassan Mahamdallie

'The problem of the twentieth century', wrote the African-American historian W.E.B. Du Bois in his 1903 treatise on racism, *The Souls of Black Folk*, 'is the problem of the colour-line – the relation of the darker to the lighter races of men in Asia and Africa, in America and the islands of the sea'. Du Bois could just as easily have looked behind him and said that the problem of the colour line had bisected the previous century during which chattel slavery in America had been ended as an institution after a nearly all-consuming civil war. Instead Du Bois looked to the century stretching before him and observed that racism was not only very much alive in his own country, codified in the segregationist Jim Crow laws, it was flourishing across the globe, embedded in the European colonial project busy carving up Africa and Asia. However, even in his darkest nightmares Du Bois could not have imagined that within four decades an ideology of racial purity and superiority would result in the Holocaust – the near total extermination of European Jewry by the Nazis.

Will the colour line dog our progress too? It seems as if we are heading that way. In his essay on Du Bois's biography of abolitionist John Brown, Gary McFarlane notes that 'we now have Black History Month, African-American history departments in the major universities of the West and an African-American president of the US, but, as we saw in Ferguson, none of that can shield us from still confronting a reality shaped by the legacy of slavery'. McFarlane is referring to the aftermath of the fatal shooting of an unarmed black teenager in Ferguson, Missouri, by the police, a case that reminds us that at the heart of America is 'a sickness that has been with the republic since its birth; a searing contradiction in the land of the free'.

Of course we know now that there is no scientific or genetic basis for race and associated notions of superiority and inferiority. Or we think we know. Just twenty years ago Charles Murray and Richard Hernnstein published *The Bell Curve* which argued that African-Americans were genetically predisposed to lower intelligence and higher levels of anti-social behaviour than other 'races'. More recently, popular science writer Nicholas Wade's *A Troublesome Inheritance* advances the argument that 'evolutionary differences between societies on the various continents may underlie major and otherwise imperfectly explained turning points in history such as the rise of the West and the decline of the Islamic world and China'.

Whenever notions of race and racism and theories of human development rear their heads, I am reminded of the Ray Harryhausen animated scene in the 1963 film *Jason and the Argonauts*. Jason, in possession of the Golden Fleece, is being pursued by King Aeetes. The King sows Hydra's teeth which spring up as an army of skeletal warriors with swords and shields who advance towards Jason and his men. Every time Jason takes a swipe at one and shatters its bones another springs up to take its place. Jason only escapes being killed by jumping off a cliff, whereupon the skeletons follow him lemming-like and sink to the bottom of the sea while he swims to the Argonaut and safety.

Today the dragon's teeth are constantly being sowed and re-sowed with the skeleton army springing up everywhere. Europe teems with xenophobic, racist and fascist parties, invigorated by a combination of imperial blowback from the Middle East and economic decline at home – as our list of 'Ten Xenophobic European Political Parties to Avoid' demonstrates. A new, but rather indistinct, phrase 'Islamophobia' has been coined to describe the hostility towards Muslims that now seems a permanent and baleful influence on Western societies. I prefer the term 'anti-Muslim racism', or even 'anti-Muslimism', the term advanced by the British political scientist the late Fred Halliday.

Indeed, in some countries racism and xenophobia are now part of the mainstream political landscape. As Jim Wolfreys argues, established political parties in France have been unable to challenge the impact of the far-right Front National on French politics with any integrity and have instead tried to outbid it: 'The blunt truth is that instead of isolating and exposing racism, and the way it has adapted under the pressure of economic crisis, the two principal parties of government, the right-wing UMP coalition (Union pour un Mouvement Populaire) and the Socialist Party (PS), have rushed to embrace it. The scapegoating of Muslims has reached unprecedented levels, with their activities subjected to relentless scrutiny.' Wolfreys shows how the revolutionary ideal of *laïcité*, originally developed to deprive the Roman Catholic Church of overweening influence in public affairs, has been co-opted as a weapon with which to beat Muslims. Both the left and the right in France have menaced Muslims with 'Enlightenment values' to justify their desire to curb their freedoms. Their great hero is Voltaire who wrote an obscure drama about the 'imposter' Mohammed. But they forget that in his final years Voltaire also campaigned in defence of religious minorities – specifically the violent persecution of France's Protestants. On hearing of a particularly awful incident Voltaire wrote to a friend: 'I am beside myself. I am concerned as a man, and a bit also as a philosopher. What I want to know is, on which side is the horror of fanaticism?' It is a question that politicians in France and elsewhere would do well to ponder.

Of course, racism is not just a problem for Western states; it is equally deeply rooted in Muslim societies as well. As Ziauddin Sardar shows, the part of the world that we are increasingly told to look to and draw our global Islamic culture from is based on the most brutal racial hierarchy that draws not only on super-exploitation but on bondage. 'Xenophobia and racism are intrinsic to the worldview of the kingdoms and emirates of the region; an element of their brand of ultra-orthodox conservatism', he writes. It is often justified in religious terms and accepted by Muslims elsewhere who perpetuate this bigotry by bowing down to the superior Muslims of the Arabian peninsula. Something similar can be seen amongst Muslims in Britain who, as Naima Khan notes, like to believe that the practice of Islam, and therefore Muslims as a 'community' (although following the historian Benedict Anderson we might more accurately term it 'an imagined community') are somehow pure of spirit and free from racial prejudice – the chosen people. It is an assertion of an ideological and social superiority against a world that considers us inferior in every respect. But, like its reverse, it is a flawed conception. It allows us to turn a convenient blind eye to manifestations of bigotry and inequality amongst us. Khan accuses the South Asian Muslims of a 'jostling for position in the racial pecking order that has not just separated Asian and black people but caused fault lines to form within our communities'. They have internalised the notion that blackness is bad, black men are criminal and that black women are undesirable. This attitude manifests itself in prejudice surrounding interracial marriages, the dismissive attitude towards young Asian boys who emulate the perceived stereotypical mannerisms of their black counterparts, and the Asian shopkeepers who perpetuate ideas about beauty by supplying Indian hair extensions to black women. 'There is a cruel ignorance in our expectation of black people to conform to their stock characters while we consider ourselves worthy of more nuanced depiction', argues Khan.

Racism in Muslim societies, like in the West, is not a recent phenomenon: it has a long history. As Robert Irwin shows in his examination of a major canon of Islamic literature, *The Arabian Nights*, which was also the Victorians' favourite tale from the East, racism was an integral part of Muslim societies. Irwin's examination of the 'morality' behind the tales 'reveal racist prejudices not only regarding blacks, but also with respect to Jews, Persians and Europeans'. Irwin traces the layers of prejudice that were added to the tales over the centuries by various translators, including the Victorian adventurer and scholar Richard Burton. We get an object lesson in the enduring but changing nature of racial stereotypes through different civilisations and modes of production. Irwin also includes the response to racial prejudice on the part of those burdened by it. How fascinating to read of al-Jahiz's eighth-century riposte to the denigration of black people: *The Book of Vaunting of Blacks Over Whites*, an early example of an articulation of what we know today as 'Black Pride'. However, not everyone wanted to fight, or could fight, racism with scholarly weapons. As Hugh Kennedy shows in his fascinating article, the ninth-century East African slaves, labelled the Zanj, chose to fight by other means – their revolt culminated in the destruction of Basra. Kennedy is careful to note that the reasons behind the revolt are complex and cannot be easily fitted into modern categories. However the rallying cry of the Zanj leader does come down to us loud and clear: 'the slaves were going to be rich and free and their masters were going to suffer'.

If history is written by the victors and the powerful, we sometimes have to use imagination to spirit up those robbed of their identity. Dorothea Smartt's beautiful cycle of poems about 'Bilal', breathes life back into 'Sambo', an anonymous slave who died within days of his arrival in eighteenth century Lancaster. We all know that Bilal was an African slave – but how many of us ask why black African slavery existed as an institution before, during and after the life of the prophet Mohammed? And what came first, the belief that black Africans were inferior beings and thus could be enslaved, or that the use of Africans as slaves needed a set of ideas, including religious dictates, to justify it? Was the racism that branded the African the spawn of Noah's curse on Ham's son Canaan the same as the racism that excuses slavery in parts of the Muslim world today? Was the treatment of the Zanj that caused them to finally rebel the same as that meted out by the police in Ferguson, Missouri?

Shanon Shah addresses this question by way of raising another question: can we construct Islam as a race, or ethnicity, or both? He explores the question by placing his fictional character, Abdullah, in a variety of different Muslim and Western contexts. Shah shows that racial, religious and ethnic categories are increasingly fused together at state and global levels, and identities imposed upon us in ways that have little or no bearing on how we see ourselves or our relations with our fellow citizens. While individuals 'might internally feel that concepts like "race" or "religion" limit their expressions of humanity, they cannot escape being defined by these concepts. In too many situations, they feel like their racial and religious identities choose them, not vice versa', he writes. This sentiment was also expressed by young Muslim women interviewed by Shabana Mir for her book *Muslim American Women on Campus*. But Mir's young students are highly intelligent and world savvy. Samia Rahman writes in her review of Mir's book that as marginal individuals they 'use the cultural resources at their disposal – including Orientalist discourse, dominant majority practices, stereotypes, and slurs – to perform and to reinvent identities, and to represent communities, ideologies and themselves'.

There are many responses to being at the receiving end of racist categorisations. For example, it is all too easy to slip into 'believing the hype', and absorbing the racial or religious characteristics imputed to you, until they become a part of you. As Du Bois wrote in the introduction to *The Souls of Black Folk*, the African-American is 'born with a veil, and gifted with second-sight in this American world – a world which yields him no true self-consciousness, but only lets him see himself through the revelation of the other world. It is a peculiar sensation, this double-consciousness, this sense of always looking at one's self through the eyes of others, of measuring one's soul by the tape of a world that looks on in amused contempt and pity'. In 2014 we saw this 'veil' literally manifested in a campaign launched by the British tabloid newspaper *The Sun* with a pull-out poster image of a woman in a Union Jack print hijab with the headline: 'As police swoop on first Islamic State terror cell in UK, *The Sun* urges Brits of all faiths to stand up to extremists.' The subtext was that Muslims must prove a false negative and publicly declare their opposition to terrorism, lest they be suspected of secretly revelling in the decapitation of hostages. As *The Guardian* 'Comment is Free' commentator Nesrine Malik pointed out, this is 'not to say that Muslims should not condemn Islamic State. Many do, and have. But to have it demanded of you is different. And to have it linked to your nationality via the Union Jack is a threat. It attaches conditions to that nationality that others do not have to meet'.

Another response is to say 'we are not like that' – we are hard-working, honest, peaceable, moderate in our temperament, good law abiding citizens, even middle-class in our values. But surely the true measure of equality in any society is to be as lazy, dishonest, lawless and 'common' as anyone else, but not to have such behaviour and attitudes attributed to your race or religion. The game of being, pardon the pun, as white as white can be, is a no-win exercise, because you can guarantee that the rules of the game will be arbitrarily changed and the goalposts shifted to make sure that yearned-for acceptance is always just out of reach. As Ziauddin Sardar has written elsewhere we have to break out of the confines of a dominant discourse that increasingly recognises 'only two kinds of Muslims: the terrorist (who has declared war on the West) and the apologetic (who claims to be liberal and defends Islam as a peaceful religion)'.

In *The Souls of Black Folk* Du Bois, even when talking about the intense racial hostility directed by whites towards the black population, is at pains to avoid categorising all whites as perpetrators and blacks as their victims. He witnesses in his travels through the Deep South that racism consumes the hater and the hated alike. In his biography of Enoch Powell – the demagogue infamous for his 'Rivers of Blood' speech – the campaigning British journalist Paul Foot pointed out that 'politics can drive the knife home or remove its menace... No-one can underestimate the danger of that choice. The tiger of racialism, once unleashed, knows no master. It devours its liberators and its prey with equal ferocity'.

How true. I can still vividly recall attending the trial fourteen years ago at Kingston Crown Court, London, of Robert Stewart, accused and found guilty of the murder of teenager Zahid Mubarek. The two boys had been locked up in the same cell in Feltham Young Offenders Institution despite prison officers knowing that Stewart was a severely disturbed young man who harboured fantasies of killing a black person. Mubarek had landed up in Feltham after being sentenced to three months in jail for stealing some razor blades worth six pounds. The day before he was due to be released and return to his East London family he was bludgeoned to death by Stewart. It was a terrible murder, and entirely avoidable as the subsequent public inquiry found.

I sat in the public benches in the court alongside other reporters and Mubarek's grieving family. In the dock sat a small, undernourished, deathly white young man – Stewart. On his forehead you could see the faint outline of a badly done amateur tattoo spelling the letters R.I.P. and a cross. Next to me sat various anti-racist activists who glared non-stop at Stewart, as if they were trying to project righteous anger towards him. I couldn't bring myself to do the same. All I saw when I looked to the dock was a victim. I didn't feel sorry for him. I knew he was a racist and a murderer and should be deprived of his liberty. But Stewart was in another way also a casualty of the drip-drip racist poison that people like the Right Honourable Enoch Powell MP MBE and others like him had been dispensing to the British people for decades. Admittedly it is not always easy to see the victim in the perpetrator – especially in the heat of the moment. Not so long ago walking home through an alleyway I was blocked by a group of aggressive white teenagers who spat insults at me: 'Paki, Bin Laden, terrorist, fuck off back to where you came from'. I confess I did not instinctively reach for Du Bois's detachment – only later could I appreciate how their jumbled insults were a fine example of the synthesis of old and new racist configurations.

In Britain the divisions that have separated those of a different 'race' or religion have been institutionalised demographically. Different communities have been engineered via social policy to grow apart. The Lancashire mill towns are an example of this. From the 1960s male immigrant workers from Pakistan and India were lured to towns such as Blackburn to work for low wages in the textile mills. They were segregated from their white counterparts by the mill owners, given different shifts and allocated to work on different floors of the factories. It was a deliberate strategy that sought to divide the workforce on racial lines. I reported on an industrial dispute in the mid 1980s at a mill in north Manchester where the workers had gone out on strike for higher wages. By this time the British textile industry was going into permanent decline, undercut by factories in South and East Asia. On the first day of the strike the workers threw up a picket line to stop lorries going in and out of the factory. Except it wasn't a picket line: the Asian strikers stood on one side of the road, the white strikers on the other, leaving a big gap in the middle which the lorries thundered through. I asked the Asians why they weren't physically joining up with their white workmates to complete the picket line and stop the trucks. 'We don't know them, we don't think they like us'. I asked the same question of their white co-strikers: 'We don't know them, they keep themselves to themselves you see.' I did see. The strike was doomed. I was not surprised to learn that in a parliamentary by-election in this same area of Manchester in the autumn of 2014 the UK Independence Party had come within a hair's breadth of defeating the shoe-in Labour candidate.

The industrial divide I witnessed was mirrored in social policy. 'Old Labour' controlled councils infected by casual 'old racism', allocated the Asian workers different housing estates in the town apart from the indigenous working class. The men were gradually joined by their wives and had children who went to their local primary school, which because of residential segregation, eventually became attended almost exclusively by children of South Asian heritage. The few white children in those schools were over time withdrawn by their parents, creating mono-racial teaching environments. I worked in a school in Rochdale, Lancashire, in the 1980s that was 99 per cent Pakistani (except the teaching staff who were exclusively white).

In his autobiographical study of the Asian population of Blackburn, playwright and poet Avaes Mohammad, paints a picture, illuminated by snatches of dialogue from his stage plays that echoes my own experiences. Mohammad was perhaps fortunate: 'my parents were wise to ensure my primary education was delivered at an all-white school on the other side of town, otherwise my only interaction with White England would have been at the hands of the National Front who would pass by occasionally to touch up their graffiti and steal our toys'. But he also tells a story of a community that, in a way, thrived in its isolation, thrown back as it was on self-reliance. He talks of 'new generations of confident and capable South Asian Blackburnians, for whom their town is their only home and any notion stating otherwise is to be whole-heartedly challenged'. This is the other side of the coin: young people who plant their feet firmly on British soil, and who assert their rights to be treated equally, by which I mean the same as everyone else. Some of them have managed, typically through the hard work, business skills and thrift of their parents, to get a foot on the lower rungs of the social ladder.

While we traverse Du Bois's colour line, we must not neglect the other divides that pull apart our common humanity – the patriarchal attitudes that seek to place women into an inferior relationship not only with men but with God. In her commentary on ibn Arabi, the thirteenth century sufi philosopher, Sa'diyya Shaikh deconstructs the gendered power relations embedded in orthodox Muslim beliefs. Shaikh points out that 'patriarchal theologies often excessively focus on elements of God's distance, majesty and transcendence' from which a hierarchy descends like rungs on a ladder. She goes on to argue that 'proponents of such patriarchal approaches may also denigrate materiality and the body and, by extension, women, whom they primarily identify with the bodily principle'. From this flows the active denial for women of leadership positions within Islam, a state of affairs that ibn Arabi described as 'a state of ignorance and spiritual negligence'.

The main reason for my wariness about using the term 'Islamophobia' is that it can be interpreted fatalistically, putting hostility towards Islam and Muslims in some kind of unique and eternal category that stretches back through time. But if the contributions to this issue of *Critical Muslim*, and W.E.B. Du Bois, tell us anything, it is that racism is a shape-shifter that moulds itself into the contours of time and place. It is not true that the Crusades and what is happening in the Middle East at the moment are one and the same thing, and that today we are just going through an asymmetrical re-run of a mediaeval conflict. We need to situate 'Islamophobia' in its modern context, otherwise we can render ourselves blind to the commonalities between different groups who are persecuted, under attack and who may potentially be our allies. For example, even though the far-right across Europe today seeks to brand Muslims as 'the problem', a deep-seated, vile animus towards Jewish people lurks within them. The journalist Gary Younge is right to point out that 'the most potent anti-Semites and bigots in Europe do not live in run-down housing projects, but grace the corridors of power. They are not Muslim, they are Christian. The continent is not suffering from some new strain of bigotry imported from the Arab world or the Maghreb – it is simply suffering from one of the oldest viruses harboured among its most established populations'.

This virus has already had serious consequences for the Muslims. The tangle of presumptions, wrong assumptions, historical fantasies of eternal nationhood, the 'othering' of your next door neighbour or people of the next town or village, has proved to be a nihilistic tool in the hands of political rabble-rousers who wield it regardless of the carnage they leave behind. Ruth Waterson's essay on Bosnia combines prose, poetry and photography to build an impression that is powerful and poignant in turn. She impresses upon us the sheer human tragedy and near obliteration of hope that overwhelms the Bosnian people twenty years after the end of the bitter, civil war fuelled by racism, anti-Muslim prejudice and ethnic rivalries.

Younge echoes Edward Said who argued that 'hostility to Islam in the modern Christian West has historically gone hand in hand with, has stemmed from the same source, has been nourished at the same stream as anti-Semitism'. However, when we rhetorically state 'Muslims are the new Jews!' we should understand what that really signifies and the responsibility it carries with it. That is why it is so tragic that anti-Semitism has so much currency in Muslim societies. Of course, one should not equate anti-Zionism with anti-Semitism: people are right, and have a right, to criticise the Israeli state but that does not automatically imply hatred of the Jewish people. Israel and its supporters are guilty of playing a dangerous game by equating the two. Some of the most vocal opponents of what the Israeli state is inflicting upon the Palestinians are Jewish people themselves, the majority of whom live outside its borders.

It is, however, alarming to see figures such as the French comedian Dieudonné M'bala M'bala playing the anti-Semitism card in his stand-up act, including inventing a stiff-armed downwards gesture, the *quenelle*, which apparently signifies an inverted Nazi salute. It is reported that some of his admirers amongst North African youth in France have taken it upon themselves to be photographed outside synagogues performing the *quenelle*. It may be argued that Dieudonné's act represents a satirical two fingers at an outraged hypocritical establishment, or an example of post-modern irony, but ultimately it is stupidly self-defeating. Why on earth in France of all places would you give succour to your common enemy, the Front National, in pursuit of the ephemeral gain of cheap popularity and notoriety?

Dieudonné's bitter retort is to say that the French media give 'special treatment' to the genocide against the Jews, whilst ignoring other 'crimes against humanity', such as the transatlantic slave trade or the treatment of Native Americans. But as Gilbert Achcar writes in his important book *The Arabs and the Holocaust*: 'there is no reason at all, in my opinion, not to submit oneself in horror and awe to the special tragedy besetting the Jewish people. As an Arab in particular I find it important to comprehend this collective experience in as much of its terrible concrete detail as one is capable: this act of comprehension guarantees one's humanity and resolve that such a catastrophe should never be forgotten and never again recur'. We must ensure that the 'the colour line' defining our century does not repeat history.

Medina in Birmingham, Najaf in Brent

Inside British Islam

INNES BOWEN

ISBN: 9781849043014
£16.99 / Paperback / 288pp

Muslim intellectuals may try to define something called British Islam, but the truth is that as the Muslim community of Britain has grown in size and religiosity, so too has the opportunity to found and run mosques which divide along ethnic and sectarian lines.

Just as most churches in Britain are affiliated to one of the main Christian denominations, the vast majority of Britain's 1600 mosques are linked to wider sectarian networks: the Deobandi and Tablighi Jamaat movements with their origins in colonial India; the Salafi groups inspired by an austere form of Islam widely practiced in Saudi Arabia; the Islamist movements with links to religious political parties in the Middle East and South Asia; the Sufi movements that tend to emphasise spirituality rather than religious and political militancy; and the diverse Shi'ite sects which range from the orthodox disciples of Grand Ayatollah Sistani in Iraq to the Ismaili followers of the pragmatic and modernising Aga Khan. These affiliations are usually not apparent to outsiders, but inside Britain's Muslim communities sectarian divides are often fiercely guarded by religious leaders.

This book, of which no equivalent volume yet exists, is a definitive guide to the ideological differences, organisational structures and international links of the main Islamic groups active in Britain today.

'After a decade of fear-mongering, when Islam was portrayed as a unitary threat to the West, here comes a book that cuts through the hysteria. In this short and very readable volume, Bowen shows the complexity and nuances of Islam in Britain. This is a must-read for all people who want to understand the changing nature of Britain and its Muslim communities.' — Marc Sageman, author of *Leaderless Jihad: Terror Networks in the Twenty-First Century*

WWW.HURSTPUBLISHERS.COM/BOOK/MEDINA-IN-BIRMINGHAM-NAJAF-IN-BRENT

41 GREAT RUSSELL ST, LONDON WC1B 3P
WWW.HURSTPUBLISHERS.COM
WWW.FBOOK.COM/HURSTPUBLISHERS
020 7255 2201

IS ISLAM A RACE?

Shanon Shah

How much does Richard Dawkins, biologist, atheist and secularist, loathe Islam? Let us count the ways. Actually, let us not count the ways because of space limitations. But let us pause at one argument he uses to defend his singling out of Islam for criticism – Islam is not a race, and therefore disparaging it is not equivalent to racism.

Is Islam not a race? Other commentators have already characterised Dawkins's stand as casuistry and taken him to task for it. For example, Nesrine Malik of *The Guardian* admits that technically Islam is not a race but points out that there is a 'strong racial dimension to Islamophobia' – Muslims in the UK are mostly African, Asian or Arab. Many suffer hate incidents or discrimination because of their intersecting racial and religious characteristics. So, Malik tells Dawkins, saying that Islam is not a race is a 'cop out', because although 'Islam might not be a race…using that as a fig leaf for your unthinking prejudice is almost certainly racist'. Tom Chivers, who blogs for *The Telegraph*, says Dawkins often goes from 'criticising the religion itself to criticising Muslims, as a vast bloc', and is thus 'failing as a scientist'. For example, Chivers argues, when Dawkins points out that the Muslim world has not produced very many Nobel laureates, he implies that this is 'because they're stupid, or brainwashed into zombiehood by their religion'. Surely, argues Chivers, a scientist should also examine other institutional or non-institutional dimensions on the lack of progress in Muslim societies, such as poverty and the scarcity of other resources? In other words, claiming that Muslims are exceptionally backward and attributing this to Islam is tantamount to racism and Islamophobia.

It is important that Malik and Chivers engage with the debate in this way, but we must also remember that Dawkins's rhetoric is not new. As the sociologist Nasar Meer points out, opponents of the British government's proposed legislation against racial and religious hatred also played a variation on the 'Islam-is-not-a-race' card. According to Meer, these opponents held that religious minorities did not deserve protection because religion is something we can voluntarily subscribe to, whereas race is an involuntary aspect of identity. Meer argues that it is unrealistic to be doctrinaire about the difference between race and religion. According to him, Muslim identity in Britain is actually 'quasi-ethnic' because for Muslims here, 'ethnic and religious boundaries continue to intersect and are rarely clearly demarcated'. What complicates matters is that the British legal system – and proponents of a particularly ideological strand of secularism – steadfastly refuses to acknowledge the intersecting nature of racial and religious identity among Muslims.

There are certainly voluntary dimensions to 'religion', and we can surely try to separate it analytically from 'race'. But the implication of Meer's argument is that we can also construct links between the two concepts in our thoughts, speech, and actions. If we start taking these links for granted, they gain an aura of truth and we blur the line between 'voluntarily' held religion and 'involuntarily' held race.

This is not to accuse British Muslims of cynically manipulating the link between Islam and race. Rather, their circumstances as racial and religious minorities are such that it is difficult for them to separate their experiences of race from religion in everyday life. For example, when a young, bearded Muslim male of South Asian background is stopped and searched by white police officers, would he think this was due to his racial or religious background, or both? Would he separate race and religion in his mind or perceive them as one?

Yet, for British Muslims, is race entirely involuntary? This is where the debate can get messy. Social scientists initially distinguished between the biological loadings of 'race' and the concept of 'ethnicity' – a group identity we can self-consciously claim based on a belief in common descent. Yet the two are now often used interchangeably. Furthermore, social scientists also point out that 'race' is as much a social construct as 'ethnicity' – we can choose to construct racial and ethnic categories to describe ourselves and others. For example, in Britain, the word 'Asian' predominantly conjures images of brown-skinned people from the Indian subcontinent, but in Australia, it usually refers to yellow-skinned South East or East Asians. In other words, there are arbitrary aspects of race and ethnicity, too. Thus, if race, ethnicity and religion are socially constructed – with voluntary, involuntary, and sometimes arbitrary dimensions – it is quite possible to either apply them discretely or to collapse and use them interchangeably.

Can we then construct Islam as a race, or ethnicity, or both? One way to answer this is to leave Britain for a moment and turn our attention to the politics of Islam in Malaysia.

In April 2014, the Malaysian Islamic Party (PAS) said it would table a Private Members' Bill in Parliament in June calling for the enforcement of *hudud* – a category of Islamic criminal law – in the State of Kelantan, controlled by the Islamic party, PAS. Under *hudud*, it would be *de rigueur* for theft to be punished by amputation, consumption of alcohol by flogging, and adultery and apostasy by stoning to death. PAS's coalition partner in the parliamentary opposition bloc, the secular Democratic Action Party (DAP), objected to this – as it had always done whenever PAS had pushed for *hudud* before. So PAS's ambitions and its tensions with the DAP over *hudud* were not new. What was new was the emergence of the Malaysian Muslim Solidarity (ISMA) – a headline-grabbing non-governmental organisation – and how it participated in what became a highly politicised and polarised public debate. Abdullah Zaik Abdul Rahman, the president of ISMA, said, 'the Islamic state would ensure power remains under Muslim control. The Islamic state would also preserve the sovereignty of the Malays in our own land…that is why we see non-Muslims reject *hudud*.' In fact, he called for *hudud* punishments to apply to non-Muslim Malaysians, too.

Abdullah's leap from espousing 'Muslim control' to defending the 'sovereignty of the Malays' was also not new. In November 2012, Reezal Merican Naina Merican, a youth leader of the race-based United Malays National Organisation (UMNO) – the senior partner in Malaysia's ruling National Front (BN) coalition – proclaimed that his party was 'chosen by God'. This did not go unchallenged, however – none other than Marina Mahathir, daughter of former prime minister and UMNO president Mahathir Mohamad, called Reezal an 'idiot' for saying this. In May 2014, Awang Selamat – the pen-name of a columnist with UMNO-owned broadsheet *Utusan Malaysia* – argued that insulting UMNO was tantamount to insulting Islam, since the party represented Malays who were also Muslim.

Here, then, we have a group of people in Malaysia explicitly equating Islam with the Malay race. It is as though we have landed on another planet, with life forms utterly different from those on the one inhabited by Dawkins, Malik and Chivers – or have we?

We could argue that it is unfair to compare Malaysian Muslims and British Muslims in this way – Muslims form the majority in Malaysia where Islam is the state religion, but are a minority in Britain where it is not. Certainly we must not forget this crucial difference, but this is precisely why it is important to compare the two countries. We need to see that unlike in Britain, for example, Malaysia's political and legal system steadfastly insists on merging race and religion for Malay-Muslims. In Malaysia, 'Islam' or 'Muslim' can and often does refer to someone's race and the word 'Malay' is automatically associated with 'Muslim'.

How is this possible? The Federal Constitution says it all in Article 160, which defines 'Malay' as a 'person who professes the religion of Islam, habitually speaks the Malay language, [and] conforms to Malay custom'. Thus, Malays are defined by law as Muslims – it is unthinkable that a Malay person might not be Muslim. Incidentally, this is why cases of apostasy involving Malays cause immense controversy in Malaysia. However, this does not necessarily mean that all Muslims are Malays, even though the constitution enables non-Malay Muslims to claim a Malay identity.

This merging of Islam and Malay-ness is actually a legacy of British colonialism. As the historian Anthony Reid argues, the idea of a Malay 'race' or nation was largely constructed by the British. Before the British arrived, there were certainly people in the region who spoke the Malay language, but they did not necessarily identify as Malay and certainly did not think of 'Malay' as a race. Instead, we can see them as having place-based ethnicities and their own local languages and dialects, but with Malay as their *lingua franca*. British colonialists, however, increasingly used 'Malay' as a catch-all label for Malay speakers of various ethnicities, such as Bugis, Aceh, Mandailing and Java. Soon enough, these Malay speakers started internalising the label 'Malay' as a self-descriptor. Thus, British colonialists imagined for themselves the existence of a Malay 'race' and gradually started behaving as though this was a given. According to Reid, in the colonial censuses of 1871 and 1881, the British still listed 'Malays, Boyanese, Achinese, Javanese, Bugis, Manilamen, Siamese and so on as separate groups'. In 1891, however, the census subsumed these under the category of 'Malays and other Natives of the Archipelago' and distinguished them from the Chinese and 'Tamils and other Natives of India'.

In the 1901 census, all occurrences of the word 'nationality' were replaced with 'race', with the British knowing full well the biological loadings of 'race'. In the 1931 census, however, the British finally acknowledged the Euro-centric bias of this fantasy by admitting the sheer difficulty they had of neatly classifying the natives by 'race'. They lamented that the 'Orientals' themselves did not have a conception of race and regarded 'religion' as a more important self-descriptor. Despite acknowledging this messiness, the colonial construction of a Malay 'race', with Islam as its key component, endured and eventually made its way into the Federal Constitution of independent Malaya (now West Malaysia). Worse, British colonialists also inferred that to be 'Malay' was to be rural, loyal to authority, conservative and relaxed to the point of laziness. Not only that: British colonialists such as Sir Hugh Clifford, a governor of Malaya, believed that it would be catastrophic if Malays were to be 'infected' with Western ideas. Rather, the Malays needed only enough education to maintain their self-respect as an agricultural peasantry – British rule would protect them from all other evils of the world.

In this context, growing numbers of self-identifying Malays internalised these notions of Malay-ness. However, instead of remaining passive colonial subjects, many began agitating for independence from the British and this is how Malay nationalist movements such as UMNO were born.

Lest there be any doubt that the Malay 'race' is a British colonial construct, we need only compare the experiences of Malaya (and now Malaysia) with the experiences of Indonesia. There, Dutch colonialists saw 'Malay' as primarily a language, not a catch-all ethnic identity; they regarded the natives as 'Indian'. The term 'Indonesian' was first used among some European anthropologists and linguists in the nineteenth century to describe what other scholars referred to as Malayo-Polynesian. According to Reid, it was eventually embraced by students in Holland and soon the concept of an Indonesian language and identity spread among anti-colonial movements in the Dutch-controlled archipelago. In fact, 'Indonesian' remains a national rather than ethnic marker – there are numerous indigenous ethno-linguistic groups in contemporary Indonesia. Unlike in Malaysia there is nothing dictating that, for instance, all Javanese have to be Muslim.

Now it gets really complicated. Is Islam a race, or is it not a race, or is it not not a race? Things will remain complicated if we do not try to understand how people make these concepts work, or challenge them, in concrete situations in their everyday lives. Of course it would be disingenuous to assume that race and religion are the only factors that govern the thoughts and behaviours of Muslims – or people of any other background. The world is more complicated than that; let's not forget issues of gender, sexuality, class, language barriers, age, and degrees of physical ability.

But we can see how these slippery concepts of race and religion intrude into our daily lives. For example, the official censuses in Malaysia and Britain ask citizens to state their ethnic and religious affiliations. Once the numbers are crunched, policy makers, community leaders and media commentators make recommendations in the public interest based on these statistics. And whether intentional or not this can lead to a sometimes subtle, and sometimes less subtle, hierarchy of Other-ness in Malaysia and Britain. A worldview informed by this hierarchy of Other-ness often goes on to assume that one can acquire truths about certain societies by focusing on groups that organise themselves within certain rigid boundaries of identity. Yet, it is really through understanding the struggles of people who do not fall into neat official designations or expectations of identity that we can witness the danger of painting things in black and white. I would like to go back to my earlier question about whether Islam is a race.

Allow me to explore this question through a character. Let's call him Abdullah: he demonstrates how rigid conceptions of racial and religious identity can fall apart. Abdullah's story pulls together the experiences of many Muslims in Malaysia and Britain, experiences that the state and many ideologues, pro- or anti-Islam, would rather see as apocryphal to their version of reality. Abdullah's father was born in Malaya, to Muslim, Punjabi-speaking parents who migrated from the pre-Partition Indian subcontinent. His mother, born in the Straits of Malacca, is Peranakan, Chinese folk religionist whose ancestors settled in the Malay peninsula in the sixteenth century. Both Abdullah's parents are not categorised by the Malaysian State as Malay. The point about Abdullah's mother is especially important, since there are many Malay supremacist arguments that dismiss non-Malay Malaysians as mere immigrants who have no roots tying them to the country. Straits-born communities illustrate the sheer inaccuracy of this dismissal, since many Straits-born families can trace their arrival in Peninsula Malaysia as far back as the founding of the Malaccan Malay Sultanate in the fifteenth century. However, in Malaysia's affirmative action policy, introduced in the early 1970s and very quickly racialised in favour of the Malays, Straits-born non-Malays are not eligible for the same benefits that Malays enjoy.

But consider that Abdullah's father is Muslim. Abdullah's mother converted to Islam upon marriage, adopting a very Malay-Muslim sounding name. Consider that on the day of Abdullah's birth, the well-meaning Malay doctor mistakenly lists both parents as 'Malay' instead of 'Indian' and 'Chinese' on Abdullah's birth certificate. Overnight, by accident of birth and a loophole in the constitution, Abdullah assumes the authentic identity of Malay-Muslim. Not Indian, not Pakistani, not Punjabi, not Chinese, not Straits-born anything, but Malay-Muslim. Bear in mind, his father remains officially 'Indian' and his mother remains officially 'Chinese'. According to economic policy they are still not entitled to certain things, for example, they cannot purchase land that is reserved for Malays. But Abdullah is now able to. This is just one of the many things that is suddenly made available to Abdullah, but systematically withheld from his parents and his other non-Malay relatives. And due to his mixed parentage, Abdullah looks more ethnically ambiguous compared to his parents. He ends up attending a school where, in cliques drawn around racial lines, he hears his Malay classmates conspiratorially make disparaging remarks about non-Muslim Indians and Chinese. They feel no danger making their thoughts known to Abdullah, whom they assume is 'proper' Malay and a 'proper' Muslim. Abdullah has to sit with other Muslim students in their daily Islamic Studies classes, while the non-Muslim students are segregated and sent to a different classroom for 'Moral Studies'. He becomes traumatised by a particularly overzealous Islamic instructor's pronouncement that all non-Muslims are bound for Hell. When he hears this, he cannot help thinking about his mother's parents and siblings, and his cousins, who are not Muslim and eat pork and drink alcohol.

Abdullah is quite a bright student, and because of this comes to realise how even a person's intellect can be racialised. After his term exams, he is sometimes approached by some Malay students or Malay teachers who congratulate him for showing the 'Chinese and Indian immigrants' what a 'real Malay' student can achieve. At this, Abdullah (again) immediately thinks of his own Chinese mother and Indian/Pakistani father. He is not aware that these racial stereotypes are actually hand-me-downs from the divide-and-rule tactics of British colonialists, and fluctuates between multiple levels of resentment – towards himself, towards the 'Malays' around him, towards 'non-Malays', towards his parents, and towards the world in general.

But here's the tricky bit. Abdullah is trapped in a certain way, but in another way he actually occupies the apex of the hierarchy of privilege in Malaysia. He is a man; his parents have built a middle class household, raising their children in an urban environment; he speaks fluent English and Malay; he is a conscientious student; and he is both Malay and Muslim. Unlike his Chinese and Indian cousins, one day academic scholarships, job offers, and promotions will be showered upon Abdullah because of how the state categorises his race and religion.

Abdullah eventually gets a government scholarship to pursue his undergraduate degree at a Russell Group university in Britain. Here, he meets non-Malay Malaysian students whose parents have to pay their way through school. He resonates culturally with the Chinese and Indians among them, but though they get along with him, they still perceive him as a privileged Malay boy. He finds himself socialising with the other Malay students, sharing a laugh now and then but always feeling neither here nor there. Soon, he develops a crush on a nice English girl whom he later discovers is Jewish, which makes him start to mull over the anti-Jewish tirades from one of his Islamic instructors at school. He also becomes a friend of the white, English, Anglican chaplain at his university, who regularly organises interfaith gatherings for equality and human rights. He even attends a few Anglican services, which remind him of attending Christmas Mass in Malaysia with his aunts and cousins on his mother's side who converted to Catholicism. Same rituals, half the guilt, as Robin Williams once said.

His Jewish love interest introduces him to the concept of equality expressed in the Talmudic question: 'Who is to say that your blood is redder than that of another person? Perhaps his or her blood is redder than yours'. His Anglican friend tells him about similar teachings on equality in Christianity, as captured in St Paul's letter to the Galatians, where he says:

'There is no longer Jew or Greek, there is no longer slave or free, there is no longer male and female; for all of you are one in Christ Jesus'. And Abdullah tells his Jewish lover and Anglican friend about the very same ethos captured in 49:13 in the Qur'an, which says: 'O humankind, indeed We have created you from male and female and made you peoples and tribes that you may know one another. Indeed, the most noble of you in the sight of Allah is the most righteous of you. Indeed, Allah is Knowing and Acquainted'. And he and they begin to see and love the bigger picture of Islam as the younger sibling of Judaism and Christianity. To them, the boundaries of 'race' and 'religion' dissolve and cease to matter.

But at the same time, Abdullah becomes acquainted with some posh, public schooled English classmates who repeatedly and casually ask him to explain the 'problem' with 'Islam'. Why is Islam so violent? Why is it so homophobic? Why are Muslim women so oppressed? Abdullah is thrown off by how the people asking these offensive questions are the same ones delighting in his exotic brown skin and foreign accent. He decides to grow a beard because he thinks it makes him look even sexier, but then immediately gets stopped and searched on the streets of London.

What does Abdullah think of his race or religion now? In Malaysia he was always conscious that no matter what people around him said, being Muslim did not automatically make him 'truly' Malay. Back then, he thought he knew the difference between race and religion. In Britain, on the other hand, he notices that having brown skin and a foreign-sounding name automatically marks him as a spokesperson for Islam in various settings. He becomes less sure of the difference between race and religion.

Let us flash forward to a few years in the future. Abdullah is now doing a postgraduate degree in Britain. The terrorist attacks of 9/11 and 7/7, and then the revolutions in North Africa and the Middle East, have made him highly sensitive to the complicated dimensions of being Muslim in Malaysia and Britain. One day, in his email inbox, he receives a message forwarded by one of his Malay friends in Malaysia who attended university in Britain. The subject of the email calls upon Muslims to pay special attention to its contents. The message is ostensibly about the systematic violence perpetrated by American and British troops in the Middle East. Abdullah is disturbed by the graphic nature of the email, and this feeds his already considerable anger at Western intervention in the Middle East. He initially empathises with the email's ferocious tone, and agrees that something has to be done. But Abdullah is also profoundly disturbed by the way the rest of the email is framed. The writer of the email talks about the need for an all-out *jihad* by Muslims against the Jews and the infidels. It calls on Muslims to be prepared to die for their faith in order to combat the enemies of Islam all around the world. It exhorts Muslims to rise up against the 'Western', Jewish-Christian-secularist conspiracy to destroy Islam.

Abdullah cannot make sense of this. He thinks about his Jewish girlfriend who now advocates justice for Palestinians. He thinks about his white, English, Anglican chaplain friend who consistently campaigns against racism and Islamophobia in Britain. He also thinks about instances when supposedly Islamic regimes have committed atrocities against non-Muslim minorities, for example, the stories his father has told him about Christians persecuted in Pakistan. Although filled with discomfort and fear of being censured, Abdullah debates whether he should respond to the email with these points in mind. But how does Abdullah figure out the positions of each of the email recipients on the Islamic compass? How can he identify those who are more inclined to agree with him, as opposed to those who would vehemently dismiss his ideas and perhaps hunt him down and attack him? Abdullah knows that diatribes against the 'enemy within' occur in other religions, too, for example, during the Spanish Inquisition or when right-wing Zionist fundamentalists target reformist, liberal, non-Zionist Jews. But consider also that, post September 11, anti-Muslim attitudes in the West are real and he feels pressured not to snitch on other Muslims.

There are many Muslims like Abdullah around the world. They fall between the cracks of rigid definitions of 'race' and 'religion'. But everywhere they go, they feel that Islam has become the central component of their identities. And whether they are African, South Asian, or Southeast Asian, they know that this is because being Muslim also means having black or brown skin. So, while they might internally feel that concepts like 'race' or 'religion' limit their expressions of humanity, they cannot escape being defined by these concepts. In too many situations, they feel like their racial and religious identities choose them, not vice versa. Is Islam a race or religion for people like Abdullah? They might want it to be neither, but often it is both.

So, in complicating the concepts of 'Islam' and 'race', Abdullah is showing us how fluid they really are. But it can be frustrating observing how politicians and other authorities in Malaysia and Britain factor, or do not factor, these complexities into their everyday strategies for mobilising citizens. For example, it is no secret that successive British governments have wanted to promote 'moderate', 'tolerant' expressions of Islam. However, they have also unwittingly started preferring some Muslim groups over others, and pitting supposedly 'liberal' Muslims against their 'traditionalist' co-religionists. This does nothing to dismantle doctrinaire assumptions about 'race' or 'Islam' — instead it creates a new layer of 'us' against 'them' between British Muslims. In Malaysia, the government also says it wants to promote 'moderate' forms of Islam. But it does nothing to stop the small gods of UMNO and groups like ISMA from throwing thunderbolts and roaring that insulting Islam is tantamount to insulting the Malays, and vice versa.

Meanwhile, Abdullah is busy living it up in London. Despite his angst about being Muslim, he is generally a happy sort of chap. This is why he eventually decides to ignore the jihadi email, and instead embarks on a quest to look for other Muslims in Britain who share his take on Islam. So, for example, he attends a conference on diversity in Islam in London in May 2014, jointly organised by the Muslim Institute and Imaan, the British organisation for lesbian, gay, bisexual, transgender, queer and intersex (LGBTQI) Muslims. He decides this is his kind of Islam, and is grateful to be in Britain because of this. On Facebook and Twitter, he shares his experiences at this conference with like-minded Muslim groups in Malaysia such as Sisters in Islam and the Islamic Renaissance Front. In a way, Abdullah has found a new 'us' among these open and inclusive Muslims, and they make him love being Muslim and Asian in ways he never thought possible.

In fact, Abdullah starts getting a bit smug about being a hip young Muslim. He now has the vocabulary to simultaneously critique both Western policies on the Middle East and Islam, and the authoritarianism of Muslim-led governments. He can juggle Qur'anic hermeneutics, feminist theory and postcolonial politics with his eyes closed. He can even rap about 'governmentality', 'homonationalism', and bio-politics on demand. He can charm and scare the bejesus out of a white, liberal audience yearning to hear from articulate, intelligent Muslims. He can hold his own among other Muslims and face them off in the Battle of the Bigger, Better Islam. He even writes articles on 'Islam and race' for erudite, sophisticated publications!

Abdullah then has to struggle with how to avoid turning his experiences of 'Islam' and 'race' into a self-advertising strategy. There is a veritable treasury of academese (numerous '-isms', '-isations', and '-ifications') he has accumulated and finds himself drowning in in his soliloquies on being Muslim. He finds himself resisting the temptation to use these to intellectualise and self-aggrandise his journey as a Muslim for a wider audience. Yet, he desperately wants to use them to smack down the likes of Dawkins in Britain and ISMA in Malaysia. So he finds he has to brace himself every time he wants to speak.

And deep down he knows that fancy academic jargon cannot persuade people to abandon their rigid notions of 'us' and 'them'. Instead, he knows that no matter how concepts like 'religion' and 'race' have become divisive dogma, we all have the potential of seeing through and past them. Given all of this, he feels that he still has an important story to tell about the challenges of growing up as a hybrid Muslim in Malaysia and then moving to Britain. Nevertheless, he still fears the price he might have to pay for criticising those in power who define 'Islam' and 'race' in Malaysia and Britain.

Certainly there are times when he thinks it is all worth it, but there are other times when he feels unsupported, afraid and unable to articulate his deepest thoughts. But mostly, underneath all the social theory and postcolonial worry clogging up his brain, he just feels like telling the likes of Dawkins and ISMA: 'Whether Islam is a race or not, could you please just see every person as fully human? Please – see me as fully human.'

We might think that Abdullah is the Apocrypha among contemporary Muslims, but his experiences speak louder and truer than that. He shows that how we see 'Islam' and 'race', and the connections between the two, is contingent upon our immediate social contexts. And that the question is not whether we see Islam as a race, but whether we construct and abuse concepts to create an 'us' that demonises a 'them', and feel justified in doing so.

THE DARK SIDE OF
THE ARABIAN NIGHTS

Robert Irwin

In an essay on toy theatres, 'A Penny Plain and Twopence Coloured', the novelist Robert Louis Stevenson recalled the evening when as a child 'I brought back with me "The Arabian Nights Entertainments" in a fat, old double-columned volume with prints. I was well into the story of the Hunchback, I remember, when my clergyman grandfather (a man we counted pretty stiff) came up behind me. I grew blind with terror. But instead of ordering the book away, he said he envied me. As well he might!' The innocent childhood delight in reading *The Arabian Nights* (or more correctly *The Thousand and One Nights*) has been much celebrated in Victorian and subsequent literature.

The stories are indeed delightful, but how innocent are they? A fisherman, desperate to make a living, casts his net out four times a day. On the particular day in question he has little luck until the fourth attempt when he finds a brass jar in his net. When he unstoppers the jar an enormous '*ifrit* (a kind of jinni) comes billowing out and the '*ifrit*, whom Solomon had imprisoned in the flask, now threatens to kill the fisherman. Yet the wily fisherman tricks the jinni into re-entering the flask and only releases the '*ifrit* on receiving the promise that he, the '*ifrit*, will not harm him, but reward him. So then the '*ifrit* takes him to a lake where there are white, red, blue and yellow fish. The fisherman takes some of these fish to the sultan's palace where he is richly rewarded. The sultan orders that the fish should be cooked, but just as the fish are put in the pan, ready to be fried, the wall of the kitchen bursts open and a woman appears who demands to know if the fish are true to their oath. They affirm that they are.

Now the sultan and the fisherman are determined to solve the mystery of the curiously coloured fish and they set out towards the lake that no one has ever seen before. Then the sultan proceeds on alone and enters a palace in the middle of which he encounters a prince who has been turned to stone from the waist down. The prince tells the sultan his story... So far so mysterious. And so innocent. But just as the leisurely flow of the Thames in Joseph Conrad's *The Heart of Darkness* carries the novel's readers to the depths of the Congo and the horrors that were being practised there, so the bizarre and meandering narratives of the linked stories of 'The fisherman and the *'ifrit'* and 'The semi-petrified prince' conduct us to a tale that is dark and cruel.

The prince relates how he used to rule over the Black Islands and believed that he was happily married, but eavesdropping on his wife's slave-girls he learned that he was being cuckolded: every night his wife had been giving him a sleeping draught before going out to visit her lover. So the following night the prince pretended to take the sleeping draught and feigned sleep before following his wife out of the palace. When she entered a hut he climbed on the roof to spy on her. She went up to a black slave. 'One of his lips looked like a pot lid and the other like the sole of a shoe – a lip that could pick up sand from the top of a pebble. The slave was lying on cane stalks; he was leprous and covered in rags and tatters. As my wife kissed the ground before him, he raised his head and said: "Damn you, why have you been so slow? My black cousins were here drinking and each left with a girl, but because of you I didn't want to drink." The prince watched his wife humble herself before the slave and cook for him, but when he saw her undress and get in the bed of rags and tatters with the black slave, he lost control of himself and, descending from the roof, he unsheathed his sword and struck at the neck of the slave with what he hoped was a fatal blow before slipping away. When his wife, a sorceress, eventually discovered it was he who had come close to killing her beloved, she cast the spell upon him that turned his lower half into stone.

There is no need here to follow this story any further. 'The semi-petrified prince' is a tale told by Shahrazad to King Shahriyar as she tells stories night after night with the aim of prolonging her life. King Shahriyar had previously resolved to sleep with a virgin every night and then have her killed the following dawn. He had resolved on this brutal measure after learning from his brother Shah Zaman that he had been the victim of sexual betrayal by his beautiful wife. '"Mas'ud," the queen called, at which a black slave came up to her and, after they had embraced each other, he lay with her, while the other slaves lay with the slave girls and they spent their time kissing, embracing, fornicating and drinking wine until the end of the day'. Shahriyar has the wife and all her slaves executed.

So a story of sexual betrayal, a fantasy of a black man secretly pleasuring a queen, provides the pretext for the long sequence of framed tales that follow concerning magic, romance, revenge, travels to distant lands, holiness, and more sexual betrayals. Daniel Beaumont, one of the few critics of the *Nights* to focus on the originating frame story's implicit taboo against black men sleeping with white women has this to say: 'The racism involved is unmistakable. The scandal is clearly worsened by the fact of the slave's blackness. The view that slavery was a divine punishment imposed on blacks was known in medieval Islam'. Beaumont goes on to cite the tenth-century historian and belletrist al-Mas'udi's account of how Noah was alleged to have cursed his son Ham and called on God to make Ham ugly and black, and to make Ham's son a slave to the son of Shem.

The sexual threat posed by black men, as well as the disparagement of their looks and intelligence, features in a significant number of the stories of the *Nights*, including 'King 'Umar ibn al-Nu'man and his family', 'Judar and his brothers', 'Gharib and Ajib' and 'Sayf al-Muluk'. The innocence of pre-modern fantasy is precisely a fantasy. The stories reveal racist prejudices not only regarding blacks, but also with respect to Jews, Persians and Europeans. Moreover, racism is not the only issue, for the stories also provide many instances of sexist and misogynistic assumptions, as well as a taste for Schadenfreude and the heartless mockery of cripples.

These ugly passions can be found elsewhere in medieval Arabic popular literature. *Tales of the Marvellous and News of the Strange* is a rival story collection to the *Nights*, though much less well known. It includes 'The Story of Ashraf and Anjab and the Marvellous Things That Happened to Them', a sustained fictional exercise in racial abuse, in which the black slave Anjab usurps the young Arab noble Ashraf's place and goes on to perpetrate monstrous crimes. As with 'The story of the of the semi-petrified prince' in the *Nights*, there is an aesthetic aspect to the racial abuse. The sadistic and villainous Anjab is described to Harun al-Rashid as follows: 'This man is black as a negro ... with red eyes, a nose like a clay pot and lips like kidneys' and his mother is no better looking for she 'was black as pitch with a snub nose, red eyes and an unpleasant smell'. There are many instances of racism and misogyny in *Tales of the Marvellous* and its anonymous author, or authors, took additional delight in mocking cripples and in piling misfortunes on them.

Of course parallels for the sort of racism found in the *Nights* and *Tales of the Marvellous* can easily be also discovered in British popular literature, in novels by Sax Rohmer, Sapper, Dennis Wheatley and Ian Fleming in which the villains customarily suffer from the dual misfortune of being ugly and not being British. In such books a swarthy complexion and a foreign accent can be used to signal criminal intentions to dim-witted readers. To stick with popular literature, the second half of Margaret Mitchell's best-selling novel, *Gone With The Wind* (1936) harped on the sexual threat posed to white women in the wake of the American Civil War, as in the following passage: 'But these ignominies and dangers were as nothing compared with the peril of white women, many bereft by the war of male protection, who lived alone in outlying districts and on lonely roads. It was the large number of outrages on women and the ever-present fear for the safety of their wives and daughters that drove Southern men to cold and trembling fury and caused the Ku Klux Khan to spring up overnight.'

The Thousand and One Nights is the product of many anonymous authors over the centuries; a version of the *Nights* existed in the tenth century. A more extensive version survives from the fifteenth century (and it was this that was translated into French by Antoine Galland at the opening of the eighteenth century), but the Arabic story collection was still being added to as late as the opening of the nineteenth century. While some of the stories are folk tales, many stories have been taken from high literature and reflect courtly or scholarly preoccupations. Therefore the stories do not present a consistent attitude towards race or towards anything else and there are quite a few positive representations of black people. In particular Masrur, Harun al-Rashid's sword bearer and executioner, features in several stories and is always presented positively. Bizarrely in one short story, 'The pious black slave', the slave in question is rewarded for his piety by being turned white at the hour of his death.

But the question of race is brought to the fore and in a most positive way in 'The story of al-Ma'mun, the Yemeni and the six slave girls'. In this story the Abbasid caliph al-Ma'mun is told of a wealthy Yemeni who possesses six beautiful slave girls. 'Of these one was white, the second dark, the third plump, the fourth thin, the fifth yellow and the sixth black.' These slave girls are like hetairas or geishas, for they are highly cultivated and consequently, when their owner asks them to first sing and then engage in a boasting contest concerning their respective merits, the result is a civilised symposium. Though the white girl disparages the black girl and, among other things, relates the story of the curse of Ham, the black girl is more than equal to this verbal contest and she cites the Qur'an as well as a string of poets in praise of darkness. She concludes by comparing the white girl's complexion to leprosy before reciting a poem:

> Do you not see how high a price is fetched by musk,
> While a load of white lime fetches one dirham?
> Whiteness in the eye is ugly in a young man,
> While black eyes shoot arrows.'

The Yemeni delivers no verdict at the end of the debate, whose implicit message must be that all races are equal. (By the way, the yellow girl will not have been Chinese, but Greek, for the Byzantines were conventionally referred to as *Banu'l-Asfar*, 'the Sons of the Yellow'.)

'The story of al-Ma'mun, the Yemeni and the six slave girls' is a specimen of *munazara*, a genre of Arabic high literature in which the respective merits of things or people were debated, for example, Kufa versus Basra, the pen versus the sword, the Abbasids versus the Umayyads. 'The dispute about the merits of men and women' is another example of *munazara* that has been included in the *Nights*. The genre of *munazara* overlapped with that of *mufakhara*, or boasting. The master of this kind of literature was the prolific and brilliant essayist al-Jahiz (c.776-868 or 9), by common consent the finest prose writer of the Arab Middle Ages. Al-Jahiz, whose grandfather is said to have been a black cameleer, composed the *Kitab fakhr al-sudan 'ala al-bidan*, (The book of vaunting of blacks over whites), a sustained defence of black people, albeit one that worked with stereotypes: 'These people have a natural talent for dancing to the rhythm of a tambourine without needing to learn it.' Blacks were also described as great singers and al-Jahiz claimed that in general they were strong, good tempered, cheerful and generous. The Arab perception of the black man had been warped by only encountering them as slaves. Al-Jahiz also argued that skin colour was not determined by heredity, but was entirely due to climate and soil and, if blacks moved into the clime, or zone, occupied by the Arabs, over time they would lose their blackness. In this he was to be echoed by the fourteenth-century philosopher and historian ibn Khaldun.

Al-Jahiz wrote that Arabs used to accept black husbands for their daughters in pre-Islamic times, but not in his own time. His perception that racial prejudice had increased in the Islamic centuries may have been correct. In pre-Islamic times and during the first century of Islam, the a*ghribat al-Arab*, or (Crows of the Arabs), poets of black ancestry, enjoyed considerable reputations in Arabia and the most famous of them, 'Antara ibn Shaddad, a warrior as well as a poet, had a popular epic devoted to him. Even in al-Jahiz's time religious, scholarly and high literature was almost entirely free of prejudice against black people.

To return to the *Nights*, the stories that form part of the early core of the story collection are fairly free of anti-Semitism and there are no disparaging comments about Jewish physiognomy. For example, the Jewish doctor in the 'Hunchback' cycle of stories is presented as the equal of the Muslim storytellers he is with. Moreover the *Nights* contains several stories about pious Israelites. But some of the stories that were later added to the corpus of *Nights* have a nasty feel. For example, in 'Three princes of China', two of the princes are murdered by a Jewish community in Iraq and rolled inside mats, but when the third prince arrives, he tricks the leader of the Jews into killing his own son. In 'Masrur and Zayn al-Mawasif' Zayn al-Mawasif's Jewish husband is cuckolded by Masrur and ends up being buried alive by a slave-girl. In 'The fisherman and his son' the fisherman gets the jinni at his command to throw a Jewish merchant into the fire. Villainous and drunken Jewish pirates feature in 'The merchant's daughter and the prince of al-Iraq'. It is possible though unprovable that growing Arab anti-Semitism was influenced by Western anti-Semitism. In *Reason and Society in the Middle Ages*, Alexander Murray has argued that anti-Semitism and the pogroms that followed in Europe got under way in the late eleventh century.

Those who read the *Nights* in English or French translations should be warned that, though there are certainly racist passages in the original Arabic, the racist abuse has been heightened or actually invented in the English translation of Richard Burton (1885–8) and the French translation of Joseph Charles Mardrus (1899–1904). Burton was a firm believer in the legend of Jewish ritual murder and wrote a treatise on it that was posthumously published. In 'The semi-petrified prince', Burton has the king imitate 'blackamoor' speech: 'he keeps on calling 'eaven for aid until sleep is strange to me from evenin' till mawnin', and he prays and damns, cussing us two'. The original Arabic gives no licence to Burton's rendering of 'blackamoor' speech. In a note to the opening account in the *Nights* of the sexual betrayal of Shahriyar by his wife, Burton notes that 'debauched women prefer negroes on account of the size of their parts'.

As for Mardrus's elegantly composed but essentially fraudulent 'translation', he imported extra '*nègres*' and '*négresses*' to serve as slaves in the stories. His work was a product of its times and, since he wrote at a time when the virulent right-wing and Catholic campaign against the Jewish Captain Alfred Dreyfus had reached a feverish pitch, his 'translation' is peppered with anti-Semitic digs. (Dreyfus was tried for treason and sent to Devil's Island in 1894. He was only exonerated in 1906.) It is possible that the ethnic prejudices that feature in many of the stories of the *Nights* gave additional impetus to the racism of Burton and Mardrus. Certainly some famous racists came to cherish the *Nights*, it was the favourite book of the racial theorist Joseph-Arthur de Gobineau (1816–82). In the *Essai sur l'inégalité des races humaines* (1853–5), for example, he wrote, 'in the Arabian Nights—a book which though apparently trivial is a mine of true sayings and well observed facts—we read that some natives regard Adam and his wife as black, and since these were created in the image of God, God must also be black....' The *Nights* was also the favourite book of the fantasy author H.P. Lovecraft and the pulp thriller writer, Sax Rohmer; instances of racist attitudes abound in Lovecraft's stories and he was also the author of a poem *On the Creation of Niggers* (1912). As for Sax Rohmer, the creator of the villainous mastermind Fu Manchu, his fictions do not betray any particular animus against the Chinese (as one might have expected), but they do show that he was virulently prejudiced against blacks and Jews.

There is no space and perhaps no need to provide a full discussion of the other forms of racist attitudes embedded in the Arabic stories of the *Nights*. Persians often feature as pagan Magians and as such they have a propensity for homosexuality, cannibalism, sorcery and piracy. Byzantines are customarily shown to be cowards. The Franks are barbarous, lecherous and not fond of washing. Yet though examples of racial prejudice are easy to find, there is little sign of the converse—that is, an awareness of and pride in an Arab self-identity. The Arabs' status as Muslims seems to take precedence over their ethnic origin. When the term 'Arab' does feature in the stories, it is often used to refer specifically to Bedouin and the Bedouin are usually, though not always, depicted as cruel and thieving. They are also portrayed as stupid, and, for instance, in 'Dalila the crafty', Dalila, who is being crucified, tricks a Bedouin into taking her place in exchange for the promise of fritters.

In recent decades there has been a marked tendency to write about racism as if it is something that was invented in the West in fairly modern times. Thus the philosopher and cultural historian Michel Foucault presented racism as a uniquely modern and Western phenomenon which originated in Europe in the seventeenth century. The electronic catalogue of the library of London University's School of Oriental African Studies lists 724 books as dealing with race and 137 specifically devoted to racism. As far as I can tell, only one book deals with pre-modern racism (in medieval Europe). In effect racism is a crime without a history.

There has also been a tendency to trace racism back to racial theorists such as Gobineau, Ernest Renan and Houston Chamberlain, but this is surely a case of putting the cart before the horse. Racism did not need theoretical articulation to serve as its midwife. In a recent book, *Racisms from the Crusade to the Twentieth Century* (2014), François Bettencourt has defined racism as 'prejudice concerning ethnic descent coupled with discriminatory action'. So in what sense can there be racist literature? Must literature call for discriminatory action before it can be termed 'racist'? Bettencourt argues that the ideological origins of systematic racism can be traced back to Europe in the twelfth century and that the expulsion of the Moriscos (the Christian Arab and Berber descendants of Muslims who had been forced to convert to Christianity) from Spain in the years 1609-14 was the first practical instance of systematic racism. But this is questionable, as it was not so much the racial origins of the Moriscos that was in question as the genuineness of their adherence to the Christian faith. Bettencourt maintains that 'discriminatory action' is a necessary part of the definition of racism. Of course no such 'discriminatory action' follows from the hostile portraits of blacks, Jews, Franks and others in the *Nights*, yet if we are not to describe those portraits as racist, what other adjective is available?

The opening story of the *Nights*, the story of Shahriyar's sexual betrayal, closely followed by the account of his brother Shahzaman's similar betrayal and then that of the sleeping jinn by the woman with a hundred signet rings, all of this leading on to the account of Shahrazad's telling stories for her life, has an undeniably potent charge. The erotic force of the opening scene, was of course, given dramatic expression in Diaghilev's production of the ballet *Schéhérazade* in 1910. The plain truth is that the stories of the *Nights*, like the Bible and Shakespeare's plays, derive much of their power from cruelty, prejudice, violence, deceit and hatred. My *murshid* (my spiritual guide) used to say '*Il faut beaucoup de noire pour voire la lumière*' — it takes a lot of black to get some light. It is an unwelcome conclusion, but is it possible that the stories of *The Thousand and One Nights* fascinate, not in spite of their sinister blemishes, but because of them?

DEMYSTIFYING THE CALIPHATE

Edited by Madawi Al-Rasheed, Carool Kersten and Marat Shterin

9781849042284 / January 2013
£25.00 / Paperback / 356pp

In Western popular imagination, the Caliphate often conjures up an array of negative images, while rallies organised in support of resurrecting the Caliphate are treated with a mixture of apprehension and disdain, as if they were the first steps towards usurping democracy. Yet these images and perceptions have little to do with reality. While some Muslims may be nostalgic for the Caliphate, only very few today seek to make that dream come true. Yet the Caliphate can be evoked as a powerful rallying call and a symbol that draws on an imagined past and longing for reproducing or emulating it as an ideal Islamic polity. The Caliphate today is a contested concept among many actors in the Muslim world, Europe and beyond, the reinvention and imagining of which may appear puzzling to most of us. Demystifying the Caliphate sheds light on both the historical debates following the demise of the last Ottoman Caliphate and controversies surrounding recent calls to resurrect it, transcending alarmist agendas to answer fundamental questions about why the memory of the Caliphate lingers on among diverse Muslims. From London to the Caucasus, to Jakarta, Istanbul, and Baghdad, the contributors explore the concept of the Caliphate and the re-imagining of the Muslim ummah as a diverse multi-ethnic community.

'This is a book of exceptional scope and erudition that is nevertheless accessible and very timely. By bringing together such a wealth of regional expertise it succeeds admirably in living up to the promise of its title. More than that, these essays throw new light on the many ways in which even a mythical caliphate can exercise a powerful hold on contemporary political imaginations.'
— Charles Tripp, School of Oriental and African Studies, University of London

www.hurstpublishers.com/book/demystifying-the-caliphate

41 GREAT RUSSELL ST, LONDON WC1B 3PL
WWW.HURSTPUBLISHERS.COM
WWW.FBOOK.COM/HURSTPUBLISHERS
020 7255 2201

THE REVOLT OF THE ZANJ

Hugh Kennedy

The story of the revolt of the Zanj slaves in southern Iraq has always been seen as a striking exception among the political and social movements of the Abbasid period. Rather than being based on religious differences and struggles for authority in the Muslim community, it seems to be based on secular concerns and class warfare. The basic facts are well-known and not really in dispute whilst the military conflict is covered in minute and sometimes wearisome details. The Zanj were able to dominate much of southern Iraq for almost a quarter of a century from 869 to 883. But beyond this apparent clarity, lie some interesting and revealing ambiguities and differences of interpretation.

Zanj was the name given to the slave population of southern Iraq, most of them of East African origin. Since early Islamic times, large numbers of slaves had been used by landowners in the marshes and deserts of southern Iraq, the breadbasket of the early caliphate, to reclaim land by irrigation. Under Islamic law, reclaimed land brought under cultivation belonged to the man who made it productive and so it was worth investing large sums in this work. Not only that, but there were tax breaks too: such reclaimed land paid much less than the state demanded from already cultivated areas. The rich and entrepreneurial members of the early Muslim elite saw these opportunities and rushed to exploit them. As in the ante-bellum American south, there was not enough local labour and work was too unpleasant (hard digging in a shadeless landscape in temperatures which regularly topped 40 degrees) to be able to entice free men from other areas of the Muslim world. As time went on the work became even harder as they were forced to dig off the large quantities of salt which accumulated on the land, backbreaking and extremely unpleasant work. This salinisation threatened the whole productivity of these valuable estates. We have no knowledge of who the slave traders were or where exactly their victims came from but we can be fairly sure that the traders were Gulfi merchants and the Zanj came from the East African littoral.

This seems to have been the only area in the Islamic world where this sort of large-scale agricultural slavery was practised: elsewhere farming was conducted by free peasants while slaves were used for domestic, administrative or military purposes. Just as in the Roman world, slaves could rise to powerful positions. There were generals, queens and even rulers of slave origin. Indeed one of the Arabic words for slave, *Mamluk*, was used to describe the rulers of Egypt from 1260 to 1517. It could even be that selling oneself into slavery could be a shrewd career move for the young and ambitious.

It was not like that for the Zanj. There is no doubt that many of these slaves lived in very bad conditions and there had been at least two minor rebellions before in Umayyad times. The revolt against the Abbasids was on a much larger scale and was made more formidable by the weakness of the government and the participation of other, non-slave elements. For almost twenty years, the army of slaves, used to living and operating in the swamps and water channels of southern Iraq, held the armies of the caliphate at bay. Only by a huge and continuing series of amphibious military operations was it eventually crushed. Nothing like this had happened before in the Muslim world, nor was it to recur later.

Not surprisingly this story has attracted the interest of modern historians. For those of a Marxist inclination, like Alexandre Popovic, whose work is the only book-length treatment of the upheaval, the story is straightforward: the downtrodden slaves raised the banner of revolt against their oppressors in the name of freedom and justice. Spartacus would have been proud of them. Unlike most other revolts and rebellions against the Abbasid regime, this did not appear to have a sectarian basis to it. It was, it could be argued, a clear example of a proletarian uprising against the rich and their supporters in government.

But as is often the case in history, the reality is not quite so clear. To begin with, there is no real evidence of any demands for social justice or freedom, and still less of any demands for an end to the institution of slavery. Instead, as far as we can tell, the ideology proclaimed by the rebels was quasi-Shi'ite, supporting the leadership of a descendant of the Family of Prophet

Muhammad whose rule would, of course, bring justice for all and riches to the exploited slaves.

But if this religious motivation does not suit the purposes of the modern Marxist historian, it did not suit the purposes of Abbasid propaganda either. For them the revolt was a slave rebellion led by a man who is consistently described as *al-khabīth* (the abominable one), a term which has no clear religious connotations and is not used of any other rebels, at the time or later. He is, in fact, the absolute 'other', representing an existential challenge to the Abbasid and hence the Muslim order. To understand why this should be, we must look at the sources and the way in which they remember and present the Zanj.

The Arabic accounts of the revolt, as has been said, are very full and detailed but they all come from one source, a long account composed on the orders of Caliph al-Mu'tadid (r. 892–902) to record the triumph of the Abbasid military. The circumstances of al-Mu'tadid's political position explain some of the reasons why it was composed. The caliph had come to power by effectively excluding his cousins, the children of the previous legitimate Caliph al-Mu'tamid (r.870–892), from power. He was, in fact, a usurper with no legal claim to lead the Muslim community. He had been neither designated by his predecessor, nor elected by a *shūra* (consultation). He had been able to grab power through the support of his Turkish military following, effectively his private army. Many of these were very recent converts to Islam and many of them were, in fact slaves themselves.

This is where the Zanj came in useful for the caliphal publicity machine. The purpose of the unusually full and detailed account of the war against the rebellion was to show that it was a jihad and if it was a jihad (a holy war against non-Muslims) it provided a justification for this seizure of power and established the Islamic credentials, not just of the new caliph himself but of the army who had supported him. The Muslim community of that time would not accept the idea that a war against a pretender from the house of Ali and his supporters, who must themselves have been Muslim to accept his leadership, was a jihad that would provide a legal justification for usurping the caliphal title. Hence the systematic attempt to disguise the shi'ite character of the revolt.

The rebellion was not a spontaneous explosion but was the work of one rather unusual man: 'Alī b. Muhammad had been born of Arab parents in a village near Rayy in central Iran. He had first tried to make his career as a poet in Sāmarrā but it would seem that his talents were not as great as his ambition and, seeing the chaos in the government, he decided to enter politics. He first went to Yamāma in eastern Arabia. Here, it seems that he claimed to be a prophet and attracted some following among the tribes of the area, but his supporters were soon routed and with a small number of loyal companions he went to Basra in 868 (now the biggest town in southern Iraq). There he made a few more converts to his cause but he soon came to realise the potential of the slaves as a source of support. Quite what his religious position was is not clear; he seems to have abandoned the idea of prophethood for himself and reinvented himself by claiming to be a member of the 'Alid family, or rather, according to his detractors, different members of the 'Alid family on different occasions. What is more clear is the strong social content of his message; the slaves were going to be rich and free and their masters were going to suffer.

The rebellion broke out in September 869. It spread very quickly and for ten years enjoyed almost unchallenged success. The first attempts to subdue the ex-slaves were made by the citizens of Basra, their former masters, but these were beaten off with ease and the bitterness of the rebels was demonstrated by their policy of executing all prisoners without distinction. The enfeebled and preoccupied Abbasid government in Sāmarrā was able to offer little support to the people. The rebels were aided by the difficult marshy terrain, ideal for guerrilla warfare conducted by men who knew the area well but almost impenetrable to a strange, largely cavalry army like the Turks. In 871 they succeeded in taking Basra itself. The destruction was horrendous. The city, a great commercial centre and one of the cultural capitals of early Islam, was destroyed by the rebels, the mosques were burned, the inhabitants massacred; once more the ferocity of the war is conspicuous. Their control spread to Wāsiṭ and beyond, and over much of the province of Ahwāz. 'Alī b. Muḥammad ruled from a new capital he founded, Mukhtāra, on a canal to the east of Basra; he minted his own coins and took the title of Mahdī. How much power the Zanj themselves enjoyed is not entirely clear. All the known leaders seem to have been Arabs, mostly men who had joined 'Alī in Yamāma or in Basra before the rebellion started and it may be the slaves, though now slave-owners themselves, had little say in the direction of policy.

When the 'Abbasid response did come, it was methodical, systematic and effective. From 879 government armies began a slow advance, concentrating on destroying the ships which gave the Zanj such mobility in the marshes. The army was large, perhaps 50,000, but the terrain meant that progress was slow. 'Alī ordered the evacuation of threatened areas and a retreat to the stronghold at Mukhtāra. There the rebels were eventually besieged before Abbasid forces entered the city, which had to be taken street by street in August 883. 'Alī b. Muḥammad was killed in the fighting. The rebellion was finally crushed but the damage caused had been enormous. Slave farming and large-scale reclamation of land were never begun again and it seems unlikely that the city of Basra ever fully recovered. Trade routes with the Indian Ocean area which had brought so much wealth to the city had been disrupted for too long. Merchants had found other ways of communicating with the east, via Sīrāf in southern Iran for example, and Basra and southern Iraq in general entered a long period of decline. Once again the social antagonisms in the area had led to large-scale popular movements which threatened the order and prosperity of society. As for the Zanj themselves, they seem to have scattered or melted into the local population. Some found work in the Abbasid administration or army. We never hear from them again as an organised group. But the trade in slaves between the Gulf and East Africa was to continue, albeit on a much smaller scale down to the twentieth century.

There is one interesting postscript to this. In 1961, an American archaeologist called H.S. Nelson was flying over the Basra region of southern Iraq when he noticed a pattern of parallel lines covering a wide area of what is now desert between the site of Old Basra and the Shatt al-Arab. On landing in the area, he found that the lines were long heaps of salt which had been lifted from the land and piled up in rows. It was evidence of, and in a way, a monument to, the huge amount of labour that the Zanj had contributed in trying to maintain the fertility of this area of southern Iraq and turn back the progress of salinisation. And, if you are curious, you can still see this pattern on Google Earth, more than eleven centuries after the Zanj revolt.

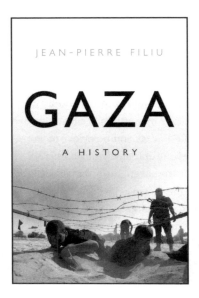

JEAN-PIERRE FILIU

GAZA

A HISTORY

ISBN: 9781849044011
£25.00 / Hardback / 424pp

GAZA
A HISTORY
JEAN-PIERRE FILIU

Through its millennium–long existence, Gaza has often been bitterly disputed while simultaneously and paradoxically enduring prolonged neglect. Jean-Pierre Filiu's book is the first comprehensive history of Gaza in any language.

Squeezed between the Negev and Sinai deserts on the one hand and the Mediterranean Sea on the other, Gaza was contested by the Pharaohs, the Persians, the Greeks, the Romans, the Byzantines, the Arabs, the Fatimids, the Mamluks, the Crusaders and the Ottomans. Napoleon had to secure it in 1799 to launch his failed campaign on Palestine. In 1917, the British Empire fought for months to conquer Gaza, before establishing its mandate on Palestine.

In 1948, 200,000 Palestinians sought refuge in Gaza, a marginal area neither Israel nor Egypt wanted. Palestinian nationalism grew there, and Gaza has since found itself at the heart of Palestinian history. It is in Gaza that the fedayeen movement arose from the ruins of Arab nationalism. It is in Gaza that the 1967 Israeli occupation was repeatedly challenged, until the outbreak of the 1987 intifada. And it is in Gaza, in 2007, that the dream of Palestinian statehood appeared to have been shattered by the split between Fatah and Hamas. The endurance of Gaza and the Palestinians make the publication of this history both timely and significant.

'A magnificent piece of historical writing: clear in its exposition, careful in its use of a treasure-trove of new sources and judicious in its analysis of competing political claims to this small and troubled strip of land. It is difficult to see how it will ever be rivalled in terms of scope, intensity and sympathetic understanding.' — **Roger Owen, Emeritus Professor of Middle East History, Harvard University**

WWW.HURSTPUBLISHERS.COM/BOOK/GAZA

41 GREAT RUSSELL ST, LONDON WC1B 3P
WWW.HURSTPUBLISHERS.COM
WWW.FBOOK.COM/HURSTPUBLISHERS
020 7255 2201

THE MASTER RACE

Ziauddin Sardar

It was on live television. The great and good of world football were announcing the winners. Australia, Japan, South Korea, United States and Qatar were in the running – all were eager to host the 2022 Fifa World Cup. Qatar does not have a rich football history, and I must admit, I did not think it had a chance. But when Qatar won the bid, I jumped for joy. At last, I thought, a Gulf state is going to do something that will be seen around the world as good. But moments later, my delight evaporated as some disturbing thoughts came to the fore. The World Cup would need a string of stadiums and new venues. Qatar can certainly afford them, but who is going to actually, physically, build them? Images of toiling South Asian labourers I had seen on various building sites around the Gulf came into mind. This is going to increase their suffering manifold, I said to myself.

Sure enough, within months news of death and distress of expatriate workers began to emerge from Qatar. Between 2010 and 2012, more than 700 workers from India died on construction sites in Qatar. Some forty labourers from Nepal lost their lives in a single month in 2013 building the new stadium, which is shaped like a well-known part of the female anatomy. And the death toll continues to rise. According to a report by the International Trade Union Confederation (ITUC), twelve migrant workers will continue to die every week, taking the toll to at least 4,000 migrant workers by the time we actually see the World Cup on our television screens.

I have watched some of these workers toiling in 50 degree heat on various building sites. They clearly work under hazardous conditions. What we can't see is that they are paid a pittance, if paid at all. Employers retain their salaries for months, and keep their passports, so they can never leave or change jobs without permission. God help them if they become sick which they frequently do thanks to their overcrowded and unsanitary living conditions. Their passports are held by their 'sponsors', who are usually their employers, and they are unable to leave the country without the – often denied – permission of their employers.

The tiny Emirate has 1.4 million migrant workers – from India, Pakistan, Nepal, Iran, the Philippines, Egypt and Sri Lanka – constituting 96 per cent of the total population. Most Qataris themselves do not perform such jobs. One would thus expect the Qataris, amongst the richest people on Earth, to treat their guest workers with humanity and dignity. So why, one could legitimately ask, are foreign workers treated so inhumanely? Perhaps the most important answer is because they are seen as less than human.

Human bondage is an integral part of both the philosophy and mental outlook of the Gulf Arabs and it goes right back to the formative history of Islam. Consider, for example, the *kafala* system that ties migrant workers to their employers. It goes back to the first civil war in Islam, the Battle of Camels in Basra, a war within the family of the Prophet, of 7 November 656. It pitted Aisha, the Prophet's youngest wife, against Ali, his cousin and son-in-law and the fourth caliph. Aisha was incensed by a number of issues. There was the question of the murderer of Othman, the third caliph, who had not been brought to justice. Indeed, there were military commanders in the army of Ali who were under suspicion. There was the rather important ongoing issue of who had the right to rule: those from the family of Muhammad or those who were elected by the whole community? After all, the Prophet had abolished claims of privilege based on blood. There was the subject of the treatment of women. And then there was this: why was it necessary for new non-Arab converts to Islam to accept the guardianship of Arab tribes? In other words, Aisha objected to the *kafala* system, which automatically made Arabs superior, simply because of their lineage and bloodlines. The tribal Arabs were the guardians of the new converts to Islam, who either could not be trusted to be good Muslims or did not have the ability to look after their own needs. As we know, the Battle of Camels was a bloody affair: over 15,000 were killed within a few hours. Aisha was defeated heavily and exiled to Medina, never to leave her house again. Some very serious questions of Islamic history were exiled with her; and the issues they have raised have been with us to this day.

One such issue is the *kafala* system, which, has since been 'ratified' using no less than hadith. We are told that the Prophet is supposed to have said that: 'The leaders are from Quraysh. The righteous among them are the leaders of the righteous, and the wicked among them are the leaders of the wicked.' In other hadith, found in the authentic collection, the Prophet says 'the people follow Quraysh' and 'this matter will remain with Quraysh as long as there are two of them alive'. So the Quraysh, the main tribe of Mecca, and by association other tribes of Arabia, are the natural leaders of Muslims. Quite why the Prophet would say this has rarely, if ever, been asked. He experienced first-hand their attempts to persecute him and torture his followers in Mecca, and wage bloody wars against him in Medina. And why would he then go on to say at his Farewell Pilgrimage that 'there is no superiority of an Arab over a non-Arab'? All questions are silenced and critical thought abandoned, once something is attributed to the Prophet.

So we also have religious authorisation for what ibn Khaldun called 'tribal chauvinism'. The Gulf Arabs are natural chauvinists. They see themselves as superior to all Muslims because they are from the birthplace of Islam, know the Qu'ran and Islam better than others, and because – allegedly – the highest authority in Islam has provided them with a special dispensation. And they see themselves as superior to non-Muslims because they possess the Truth of Islam which makes them somewhat special in the eyes of God. In their mental outlook, the world is structured as a hierarchy of beings – with the Arabs born in Saudi Arabia or the Gulf at the apex.

It is interesting to note how many Saudi and Gulf clerics still hold that slavery is an integral part of Islam. Indeed, slavery has been an important element in the life of Mecca and Medina for most of history. It was not uncommon for households to have several slaves and Arab men to have slave girls as concubines. The slave markets were the most thriving parts of the cities in the Arabian peninsula. When the Ottomans banned slavery in a series of edicts issued in 1830, 1854 and 1856, there were riots in Mecca. The Ottoman Sultan Mahmud II (r. 1808–1839) thought that it was 'a shameful and barbarous practice for rational human beings to buy and sell their fellow creatures', and abolished the trade of Circassian children. The last edict, known as *Hatti-Humayun* (the Turkish Magna Carta of the nineteenth century), gave equality to Jews and Christians before the law and contained strong anti-slavery measures. But the Meccans regarded slavery as part of the natural order of God. They believed, as many still do, that the Qur'an and the Prophet sanctioned slavery, a timeless and eternal institution. It was only in 1962 that slavery was finally abolished in Saudi

Arabia by King Faisal. It may have been abolished but it is still practised. Anyone in any doubt should look at the YouTube videos of servants in the Gulf states being abused like slaves; and the conveyor belt of cases in the English courts of bruised servants and maids having been beaten by princes and princesses in London hotels.

Thus, Human Rights Watch is not quite right when it describes the conditions of guest workers in Saudi Arabia as 'resembling slavery'. In fact, it is slavery. That there are actual slaves in the region can be easily confirmed by looking at Facebook pages selling castrated slaves. And the fact that guest workers are seen as slaves can be easily established by listening to locals engaged in ordinary, everyday conversations. Africans would be referred to as *abds* (slaves). South Asians would be described as *rafiqs*, which originally means 'friend' but has been turned into a derogatory term akin to servant or slave in contemporary parlance. The Gulf needs its *abds* and *rafiqs* to build it great metropolises: after all, the pyramids were built by slaves. Indeed, if you are black then you are automatically associated with being a slave. This is precisely what happened to Nawal al-Husawi, who is an unusual woman in Saudi Arabia for being a pilot. She is also black. Three women, who are said to be her friends, called her '*abda*' – slave – during friendly banter while celebrating the Saudi National Day in a shopping mall in Mecca. The 'Rosa Parks of Saudi Arabia', as the local newspapers called her, took her grievance to court but dropped the case after receiving an apology. But she did start a social media campaign on Twitter – #abda – to make her point.

A widely accepted myth has it that the Saudis and the Gulf Arabs are very hospitable people. Go tell that to the countless pilgrims who have been looted, decimated and mercilessly slaughtered by the Bedouins throughout history. Or better still, visit Mecca and Medina today, or find work in the Kingdom and emirates, and you will soon confirm that the Arabian Peninsula is indeed a special place: a place where outsiders, even pilgrims and devout Muslims, are not welcome. Far from being gracious and generous, most of their inhabitants are greedy and reserved. Far from being hospitable and humble, most are excruciatingly arrogant and spiteful. Notice, I say most; not all. For amongst the conceited and the vindictive, you will also find some of the finest human beings on God's earth. Unfortunately, such individuals are a distinct and silent minority.

Those who have been fortunate enough to get employment soon discover that on the whole the locals – Saudis, Qataris or Kuwaitis – are superior to everybody, and the scale of superiority moves, in careful graduation, from Arabs to non-Arabs, taking race and wealth into full consideration. I call it the 'Saudi sandwich' or the 'Gulf sandwich' – in fact, a large, multi-layered club sandwich. The top layer of the sandwich is occupied by the royal family, or the rulers of quasi-totalitarian dynastic states, based on the absolute supremacy of a single clan. In the case of Saudi Arabia, the Al Saud; in Qatar it is the Al-Thani clan that has ruled since 1859; in Sharjah, it is al-Qasimi clan; and then you have the al-Maktoums, Al Nuaimi and so on. Right next to the royal family, and often quite indistinguishable from them, are the wealthy families, who are often related to the ruling families through marriage or connected to them through some convoluted way involving business deals, loyalty oaths, and other tribal rituals. At the bottom layer of the sandwich we find the poor outsiders – the nomads in Saudi Arabia, the Shia in Bahrain, and the even poorer Yemenis who want to be Saudis or Qataris. Most Yemenis work as *farashs*, being caretakers, gate-keepers and tea makers.

Between the two layers of 'the bread' are the expatriates, also arranged in strict hierarchal order. At the top, just underneath the privileged families, are the Americans, commanding the highest salaries and perks. Underneath the Americans, come an assortment of Europeans: British, Germans, French, Swiss and Scandinavians. The Western expatriates enjoy a luxurious, carefree lifestyle. They come for money, sunshine and the renowned whiskey-driven (illegal) parties. But if they are doing business in the region, they have to be shown their position in the hierarchy: that invoice will only be paid once they have been made to suffer and humiliated for endless months. The American and European expatriates live in their exclusive compounds, complete with all mod cons. In the Aramco complex in Dammam even the ordinary Saudis are not allowed in.

What the Americans and Europeans seldom notice is that the non-white locals and foreigners in the region have a totally different status and lifestyle. In the club sandwich, the Egyptians and the Palestinians are placed well beneath the Western expatriates. They are superior to Pakistanis, Indians and Bangladeshis because they speak Arabic, which we all know is the language of God, and which also enables them to get close to the locals and become their leading functionaries. Currently, given the state of affairs in Gaza and the West Bank, the Palestinians are being shuffled down the pecking order. Then we have the Afro-locals, black Saudis and Gulf folks, followed by the South Asian expatriates who perform clerical and menial office jobs. Beneath South Asians, come the rest of the varied hired help: the Filipinos, contracted either as taxi drivers or as maids; the South Koreans who build most of the road networks and are confined to their special quarters; and the foreign *takrunis*, or blacks, Africans mainly from Ethiopia, Somalia and the Sudan, who came for pilgrimage and stayed, often illegally. They are despised in every way.

It is a common sight in Mecca to see Saudis emerging from the Sacred Mosque after prayer, worry beads in hand, cursing the *takruni* men and women, covered head to toe in a black *abaya* in scorching heat, who beg just outside. A Saudi in position of authority will talk to his Indian and Pakistani staff with disdain; but will show due respect and decorum to a Westerner. There is also the distinction between ordinary whites and white converts to Islam. White converts have a slightly higher status because they prove the superiority of Islam. In contrast, the Asian foreigners who are not Muslim are openly seen as inferior beings, only good for slavery. It is not an uncommon sight to see a Hindu Indian or a Christian Filipino harassed into converting. And many patriarchs consider a Filipino maid – foreign, non-Muslim, female – to be fair game for everything from beatings to sex.

So xenophobia and racism has been internalised within the worldview of the kingdoms and emirates of the region; an element of their brand of ultra-orthodox conservatism. Indeed, xenophobia is actually enshrined in the legal frameworks. The labour laws are in fact the laws of slavery. They define the foreigner as intrinsically untrustworthy, someone to be watched at all times, an echo of the system that tied non-Arab Muslims to Arab tribes that enraged Aisha so much. Before an expatriate can enter Saudi Arabia, or any of the sheikdoms, he or she has to be tied to a *vakeel*, ostensibly a representative who would look after their interests in the Kingdom but also watch over them and control their movements. The work visa is actually issued not to the expatriate but to the employer, who is often the *vakeel*, the absolute lord of the employees. The foreigner cannot leave or enter the country without the permission of the *vakeel*, nor indeed, travel anywhere, even for *umra*, without the consent of the *vakeel*. The *vakeel* actually holds the expatriate's passport. The *vakeel* can do anything to his workforce, just as though they were slaves in a chain gang. The workers have absolutely no rights. They cannot even complain; if they did, they would soon end up in prison where torture is obligatory. Even raising your voice to a local would be regarded as slander, punishable by a long spell in prison. The so-called Shariah courts regard the utterance of the *vakeel* as sacrosanct; the word of the expatriate is by definition unreliable and unworthy of attention. When the workers are not needed, they are summarily dismissed.

I have seen and heard stories of exploitation that defy all notions of humanity. I have seen grown men cry and grovel before their *vakeels* simply to be allowed to go and see their families back home after years of service. I have known of a Bangladeshi man who died in an accident in a cement factory, unceremoniously buried within hours of his death, while his wife, confined alone to her house, waited for weeks for her husband to return – the *vakeel* did not deem it necessary to inform her of the tragedy let alone provide some compensation. I have seen local businessmen scolding and abusing their employees. I have watched highly-qualified South Asian expatriates grovelling in front of their employers, or suddenly being dismissed with their passport held thus making it impossible for them to return to their homeland or find an alternative job in the Kingdom. I have witnessed labourers toiling in unbearable heat and crying for water which is denied to them. I have watched as domestic Asian workers were abused and humiliated in front of my eyes.

Also enshrined in the legal framework is the treatment of the indigenous black population, such as Afro-Saudis, the descendants of African slaves who gained their freedom by converting to Islam. An estimated 10 per cent of the local population of the Middle East is of African heritage. There are three million Afro-Saudis. All are banned from holding government positions; joining the diplomatic service; becoming judges, mayors, or clerics; acquiring a post in the media or education; or even becoming security officials. Black Saudi women are not allowed to appear on television as presenters or reporters, or hold a job with responsibility such as running a school. These bans are institutionalised by royal decree. The royal family moves quickly to sort out any infringement or to block any appointments of black Saudis in government and civil service.

Moreover, the bloodlines have to be kept pure. So anyone with *takruni* blood is not allowed to marry someone from the master race – genealogical records are meticulously maintained and are inspected before a marriage can take place. If it is suspected that a racially inferior person has married a superior being – accidents do happen – then the law of *kafa'ah* (equality in marriage) is invoked. There has to be proportionality between a man and his wife in terms of social status and lineage. That means the racially inferior partner must produce 'proof of equality' from their genealogical records, plus witnesses for good measure. If the court rejects the proofs, the marriage is annulled and the custody of the children, if any, is given to the 'racially superior' parent.

Still, the local *takruni* has a modicum of protection as the case of Nawal al-Husawi demonstrates. But if you are a foreigner, no matter where you are in the pecking order, you are in danger. Most expatriates, including Europeans, live in perpetual and abject fear. They hardly go out at night; and limit their 'entertainment' to parties at each other's houses in protected compounds. Even during the day, a white face, particularly a female one, attracts abuse and scorn from passers-by. When people do go out, they prefer to take a taxi rather than drive: your life is finished if you have an accident involving a local. On a trip to Jeddah, a few years back, I was horrified to see a group of Saudi youth throwing stones at a couple of European women shopping in the more affluent part of the city as though they were leading some kind of intifada.

There is an inverse side to this ideology. Far too many Muslims do not see any of these abuses as something to be concerned with, let alone protest, take action against, or try to change. It is as if everything that happens on the soil that gave birth to Islam must be sacred and therefore above criticism, question or inquiry. According to a 2013 Pew Research Center survey, 95 per cent of Pakistanis adored Saudi Arabia, 60 per cent of Indonesian and Malaysians have a highly favourable opinion of the police state, and even the Muslim African countries think the Kingdom is a piece of paradise on earth. Notice how many South Asian Muslims want to dress like Arabs: men eagerly wearing the ridiculous *thoupe*, women covering their faces with *niqab*, as a sign of Saudi-inspired piety. There are shops on the internet that sell these garments as 'Islamic dresses'. The whole of the Indian Muslim community went into frenzy when the Imam of the Sacred Mosque in Mecca, Al Sudais, visited India in March 2011 to lecture at the Deoband seminary. It was as though God's personal envoy had descended from heaven. He was addressed as 'His Holiness, Imam-e-Haram, Dr Sheikh Abdul Rahman Al Sudais', the details of his degrees in Sharia from third-rate Saudi universities were read out at every opportunity, and it was repeatedly emphasised that he had received 'The Islamic Personality of the Year' award, which is handed out by the rulers of Dubai. The Deoband clerics asked that the good Imam, 'the highest religious leader of Muslims', should not be frisked during his visit to the Indian Parliament as this will violate his sanctity! Over the border in Pakistan, they get just as intoxicated by the beneficent gaze of the denizens of the Holy Land. Saudi Arabia routinely sends ultra-conservative Imams to Pakistan to educate the ignorant Pakistanis in the ways of Islam. As though Pakistan, a country that has been virtually destroyed by Saudi interventions, and where the Saudis have supported and promoted the Taliban and murderous terrorist groups such as Lashkar-e-Taiba, was itself short of hare-brained Mullahs. The arrival of these mediocrities is greeted with much fanfare and they are officially received by the Minister of Religious Affairs. Even the abuse the Pakistanis regularly receive from visiting Arabs is seen as a blessing. In honour of Arabs, the Pakistanis have abandoned their traditional term for good bye: *Khuda hafiz* (may God look after you), because *Khuda* is a Persian word. They now say *Allah hafiz* – an indication that the process of enslavement is now complete.

Given their 'love and reverence' for the people of the Arabian Peninsula, it is little wonder that hardly anyone ever criticises the Saudis of the Gulf Sheikhs. If you listen hard, you may just detect whispers of discontent coming out of Turkey and Tunisia. The rest of the Muslim world is silent; or stooped in awe and wonder. Witness how freely and easily the Saudis have eradicated the history and cultural heritage of Mecca and Medina, without a word of complaint from any quarter. The Meccans themselves now refer to the Holy City, in hushed tones during private conversations, as 'Saudi Las Vegas'. The birthplace of the Prophet, where he insisted that all men are created equal, is now a playground for rich Arabs. In comparison, imagine what would happen if the Israelis destroyed a historic site in Jerusalem – demonstrations and riots would occur on a global scale, buses would be burned, embassies would be attacked, and Mullahs would be foaming in the mouth denouncing 'the Jews'.

Yet, the evil within us is so hard to see.

In their excessive zeal to be guardians of their brand of hyper-orthodox Islam, the Saudis and the Gulf Arabs have returned to their pre-Islamic period of ignorance. Everything that the Prophet insisted on abolishing is now widely practised in the Kingdom and the sheikhdoms. Indeed, these nefarious practices are often justified in the very name of Islam. If you see yourself as superior to others you forget how to be human. The Gulf Arabs treat others with inhumanity because they don't have any humanity themselves. Moreover, if you prevent intermarriage between different ethnic groups, and insist on marriage between blood relatives, you can, the law of nature tells us, expect but one consequence: Saudi Arabia now has the second highest rate of birth defects in the world. The gene pool is moving rapidly towards imbecility. A highly revered Saudi Sheikh blamed this on female drivers – who, as the world knows so well, do not actually exist. Clear evidence, if it were needed, that the bloodlines of the master race have totally corroded its mind. Expect a mass outbreak of 'mad cow' disease.

BLACKBURN

Avaes Mohammad

I was born and raised in Blackburn. Though set in deepest Lancashire, growing up in the city felt like a mini-India or Pakistan at times, divorced from the rest of Britain by place, race and time. I lived amongst a mainly Muslim Gujarati community; all my local streets were inhabited by South Asian families. Even in the early 1980s there were three main mosques in our area alone, split along lines of ideology as well as national, sometimes regional, South Asian identities. All meat was halal and every grocer sold the curry essentials. The bygone era that teachers would reminisce over in school, where doors were left open and children would be free to safely walk in and out of homes, was still a lived reality in our area. As a result, by the time I was five I was fluent in English, Gujarati and Urdu, as well as my own mother-tongue, Kutchi. At school I would learn of the town's proud industrial heritage; a time when every home was a mini-factory. I would return home to live that reality too as my mother sewed cloth and my father and I would cut the threads, delivered and collected by wealthier immigrants with more business sense. We would go to school during the day, attend mosque to learn the Qur'an in the evening, and play the South Asian street game, *Galli-Danda* (a kind of cricket but with sticks) in between. My parents were wise to ensure my primary education was delivered at an all-white school on the other side of town, otherwise my only interaction with White England would have been at the hands of the National Front who would pass by occasionally to touch up their graffiti and steal our toys.

Integration and the far-right were the major challenges facing the working class Muslim community in Blackburn, at least while I was growing up. Integration and the far-right, with, I must add, dashes of poverty. Naturally, my experiences of growing up are inextricably linked to the history of the area. A former mill town, Blackburn sits nestled between solid Lancastrian hills, visible demarcations defining natural limits. It became one of the world's first industrialised towns, off the back of its thriving textile manufacturing industry, a proud trailblazer and boom town of the industrial revolution. Since the mid-twentieth century however, it has suffered greatly, like many other northern England post-industrial towns, with issues of deindustrialisation, unemployment, poor housing and poverty. There was another feature which would, inevitably, exert upon the town yet another dimension of transformation. From as early as the 1950s, Blackburn began experiencing steady migration from a significant number of mainly Muslim migrants from India and Pakistan. The large majority of this migration originated specifically from the Bharuch or Surat areas of Gujarat in India and the Mirpur region of Pakistan-administered Kashmir. Both are rural areas of the Subcontinent and, in some ways, share similarities with the general landscape of East Lancashire: Mirpur has hills of its own and Gujarat had a thriving textile industry, which Blackburn would have sought inspiration from during the period of the Raj.

The steady stream of migration has now become a notable feature of the town. Today, Blackburn hosts the highest proportion of Muslims in the UK outside London. The 2001 census showed that 25 per cent of the town's approximately 100,000 inhabitants were Muslim – the national average is only three per cent. The population has now risen to an estimated 44,000 Muslims – an impressive figure but one with social consequences. Not surprisingly, Blackburn has attracted growing media interest over the years.

Most of the immigrants lived in deprived areas of Blackburn. Upon arrival, they found the local community was anything but a 'keen host'; 'White Flight' is the term academics use. It was almost a running joke that the arrival of an Indian or Pakistani family caused every other house in the street to go up for sale. And it would have been funny if it wasn't so true. Whether from fear or ignorance, local white families fled leaving whole new communities to be formed in the voids they left behind. This was of course something each group enjoyed; each community having its own space to live in as it wanted. But this approach of 'avoidance' rather than 'acceptance' was also engineered by the new South Asian community itself: mainly economic migrants from rural backgrounds, with little or no formal education, and a principal motivation of making money to be sent 'back home' and benefit families left behind. Many had extravagant houses built in their native villages and towns in the hope they would one day return. No one was particularly well-versed with the dictums of immigration and so no one knew just how implausible that dream was about to become. Of course not being proficient in English, a common feature of that generation, also didn't help with initial introductions.

Multiple identities had to be quickly adopted as my generation found ourselves navigating between several different cultures through the course of a single day: at school a Britishness was desperately instilled into us by our teachers, whilst at home and in the mosques we were generally expected to demonstrate an untainted Muslim South Asian identity. Most curious of all though, were probably the streets in which we played. Having no one but ourselves to watch over us there, a third intermediary culture was evolved completely by ourselves, meant only for ourselves, where English was woven with Gujarati and Punjabi, referencing terms from all our different worlds in a single sentence only fully discernible to us alone.

I left Blackburn sixteen years ago, but I visit the city quite often as my parents still live in the same area I was raised in. On a recent visit, I wandered around the city talking to young people and recording what they said. Our street language has survived. I encounter a group talking about rings of the city's Pakistani male gangs preying upon young and vulnerable white girls who are forcibly coerced into prostitution – the subject of a recent BBC documentary.

Chief: He's got her by 'er air! She can't fuckin' leave.
T: Wow man! 'er 'ead's proper bobbin now! Get in there!! Get in there you fuckin' bastard!
Chief: D'you think 'e knows we're watchin'?
Iky: They both fuckin' do! They love it!!

The city is as divided as ever. The segregation which began with the first South Asian arrivals has continued and not lost importance over time, to the extent where an aerial view of the town will enable one to determine the racial and religious makeup of an area. Proud minarets that clash against the red-bricked landscape of the valley stand as flagpoles; domes as flags. Newer generations of British South Asians born and raised in those ghettos have sought to maintain the way of life they have become accustomed to, as have their white counterparts, all the while reinforcing feelings of mutual distrust and misunderstanding. Interestingly the few who have sought to break out of their ghettoised existences and move to more affluent, traditionally white middle class areas with better housing and general provisions, have largely experienced a repeat of the 'White Flight' behaviour originally witnessed by their parents. The difference being that in the 1970s the white families leaving their homes were of working class backgrounds whilst those selling up today are from the middle classes, causing more and more original white communities to move and be schooled in the villages that surround the actual town itself.

The schools themselves are mainstays of isolation. A study by Bristol University in 2003 found Blackburn, Bradford and Oldham to host the most segregated secondary schools in England along lines of race. In Blackburn, this mirrors exactly the distribution of housing. Children from South Asian backgrounds attend schools together. Children from white, native English backgrounds attend schools together. Most British South Asian children, therefore, will only ever have their teachers to draw upon as positive examples of the white community whilst growing up; yet most children from native English backgrounds may not have any such positive examples to draw upon from the South Asian community. It is in such absolute isolation that the two communities exist even today, as two parallel universes sitting side by side in perfect absurdist bliss. Almost.

Muzz: Brothers! Muslims are on one side and whites on the other. Even in this college, this supposed abode of western secularism we fail to stand side by side. Even in this bastion of liberal education [...] No matter what it is we do, what it is we wear, how we look, talk, no matter who we have on our arm even. We'll always be found lacking!

What's most peculiar about this extent of community separation is its latent quality. Although buildings and geographical space visually demonstrate the starkness of issues between these communities, few platforms actually exist where any concerns or questions can be effectively aired. Enter then, the ever-willing voice of the white dispossessed. The far-right in their various manifestations have held Blackburn as a focus since the 1970s, during which time National Front activity prevented many South Asians from wandering freely outside their areas for fear of violence – a fear by no means unfounded. During this time National Party councillors had also made a brief political presence in council chambers. It would be another twenty-six years, in 2002, when BNP councillors would be re-elected in the aftermath of the attacks in the USA in 2001, and the sudden, brazen legitimisation of Islamophobia which resulted in general media and politics. Until recently the council also hosted two members of the England First Party and has attracted marches by the English Defence League (EDL). It is notable, however, that relations between the far-right and the South Asian Muslim community in the 1970s differed markedly from the nature of those relations today. The Muslim community is far stronger than it had been in those early days of settlement. Economically, an array of Muslim businesses now exists, willing to donate to counter-demonstrations and social initiatives which serve to foster links between communities. Politically, there are a number of long-established South Asian Muslim councillors representing their respective communities, while socially, initiatives from the Muslim community such as the Lancashire Council of Mosques (LCM) and Ethnic Minority Development Association (EMDA) also provide platforms of representation.

But the most distinguishing difference is the attitude of the general South Asian Muslim community today. The community no longer consists of first generation displaced immigrants embodying natural fears and insecurities of being foreign in a foreign land. Blackburn also has one of the highest ratios of youth to adults in the country. For the South Asian community, this means new generations of confident and capable Muslim Blackburnians, for whom their town is their only home and any notion stating otherwise is to be whole-heartedly challenged. In short, the far-right, although still significantly active in the town, is considered far less of a threat to South Asian Muslims today than in the 1970s.

T: They din't achieve jack in Oldham. They got their 'eads kicked in and legged it. Same thing'll 'appen if they try it 'ere too!

There are other noticeable differences that strike me though, only to be expected as subsequent generations contribute to the town's constant evolution. Few families in my areas owned cars and those that did mainly drove the Datsun 120Y. Of course by the time I left, more and more people were becoming noticeably better off after years of hard work, preserving their original ethos of making money. The same ethos has been successfully inherited and celebrated by the younger generation as today in the very same terraced neighbourhood you would struggle to find parking amongst the abundance of BMWs and Mercedes.

T: I'm thinkin' sortin' the car straight out new like. Gettin' it repainted. That two-tone colour. Metallic orange and green. Recaro bucket seats up front…Keep the alloys but get it lowered. What yer sayin'?
Chief: I'm sayin' you can join the wacky racers wid a cartoon car like that.

Mosques have also increased. Blackburn now has forty-six mosques; my old neighbourhood alone boasts eight. The number of visibly 'practising Muslims' has also increased substantially. Moreover, the mosques are now the centre of political activity – or more precisely, bastions of the Labour Party. The Muslim vote in Blackburn can easily win you an election, a point not lost on Jack Straw, the former Foreign Secretary, and local MP since 1979. In fact, Straw has been a considerable source of tension within the Muslim community. His support of the invasion of Iraq and the war in Afghanistan was considered an unsavoury act by many; the abhorrent injustice perpetuated in Afghanistan and Iraq was strongly felt by members of the South Asian Muslim community as equally as it was felt generally by many Muslims around the world. During the 2005 election, a group of young Muslims decided to try and unseat Straw as a political gesture of their disapproval. A lobbying group called Muslim Public Affairs Committee United Kingdom (MPACUK) campaigned amongst the Muslim Community in Blackburn to vote tactically, to engage in a 'political jihad' against the Foreign Secretary who had sanctioned the two wars. MPACUK took its campaign to streets, homes and mosques. But they met volatile, unexpected responses. Not only were they told to leave the town and cease campaigning but they were also physically assaulted by local young Muslim South Asian men outside one prominent Blackburn mosque after Friday prayers. What was brought to light was not support of Jack Straw's actions in Afghanistan and Iraq, but rather the silent, vice-like influence of the MP on mosques in Blackburn and, by default, the town's Muslims.

The mosques are attended by worshippers of all ages contributing to a general feeling of an 'Islamic society'. Blackburn hosts a significant number of *alims*, or Islamic scholars. It even has a *Darul-Uloom*, an Islamic higher learning institution where such scholars are produced. That all these mosques and *alims* are strongly influenced by the Wahhabi brand of Saudi

Islam is evident from the fact that Shaykh Abdul Rahman Al-Sudais, the Imam of the Sacred Mosque in Mecca, is said to visit the town 'whenever he's in the UK', according to one local source.

Yet how the mosques are managed and controlled is quite problematic; the MPACUK incident is only one example of questionable practices that have been institutionalised. While each mosque has its own Imam, they play no role in its governance. The mosques are run by committees elected by paying 'members' only. Not only are these committees responsible for the day to day operation of the building and events, but they also commonly dictate what can and can't be preached from the pulpit. The mosque outside which campaigners from MPACUK were physically assaulted whilst distributing leaflets against Jack Straw's reinstatement, has the Labour Party peer Lord Adam Patel as its committee president. Similarly, another mosque in the same area where campaigners were condemned and dissuaded from activity had prominent Labour member and campaigner, Ibrahim Master, as its president. Notably, both these individuals have also held prominent positions in the Lancashire Council of Mosques, which itself is dominated by Labour activists and councillors.

This stranglehold has caused a great deal of dissent within the Muslim community. In 2006, for example, Jack Straw invited Condoleezza Rice, the then US Secretary of State, for a guided tour of his constituency. The mosque where Ibrahim Master is President was keen to host the Secretary of State. But only 50 per cent of the mosque committee voted in favour of this plan. The other half joined a national campaign against her visit, primarily as an anti-war gesture, but also to highlight the hypocrisy of the committee members in arranging a specially conducted personal tour for a female Secretary of State, whilst denying Muslim women of their own neighbourhood regular access to the building even for prayers. The campaigning was successful and the tour was eventually cancelled, though not without expressed regret from Master who was quoted in the press as saying, 'we have to use these type of visits – very high-profile visits – for our benefit and that's what we proposed to do.'

Muzz: This is why! D'you get that? This! This is why! Coz none of you village goons get it? None of you lot get any of it. Any of us! This! You lot! You lot are why!

With such active Labour supporters holding significant positions within the general mosques' infrastructure, it has been argued by opposing political campaigners that the mosques unofficially serve the needs of Jack Straw and the Labour Party amongst the electorally significant Muslim community. But there is also a genuine goodwill towards the local MP, according to Labour councillor Salim Mulla, an original founder of the Lancashire Council of Mosques. Mulla points out that Muslim Labour councillors of Blackburn raised their collective voice against the invasion of Iraq and many actually resigned from the party in protest. But the critics point out that through the use of 'community leaders' and the mosques' infrastructure they control, the Muslims of Blackburn can be manipulated as one entity. This fact, it is argued, does and has served the political needs of Jack Straw and his councillors.

The organisational structure of mosques also enhances nationalistic and ethnic divisions. Membership of mosques throughout the town is strictly available only to specific national groups and sometimes even regional ones. Separate mosques exist for Pakistanis and Indians, as well as for the Gujarati Muslims from the Bharuch area and the Surat area of the same Indian state. This extends also to children enlisted in the *madrasas*, or Qur'anic schools, which run in the evenings. *Madrasas* in Indian mosques will not receive children from Pakistani backgrounds. The Subcontinent is so accurately recreated in Blackburn that it also replicates the original conflicts of the region, brought as baggage amidst the bags of the original settlers. The fact that such attitudes and behaviours have been maintained suggests that the leadership is not amenable to new ideas and that the British-born generations within the community lack influence.

'Lack of effort to encourage integration with white counterparts, exacerbation of tribal divisions within the Muslim community, scant community resources for women, especially from the mosques, and poor engagement with the youth can all be attributed to the bad leadership which has remained in place for the past twenty or thirty years', says Maulana Khan, a local Muslim scholar, born and raised in an exclusively Muslim South Asian area of the town. He thinks that the Muslim leadership has been largely self-serving. The community thus operates on a superficial level. Outwardly, a model of an ideal Islamic living has been created; yet internally the community is ridden with dissent and disputes. 'As well as providing equal women and youth engagement, a truly Islamic society should look to its Imams for independent leadership and civic engagement, rather than community leaders impressing their own political agendas', Maulana Khan told me. The Imams, he says, should be educated, have counselling skills, understand the environment in which they work, and should be able to give advice on issues such as EDL marches. Yet, the Imams from the Subcontinent, historically favoured by mosque committees, have little or no understanding of their congregation's daily experiences. Indeed, no one from within the community has the ability to provide counsel on the growing issues of marital breakdown, domestic violence, abortion, gangs and drugs. These issues are brushed under the carpet and forgotten so the collective illusion of outward piety can be maintained. When one of these issues comes to the fore, screaming for attention, it usually creates little more than a hushed murmur. During one of my visits to the city, a married Indian woman committed suicide by setting herself alight in her own home – unfortunately not the first of such incidents.

The elders of the community insist in maintaining the cultural baggage they supposedly left behind an age ago. The younger generation is forced to comply with their cultural standards. Marriages of the British-born Indian and Pakistani generations occur strictly within their own regional groups, even to the extent of returning to the 'mother-country' to choose spouses of purer ethnicity. No doubt influenced by the extreme racism they were made to feel when they first arrived but also as a consequence of their own prejudices too, the general attitudes instilled amongst the British born South Asians by their elders have been of an irreconcilable inherent conflict between themselves and the white communities surrounding them. It is an attitude that the young generation often reject.

Muzz: Just like Oldham has shown and now even our own town; like day and night you can't have the two at the same time. Our civilisations clash!!
Major: You're chattin' shit!

For my generation, the extent of the difference between our parents and ourselves was just an accepted norm: another arena in which to learn how best to navigate. But for the younger generation, the difference has been too overwhelming with neither side knowing how to relate to the other or how to meet the other's demands. Such frustration has caused generational rifts, attributed by some in my conversations as one of the causes of the increasing gang culture amongst the British-born, Muslim South Asian youth.

There is one thing that does bring all the generations together: solidarity for oppressed Muslims everywhere. The Muslim community of Blackburn has an excellent record of giving and collecting for charity and good causes. Palestine, Kashmir, Syria; floods, tsunamis, earthquakes; cancer, heart diseases, refugees – Blackburn's Muslim community has raised funds for all. The Muslim Welfare Institute and Ummah Welfare Trust are just two examples of local charities founded and maintained by members of the local community to provide sustained aid to Muslims everywhere. During the Bosnian War one local businessman, Musa Patel, collected aid in his own van, which he then personally drove to Muslim victims of the war at the height of the conflict.

Chief: What the fuck has Chechnya got to do with Blackburn?
Muzz: Everything!

There is another success story that deserves a mention. The local secondary school, Tauheedul Islam Girls High School, consistently achieves some of the highest performance targets in the UK and has been officially recognised as an 'Outstanding School' – the first secondary school in Blackburn to receive such an award. Notable also is a new progressive *madrasa* called the Abu Hanifa Foundation, recently established by a group of young local professionals who aim to provide a more holistic and contemporary approach to education, offering playtime between classes, meditation and an iPad for each pupil, along with traditional subjects such as Arabic, learning to read the Qur'an and the basics of Islamic jurisprudence. Needless to say, corporal punishment is not a feature of this institution.

The need for progressive change is widely acknowledged by Blackburn's younger generation of Muslims. As second and third generations become increasingly financially independent, my old neighbourhood isn't the same economic ghetto I was raised in. Unfortunately, it still remains a ghetto in cultural and intellectual terms. There is limited contact between Muslim and white communities. This has inhibited each community's potential to mutually develop and become culturally enriched with the positive aspects of what the other has to offer. Without such natural flows, both groups are in danger of cultural stagnation. Intellectual ghettoisation is a product of rigid adherence to tribal norms, patriarchal values, and obscurantist religious ideals and ideas. Little opportunity exists for such ideas to be challenged or readdressed, as significant younger members of the community remain active in perpetuating these norms.

'The problems created within reflect on our relationships outside the community' – a sentiment expressed frequently by a number of people I talked to. Yet, there is also a strong feeling that not much can change while Indians and Pakistanis fight amongst themselves, often within the space of a single mosque. So entrenched is this division, in the newer generations too, that the community is seldom able to celebrate Eid together as one unit.

My memory of 1980s Blackburn is of an exciting and inspirational place in which to grow up. It was rich with community spirit, there was opportunity to absorb from a spectrum of cultures and ideas, if you wanted to. My schooling in an all-white primary school enabled me to have white English friends, through whom I discovered a culture and way of life entirely different, though equally valuable, to that of my parents. I grew up into two cultures and had enough confidence not to know what the letters N and F, which I saw painted all over our walls, even meant. Perhaps the experiences of my parent's generation – mocked, attacked, insecure – embedded them in an entrenched mentality that they could not escape. They were partially successful in combating the racism of the time. But the isolationist bubble consequently created is now suffocating the Muslim community of Blackburn.

Mr. Malik:	I worked just. I worked hard. This house and everything in it. Everything you broken here now, I worked for it. I made it. Worked day and worked night. Nobody here wanted to give me work I still worked. Worked weekday worked weekend. I worked and I told my kids work. Work this is a new country. Better country. Free country. Work. More opportunity here I say to them. Safer. We never done nothing wrong. I never done nothing wrong. I just worked. I prayed and I worked. You think maybe I work too hard? You think this? I work too hard maybe?

THE INEVITABLE CALIPHATE?

A History of the Struggle for Global Islamic Union, 1924 to the Present

REZA PANKHURST

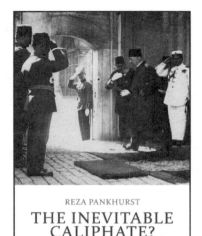

REZA PANKHURST
THE INEVITABLE CALIPHATE?
A History of the Struggle for Global Islamic Union, 1924 to the Present

ISBN: 9781849042512
£18.99 / Paperback / 256pp

While in the West 'the Caliphate' evokes overwhelmingly negative images, throughout Islamic history it has been regarded as the ideal Islamic polity. In the wake of the 'Arab Spring' and the removal of long-standing dictators in the Middle East, in which the dominant discourse appears to be one of the compatibility of Islam and democracy, reviving the Caliphate has continued to exercise the minds of its opponents and advocates. Reza Pankhurst's book contributes to our understanding of Islam in politics, the path of Islamic revival across the last century and how the popularity of the Caliphate in Muslim discourse waned and later re-emerged. Beginning with the abolition of the Caliphate, the ideas and discourse of the Muslim Brotherhood, Hizb ut-Tahrir, al-Qaeda and other smaller groups are then examined. A comparative analysis highlights the core commonalities as well as differences between the various movements and individuals, and suggests that as movements struggle to re-establish a polity which expresses the unity of the ummah (or global Islamic community), the Caliphate has alternatively been ignored, had its significance minimised or denied, reclaimed and promoted as a theory and symbol in different ways, yet still serves as a political ideal for many.

'Reza Pankhurst provides a unique and probing examination of modern thinking on the caliphate. ... This detailed analysis of the ways in which the Muslim Brotherhood, Hizb ut-Tahrir, and al-Qaeda as well as smaller groups reformulate and use the concept today is both judicious and informed. It provides the most reliable guide available to an idea and political symbol that holds attraction for many Sunni Muslims while inciting anxiety, even fear, among others, including many non-Muslims and Shi'a.' — Professor James Piscatori, Durham University

WWW.HURSTPUBLISHERS.COM/BOOK/THE-INEVITABLE-CALIPHATE

HURST PUBLISHERS

41 GREAT RUSSELL ST, LONDON WC1B 3PL
WWW.HURSTPUBLISHERS.COM
WWW.FBOOK.COM/HURSTPUBLISHERS
020 7255 2201

THE REPUBLIC OF ISLAMOPHOBIA

Jim Wolfreys

An openly racist party with deep roots in France's fascist tradition, the Front National (FN), won control of a dozen local authorities, in March 2014. Two months later it gained more seats than any other party in the European elections with a quarter of the vote. Some opinion polls in 2014 even identified its leader, Marine Le Pen, as the figure most likely to win the first round of the 2017 presidential election. Le Pen has vowed to put mosques under surveillance, tap the phones of 'proselytisers' and ban 'ostentatious' religious symbols from all public services. She has compared the sight of Muslims praying in the street to the Nazi occupation of France and promised to bring the 'gangrene' or 'green fascism' of radical Islam 'to its knees'.

In areas now under FN control, the party's mayors have lost no time in making their mark. In the southern town of Pontet, free school meals have been scrapped. In the town of Hayange, north-east France, the mayor forced a halal butcher to close on Sundays or face arrest before inaugurating a new event on the town's calendar: a Pig Festival. In the seventh district of Marseille the FN has imposed French as the only language that the mayor's collaborators are permitted to speak. Personal interventions from the mayor include halting a marriage ceremony because the Muslim bride's face was covered by a veil, and ensuring that the quiche served at an annual city hall function contained bits of bacon.

As part of her campaign to 'save secularism' Marine Le Pen herself has turned her attention to the issue of pork meat and its derivatives. Typical of the false polemics the FN has made its speciality was her vow to lift an apparent 'ban' on pork in schools. Yet pork was already on the menu in FN controlled towns, with alternative menus available, as had been the case in most schools for decades. There was no evidence that religious organisations had been attempting to intervene on the question.

Faced with the advance of an increasingly aggressive Islamophobic party, how has the mainstream political establishment responded?

The blunt truth is that instead of isolating and exposing racism, and the way it has adapted under the pressure of economic crisis, the two principal parties of government, the right-wing UMP coalition (Union pour un Mouvement Populaire) and the Socialist Party (PS), have rushed to embrace it. The scapegoating of Muslims has reached unprecedented levels, with their activities subjected to relentless scrutiny. Insulting acts that would once have invited scorn or ridicule are increasingly tolerated, even welcomed. The petty bigotry that imposes pork on menus, for example, found expression in attempts by far-right activists to organise cocktail parties serving red wine and dried sausage ('*Apéros saucission-pinard*'). This crude anti-Muslim provocation eventually found its way into the national assembly via the 'Popular Right' grouping of deputies in the mainstream right UMP coalition.

Attitudes towards diet, and meat in particular, are shaped, like most anti-Muslim prejudice in France today, not just by ignorance but by outright fantasy. In 2012 Marine Le Pen declared that she intended to ban halal meat from school canteens. The fact that virtually no schools had ever adopted a policy of serving halal meat did not prevent President Nicolas Sarkozy's prime minister, François Fillon, from warning that communitarianism was putting the Republic itself in danger, musing that perhaps religions ought to show greater awareness of health issues and update their traditions in line with advances in science and technology.

In November 2013, when a court ruled that Muslim inmates at a Grenoble prison could be served halal meals, on the grounds that secularism meant that everyone should have the right to practise their religion, the Socialist government intervened to contest the decision, which was overturned the following July. Interior minister Manuel Valls warned of the need to be vigilant, in a time of economic crisis, about anything that called into question 'our own identity' or gave the impression that 'fundamental principles' were being undermined. Secularism, he was at pains to stress, was one such principle.

Attempts to prescribe what Muslims can and cannot wear have produced three major flashpoints. In 1989 the first 'headscarf affair' saw three Muslim school students expelled for wearing the hijab. In 1994 a circular issued by education minister Francois Bayrou offered guidance on the wearing of religious symbols in schools, distinguishing between acceptable 'discreet' religious symbols, like the crucifix and the kippah, and unacceptable 'ostentatious' ones, like the hijab. In 2004 this guidance became law. Later, in 2011, the burqa and niqab were banned in public places, as were prayers in the street, the consequence of overcrowded mosques and a lack of suitable alternatives for prayer. The interior minister at the time, Claude Guéant, went out of his way to warn that his government would use force, if necessary, to outlaw this infringement of secularist principles.

During the 2012 presidential election campaign both leading candidates, François Hollande and Nicolas Sarkozy, devoted time in their speeches and interviews, and even the televised presidential debate, to the decision of a municipal swimming pool in Lille to allow a group of obese women (some of them Muslims) to be allocated a separate aqua gym class. The two candidates were extremely concerned at this apparent violation of secular principles, with Sarkozy identifying the swimming pool timetable as a threat to the Republic itself. Those advocating differences between men and women or non-compliance with the principle of equality had 'no place on the territory of the Republic'. That the president of one of the world's leading economic powers felt compelled to set such store by the defence of mixed aqua gym classes in municipal swimming pools underlined the extent to which things were getting wildly out of perspective.

From the conservative right to the socialist left, politicians have lost no opportunity to stress their commitment to secularism. Claude Guéant, chief of staff to Sarkozy who served as Minister of Interior between February 2011 and May 2012, revealed that his opposition to granting immigrants the right to vote in local elections was motivated by fears that if elected to local office, foreigners would make halal meat compulsory in school canteens or run swimming pools without taking into account the principles of diversity. In February 2013 his successor, Socialist Manuel Valls, personally intervened in the case of a nursery worker who had been sacked for wearing the hijab. Her dismissal was justified, he argued, because the headscarf remained 'an essential battle for the Republic'.

Later that spring a fifteen-year-old school student became the subject of a Council of State decision to expel her from college. She had been wearing a long skirt over her trousers and a black headband between one and three inches wide that covered about a third of her hair. Her college's disciplinary panel believed the combination constituted a religious symbol and made her study in a separate room away from her classmates. She was not allowed to speak to her fellow students or take part in recreation. The deputy for the area concerned raised the matter in parliament, arguing that a 'latent war' was taking place, waged by 'ideologues' who claimed to be fighting Islamophobia but were in fact trying to impose their values on French society. Although, he said, most Muslims condemned such behaviour, its effect was to increase mistrust of them.

The law itself banned symbols and dress that are 'immediately recognisable by their religious affiliation'. Of course, if the outfit's meaning was subject to interpretation then it is reasonable to question whether it could really be considered 'ostentatious'. As one Socialist deputy, Christophe Caresche, argued in the wake of the affair, the recurring debate over the hijab was less a sign of the rise of 'communitarianism' than a consequence of a narrowing of views around the question of identity in French society. This hardening of attitudes among a section of French society was producing an 'obsessive desire' to render invisible any sign of affiliation to Islam.

Racism becomes respectable

Part of the problem was that voices like Caresche's had become marginalised among mainstream parties. Instead it was the FN line that increasingly held sway. In May 2014 FN deputy Marion Maréchal Le Pen, grand-daughter of former FN leader Jean-Marie Le Pen, returned to the issue in parliament. She was concerned that in schools an increasing number of 'Islamic outfits', like sarouels and long dark skirts, were being worn. She believed this to be a subversion of the principal of secularism enshrined in the 2004 law that forbad 'ostentatious' religious symbols. How could staff verify where these clothes had come from? Would extra measures be implemented to reinforce the law?

Such interventions underline a shift in public debate. For over three decades Jean-Marie Le Pen had been railing against the 'two hundred million Muslims' south of the Mediterranean, at France's gates, and the immigrants rendered incapable of assimilation by the differences in race, religion and values that distinguished them from the 'born and bred

French'. Such rhetoric is no longer confined to the fringes of public debate, as the FN poses as the champion of secularism while the 'respectable' political establishment takes on the task of policing the behaviour of France's Muslim population.

In theory, *laïcité* (secularism) in France is the principle of religious neutrality, allowing for the maintenance of religious freedoms in public space. Initially concerned with those who worked in public education in the late nineteenth century, in order to shift control of education from the Catholic church to the state, since the late 1980s it has become increasingly directed towards school students and Muslim women. Politicians of all parties have in the process transformed secularism into a tool that hampers diversity in public space, based on increasingly arbitrary distinctions about how particular symbols are perceived. The law that banned the wearing of the niqab and the burqa in public, for example, was framed not in religious terms but on the basis that covering the face in public undermined the concept of 'living together'. Balaclavas were therefore added to the list of proscribed items and exceptions made for motorcycle helmets and masks worn at festivals.

Lawmakers in France were trying to put a rational gloss on legislation inspired purely by the desire to eradicate overt expressions of identification with Islam. If Muslims wanted to integrate they must prove their allegiance to the Republic and dispel suspicions that they may fall prey to fundamentalism, by adapting to the stipulations that, piecemeal, were refining the Republican dress code. Politicians from across the spectrum argued that Muslim women must remove these 'muzzles', 'walking coffins', 'Mickey Mouse masks'. When it came to legislation, then, it was emotion, instinct and prejudice that took precedence over rational debate, something implicitly acknowledged by François Hollande who, in his first major campaign speech of the 2012 presidential election, won tumultuous applause from his supporters as he punched the air and declared that to be president of the Republic was to be 'viscerally attached to secularism'.

Islam has for a long time been France's second religion, although the number of Muslims in France is often over-estimated. The figure is most frequently put at five to six million, although more careful estimates range from 2.1 million to 4.2 million. In other words, it is generally assumed that France's 'Muslim population' equates precisely to the numbers of people of North African background living in France. 'Islam', then, frequently describes a diverse community of millions of people as if it were a homogenous entity. Such slips contribute to the process of essentialisation that underpins the construction of the 'Muslim threat'. There is no more a fixed identity that can be labelled 'Islam' in France than there is a single entity that can be called 'French'. The history of immigration and citizenship in France shows that it is possible to exist in more than one culture, that identity is a fluid concept and that individuals engage in multiple relationships with society that can contradict, modify, reinforce or transform a sense of self.

Reducing Muslims to an identity defined primarily by their religion and calling upon them to conform to 'norms' arbitrarily imposed by the 'host' nation impacts upon both perceptions of Islam and France itself. The Republican model of citizenship, historically based on shared identification with a set of political values, is becoming more and more aligned with ethno-cultural notions of Frenchness, which emphasise differences based on religion, culture or 'tradition' that threaten national identity. The implication that there is something innate to Islam rendering Muslims incapable of assimilation fosters the notion that they represent an 'enemy within', posing the kind of threat characterised by Samuel Huntington as a 'clash of civilisations'. In 2012 interior minister Guéant explicitly endorsed this view, announcing that he considered some civilisations to be superior to others. France, for example, respected women more than others – such as, by implication, Islam.

Debate had well and truly moved onto the FN's terrain. For the FN, France's problems derive in part from the Republican notion of 'residence rights', granting citizenship to people born in France. This, argues Jean-Marie Le Pen, means that the promise of integration is held out to inassimilable elements, tantamount, according to his bombast, to arguing that 'a goat born in a stable will be a horse'. Although most mainstream politicians would avoid such rhetoric, the 'respectable' political establishment's efforts to police the behaviour of France's Muslim population only serves to reinforce the ideas that inform it, generating a sense that a section of the population requires permanent disciplining in order to conform to society's 'norms'.

Social effects

Some of the effects of this accelerating Islamophobia were highlighted by the National Consultative Commission of the Rights of Man (CNCDH) in

2012. Noting that racist acts towards Muslims in France rose by 33.6 per cent in 2011, a report by the Commission identified 'an increasing mistrust of Muslims'. Racist language was becoming commonplace, feeding off the exploitation of issues like national identity, immigration and religion in political debate. Reporting on its findings for 2013, the Commission noted the creation of new scapegoats: Muslims and Roma people. Both were identified as isolated groups in French society. Polarisation and distortion around questions of racism was underlined by a new phenomenon, the sense that it is the French who are the principal victims of racism, a view shared by 13 per cent of respondents. For the third year running there was a reported increase in Islamophobic acts, up 50 per cent in 2013. Women were the primary victims, subject to 78 per cent of attacks, with those wearing the hijab the principal target of Islamophobic acts and discrimination, including a pregnant woman in the Parisian suburb of Argenteuil who suffered a miscarriage following an attack.

The coming together of right-wing intolerance of Muslims with 'visceral' left-wing secularism, often bolstered by feminist objections to the hijab, has led to a process of essentialisation and dehumanisation of Muslims. What many of those who decried young women wearing bandanas or long skirts did not see was the possibility that such attire could also represent an attempt to negotiate a place for their beliefs in the context of a law that forbad 'ostentatious' religious symbols. While other students wore bandanas and long skirts as a fashion statement, a Muslim classmate was singled out and ostracised because her clothes were interpreted as an 'ostentatious' evocation of Islam in the minds of others. She was punished for being perceived as Muslim. The Republican orthodoxy that excludes Muslim students from the public space they are seeking to find or preserve a place in thus creates a self-fulfilling prophecy. By isolating Muslims, this orthodoxy is achieving through 'secular' dogmatism what it routinely denounces as the product of 'communitarian' impulses.

The CNCDH reports confirmed a trend underway in French society for some time. Two or three decades earlier 'Arabs' were more unpopular in opinion polls than Muslims. Organised racists, in the form of a group of right-wing think tanks collectively known as the New Right, had attempted since the 1970s to mask biological racism in cultural terms. According to Maurice Bardèche, one of the leading figures in efforts to revive fascism in post-war France, this would allow the right to renew itself. It would even, he claimed, allow the right to declare itself anti-racist.

In contemporary France the word 'immigrant' conveys a whole series of often unspoken racial prejudices about France's North African population and its descendants but racist rhetoric has generally focused on the claim that immigrants share a different culture, notably the Muslim faith, and are therefore incapable of assimilation. Resentment towards immigrants thus increasingly finds expression in the targeting of Islam. The opposition between Republican values and Muslims set up by actors across the political spectrum serves to legitimise prejudice in wider society. So with the collusion of mainstream parties, the Front National has achieved the ultimate objective of a strategy that set out to emphasise cultural rather than racial differences: it has made racism respectable. In the process, as Marine Le Pen has observed, the 'anti-FN wall' – the so-called 'Republican front' that bound mainstream parties, regardless of their concessions to racism, into electoral combines to exclude the FN from office – has collapsed.

The consequences of this are not simply electoral. By 2012 a leading conservative politician, Jean-François Copé, was proving Bardèche right by complaining about 'anti-white racism' in his successful campaign for leadership of the UMP. A leading Socialist, Arnaud Montebourg, spoke of the consensus shared by the PS, the UMP and the FN on the question of immigration. Sarkozy, meanwhile, declared that the FN, hitherto considered beyond the pale, was now 'compatible with the Republic', a declaration that said more about the drift of Republican values than any progressive evolution on the part of the FN.

Why did Islamophobia take hold in France?

Over the past three to four decades mainstream parties in France have experienced a hollowing out of the ideas and values that once defined their respective political traditions. Neither of the two mainstream political formations, the Socialist Party and the UMP, have succeeded in providing a positive rallying point for supporters around the market values that underpin every aspect of policy, but all parties participate in a consensus that sees these values as the best framework for shaping French society. The call to respect Republican principles has increasingly filled the void left by this absence of positive affiliation to neo-liberalism. This has led to the convergence of various strands of agitation that, from the Socialists' attempts to define and regulate respect for 'secular' values in an increasingly multicultural society to the growing reliance on racist scapegoating by the right, have left Muslims in France with few allies in public debate.

Recent history has also seen France experience long-term social decline. Unemployment hit 8 per cent in 1982 and would remain above that level for all but one of the following thirty-two years, with youth unemployment increasing fourfold since the mid-1970s, affecting a quarter of under-twenty-fives in 2012. In the late 1960s close to three-quarters of those who passed the *baccalauréat* went into professional or managerial jobs. By the early twenty-first century only a fifth were so lucky. Social mobility has stalled with the result that today it is less likely that people will surpass the social situation of their parents than it was in the 1960s and 1970s. Growing inequalities mean that in the years following the 2008 banking crash, incomes for the richest 10 per cent rose, while those for the poorest 10 per cent fell. Over the same period unemployment rose by nearly two million, the sharpest rise since the recession of the late 1970s and early 1980s.

People of North African backgrounds have suffered disproportionately from social decline. As university graduates their chances of being unemployed are five times greater than the national average. School leavers from non-French backgrounds are more likely to be unemployed than those from French backgrounds with equivalent qualifications. Research has also shown that people with non-French names are systematically discriminated against when applying for jobs. Yet studies have also provided evidence indicating strong identification with French citizenship and Republican values by Muslims in France, conflicting with the widespread view that it is Islam that generates segregation. As the uprising that swept France's *banlieues* in 2005 demonstrates, however, anger and resentment produced by discrimination is also likely to find expression.

Accusations of 'communitarianism' serve to mask the reality that Muslims from North African backgrounds find themselves living in areas like the *banlieues* not because their religion dictates that they must separate themselves off from the rest of society, but because their prospects of social mobility are blocked, relegating them to life in impoverished housing estates. The social and economic pressures that create such situations are obscured by the focus on religious and cultural differences which, as some commentators have observed, contributes to an 'ethnicisation' of social relations.

Nowhere was this more apparent than in reactions to the urban uprising that swept the *banlieues* for three weeks in the autumn of 2005. Around 300 areas were affected nationally, 10,000 cars were burnt out, 5,000 arrests made and over 100 million pounds' worth of damage caused to property. The riots were sparked by the characterisation of *banlieue* youth as 'scum' or 'rabble' by the then interior minister, Nicolas Sarkozy. These are areas of profound social deprivation: in 2005 over 700 of them, with a combined population of 4.5 million, were officially classified as 'in difficulty'.

According to a secret service report circulated in the aftermath of the uprising, the protagonists were motivated by a strong sense of identity, not primarily based on ethnic or geographic origins so much as their social condition, notably their exclusion from French society. The state's preoccupation with Islamic fundamentalism and terrorism meant that it had neglected the problem of the *banlieues*. The heads of both branches of the secret service units administered by Sarkozy went on to assert that the part played by Islamic fundamentalists in the violence was 'nil'.

Such voices were ignored, drowned out by a much louder chorus. The philosopher and media personality Alain Finkielkraut argued that the roots of the rioting could be traced not to reactions against racism in France but instead to hatred of the west, just like the 9/11 attacks. It was therefore an 'ethno-religious' revolt, an 'anti-Republican pogrom' carried out by Arabs and blacks of 'Muslim identity'. The head of the police officers' union wrote to Sarkozy complaining that forces in the *banlieues* were faced with 'a permanent intifada', a civil war orchestrated by 'radical Islamists'.

Fox News ran televised reports of the upheaval with the strapline 'Muslim riots'. According to Prince Alwaleed bin Talal bin Abdul aziz Al-Saud, a Saudi Arabian shareholder in News Corporation, his phone call to Rupert Murdoch complaining about the coverage resulted in the strapline being changed to 'civil riots' within half an hour. If any calls were being made to government ministers in France, however, they weren't having any impact. Sarkozy declared that, 'To try to understand is already to excuse'. As if to reinforce this view a number of prominent politicians, including the employment minister, the head of the ruling UMP's parliamentary party and Sarkozy himself, identified what they believed to be the cause of the riots:

polygamy. It was the absence of father figures in polygamous families that left children prone to anti-social behaviour, rendering them unemployable.

France is not alone in experiencing social and economic problems, a crisis of identity relating to loss of empire or a mutation of its political traditions. Yet few countries have seen racism, and in particular the scapegoating of Muslims, become a feature of mainstream political life quite so emphatically as in France.

There are three main reasons for this. First, the emergence, growth and durability of the Front National, a party dedicated to isolating and denigrating immigrants and their descendants at a time of economic crisis, a party that poses a genuine threat to democratic values but which has managed to shift public debate onto its terrain by establishing the defence of 'national identity' as a political prerogative. Second, the incapacity of mainstream parties to counter this scapegoating, partly in the mistaken belief that by proving its own 'get tough' credentials on immigration and Islam it would undermine, rather than bolster, the FN's credentials to do the same. This vicious circle has seen these parties imprison themselves in a logic that can only benefit the FN. In linking arms with the FN to defend 'the Republican tradition', mainstream parties have contributed to the shrinking of a set of ideas that once provided a reference point, however flawed, for anti-racists, into a disenchanted and defensive reflex. Significant steps will have to be taken for these parties ever to come to terms with, let alone defend, multiculturalism. Third, this alarming drift has been allowed to accelerate due to the lack of an anti-racist movement able to provide united and consistent opposition to the FN and the accommodations of the mainstream. Here, affiliation to the Republican tradition has created a blind-spot when it comes to defending a victimised minority: at key turning points this most basic function of anti-racism was subordinated to the need to uphold 'Republican values', putting the onus on Muslims to integrate while the institutions of the Republic, and its pathways to integration – the school, the workplace, public space – failed them. Their relentlessly stigmatised lives and behaviour were then held responsible for this failure.

Conclusion

This process has taken place amid wider international developments. The 'headscarf affair' first emerged in 1989 in the wake of the 'Rushdie affair' when the Ayatollah Khomeini issued a *fatwa* against Salman Rushdie and those involved in the publication of his *Satanic Verses*. Likewise, the rise in Islamophobic acts and rhetoric following the 9/11 attacks provided a context and justification for those who saw Islam as a threat to a 'French identity' and were already struggling to come to terms with the disorienting effects of decolonisation and globalisation. Structural unemployment, falling social mobility and rising tensions in the most deprived urban areas have further contributed to this atmosphere of permanent crisis and national decline. The emergence of a racist authoritarian party, in the form of the Front National, as a fixture of the political landscape, awakening suppressed memories of the Vichy regime, has both reinforced this sense of decline and contributed to the identification of France's Muslim population as its cause.

The divisive and discriminatory interventions of FN mayors since its local election gains of 2014 offer a glimpse of the kind of narrow, racist communitarianism that the organisation is seeking to impose nationally. Concessions to the Front's politics and, increasingly, attempts to outbid it by mainstream parties have been shown only to favour the development of an organisation that poses an immeasurably greater threat to social cohesion in France than Islamic fundamentalism, which remains a limited and marginalised phenomenon. 'Getting tough' on Muslims or immigrants on the basis of myths that hold them responsible for unemployment, crime or rising social tensions only exposes the impotence of mainstream parties. Since these groups are not the cause of social decay it will not be eradicated by targeting them. Scapegoating is a perpetual spiral; it has no end point. Ultimately frustration at the persistence of problems that 'getting tough' is supposed to resolve risks only increasing the attraction of 'outsider' parties like the FN, always ready to propose going one step further.

The persistent targeting of Muslims is preventing the effective management of diversity in French society. It is exacerbating tensions and obscuring the fundamental social and economic problems besetting France. It is encouraging the growth of the Front National. The only way to escape this vicious circle is to target and isolate the very real threat posed by the FN. The principal obstacle to this remains Islamophobia, in all its guises.

JOHN BROWN REVISITED

Gary McFarlane

The United States is still the world's hyper-power. No other state on the planet can challenge its combined economic and military might. But take a closer look and the observer will notice that despite the bluster and arrogance of imperial grandeur, it is a country that seems to be losing its way, or at any rate its self-confidence. Abroad that's easy to see in the wars it keeps losing, from Iraq to Afghanistan, but at home, too, the story is the same and has come sharply into view through recent events. Mention Mike Brown and Ferguson, Missouri, and you start to get the picture. At the heart of the beast is a sickness that has been with the republic since its birth: a searing contradiction in the land of the free.

America became the world's dominant power in no small part because of its original sin, and its Achilles heel is sourced from the same root: slavery and the racism it developed to justify it that still flourishes today. And racism continues to live and thrive precisely because it was formative to the revolution that freed white Americans from tyranny but went on to fasten the chains ever more tightly to the limbs and minds of African-Americans. Another revolution was needed to uproot the evil of slavery if the 'free republic' was ever to live up to its name. That revolution did eventually come, after 300 years of slavery – and the timing of that second coming was in no small part assisted by the work of one man: John Brown.

You may know his name from the civil war song *John Brown's Body* – a song whose tune was adopted by both North and South, but with distinctly different lyrics. After two years of war John Brown was transformed in the public psyche of the Northern populace from villain to prophetic hero. His body indeed still 'lies-a-mouldering in the grave but his soul went marching on' and as for one of his tormenters after his capture, Jefferson Davis, the massed ranks of the Union army sang 'they will hang to a tree as they march along!'

Or perhaps you know his name from a famous speech by the African-American revolutionary and Muslim convert Malcolm X that we must, in part, here repeat at some length:

> We need allies who are going to help us achieve a victory, not allies who are going to tell us to be nonviolent. If a white man wants to be your ally, what does he think of John Brown? You know what John Brown did? He went to war. He was a white man who went to war against white people to help free slaves. He wasn't nonviolent. White people call John Brown a nut. Go read the history, go read what all of them say about John Brown. They're trying to make it look like he was a nut, a fanatic...

> They depict him in this image because he was willing to shed blood to free the slaves. And any white man who is ready and willing to shed blood for your freedom – in the sight of other whites, he's nuts. As long as he wants to come up with some nonviolent action, they go for that, if he's liberal, a nonviolent liberal, a love-everybody liberal. But when it comes time for making the same kind of contribution for your and my freedom that was necessary for them to make for their own freedom, they back out of the situation. So, when you want to know good white folks in history where black people are concerned, go read the history of John Brown.

John Brown was indeed someone who fought to overthrow the foulest oppression and who did so from a position of unflinching principle. He was above all a man of action. It was because of these traits that, as Malcolm points out, he came to be derided and rejected as a lunatic. But the legacy of his life and times echo down the ages in ways that resonate powerfully in the twenty-first century.

His life's work throws up, and answers, many questions that can be readily related to today. Is it ever right to use violence to further the fight against injustice? What is and who is a terrorist? Can religious fundamentalism be a force for good? Do all whites benefit from racism, is there such a thing as 'white privilege', and if so how do we explain John Brown laying down his life in the struggle to free the four million enslaved black people of America? What is the role of the individual in history? Can the action of one person, or a handful of them – organised in secret to bring forth a shocking 'spectacular' of such explosive power that it forces an entire society to face up to the oppression in its midst – set in motion revolutionary events that truly turn a country upside down? Finally John Brown's legacy places centre stage the question: can racism ever be uprooted in the United States of America?

All these questions, and others no doubt, are forced upon us when we consider the startling and inspiring career of John Brown. Which is why the Oxford University Press is doing us all a great service by making sure that the entirety of the collected works of another fighter for justice, W.E.B. Du Bois, perhaps the pre-eminent African-American intellectual of the twentieth century, is brought back into print. Among his many writings – chief among them the seminal *Black Reconstruction in America 1860-1880* – is a little-known biography of John Brown; a book, in common with his other volumes, that sought to counter the entrenched racism of his times that so degraded all things black and suppressed the rich heritage of struggle and achievement against the odds that was, and continues to be, the hallmark of the African-American experience of survival in America. Du Bois's was not the first biography of John Brown but it was the first that placed him in his real social context, as a true friend of Black people in nineteenth century America. It is a biography that explicitly aims to give voice to African-Americans – to allow slaves, ex-slaves and the free black people of the North to reclaim their place in history as active self-conscious participants – the subjects of history, not the docile, submissive objects kept mute in the accounts of the oppressor. It was a goal Du Bois's biography achieves splendidly, providing the contemporary reader with a rich discourse on the character and meaning of racism in America.

At the end of the biography, Du Bois is forced to tackle racism as it then existed and the reader may be shocked that he has to confront the early twentieth century in all of its backwardness, specifically the social Darwinism that gave a 'scientific' veneer to the racist theory of white supremacy and its necessary opposite – the inferiority not just of those of African descent (although as we know today from the modern science of genetics, all human beings are ultimately of African heritage) but of all 'non-whites', in other words the rest of humanity. On this Du Bois remarks 'we can point to degenerate individuals and families here and there among all races, but there is not the slightest warrant for assuming that there does not lie among the Chinese and Hindus, the African Bantus and American Indians as lofty possibilities of human culture as any European race has ever exhibited'.

Thankfully, after years of anti-racist struggle and the calamities brought on by Western imperialism and the Holocaust, we have moved on from having to rebut the vile racial inferiority common sense of Du Bois's day, yet under the hood those ideas still linger or at least are transmitted with new words and codes we know today as 'dog whistling'. But the fact that they are coded means they have lost respectability, although the Islamophobes, for example, are seeking to rehabilitate those discredited ideas, admittedly in different form.

Yes, we now have Black History Month, African-American history departments in the major universities of the West and an African-American president of the US, but, as we saw in Ferguson, none of that can shield us from still confronting a reality shaped by the legacy of slavery – a legacy denied by the 'anti-PC' crowd who sought to roll back the gains of the civil rights and Black Power movements in America almost as soon as the Civil Rights Act and Voting Rights Act of the 1960s were passed. Against this background, Du Bois's slim volume should not to be viewed merely as an interesting artefact of historical research, for it is still a politically pertinent and profoundly educational excursion through the trials and tribulations of the African-American fight for justice and equality that leads the thoughtful reader to question the kind of society that could give birth to such oppression and maintain it for so long.

Before we consider who was John Brown, let's briefly consider what he did and why it was so important. Du Bois approvingly quotes from Frederick Douglass, the first national black leader to emerge in the US and a scion of fight for liberation during the civil war era, on the subject of John Brown: 'If John Brown did not end the war that ended slavery, he did, at least, begin the war that ended slavery.'

It was John Brown's raid on the federal armoury at Harpers Ferry in the slave state of Virginia that set the fire that hastened and ignited the war. As other biographers of the man would agree – among them George Novack who describes him, in a positive light, as a 'revolutionary terrorist' - he succeeded both in polarising opinion even more than it already was, and in encouraging the slaveocracy to the view that the abolitionists wanted to destroy the 'Southern way of life', which was true, and that therefore the South must strike first – hence the growing popularity of the idea of secession from the Union if needs be. But Du Bois takes the argument further, as the introduction to the Oxford University Press edition rightly highlights. Du Bois sees John Brown's masterstroke as opening up the process of an accelerating 'general strike' of African-Americans in the South who increasingly fled to freedom through the Underground Railroad, and later to the lines of the Union army when the war broke out, and went on to fight for their freedom as the shock troops of that army when it became an army of liberation after the emancipation proclamation of 1863. Without the freeing of the slaves the war could not be won, as President Abraham Lincoln came to see, and it was the slaves themselves who asserted this truth in practice by fighting for their freedom. And how did Brown contribute to this development of a revolutionary war of liberation? As Du Bois puts it: 'in the first place he aroused the Negroes of Virginia.' He continues: 'although Brown's plan failed at the time, it was actually arms and tools in the hands of a half-million Negroes that won the Civil War.' And in his death, in true martyrdom fashion, he did more for the cause of abolitionism than he had achieved in his lifetime, notwithstanding the audacity and heroism embodied in the act of the raid itself, which we will come to shortly.

Although Brown's plan failed, it wasn't because the plan was insane or unrealistic. Indeed, Brown had spent years formulating it and just as long studying insurrectionary war and slave rebellions – from the guerrilla warfare conducted against the British in the Iberian peninsula during the Napoleonic wars, to the great, and successful, slave rebellion led by Touissant L'Overture in Haiti or in earlier times the wars against the legions of Rome conducted by the slave general Spartacus. Du Bois relates how Brown especially paid attention to the most famous slave rebellions of America and their leaders: 'he learned of Isaac, Denmark Vesey, Nat Turner and the Cumberland region insurrections in South Carolina, Virginia, and Tennessee; he knew of the organised resistance to slave-catchers in Pennsylvania, and the history of Haiti and Jamaica.'

Brown noted how the rebellions in the US were necessarily different in character to those in the Caribbean where the slaves were the overwhelming majority. In his time the blacks were only a majority in two states - South Carolina and Georgia. From these studies he correctly appreciated the primacy of good ground, as any accomplished general before and since would. He noticed that the geography of the US had a mountain range that penetrated the Deep South and that could provide runaway slaves with formidable natural redoubts that would allow small numbers of defenders to beat off attacks from far larger forces. Mountain warfare was the secret of the success of the Maroons of Jamaica, who used the mountainous Cockpit country of the interior of Jamaica to destroy regiment after regiment sent by the British to re-enslave them on the coastal plantations from which they had escaped. The mountain range he identified was the Alleghenies – which he dubbed the 'Great Black Way' and which to him, a man of deep religious belief, seemed to have been divinely created for the sole purpose of effecting the liberation of the slaves of the South. The Blue Ridge mountains – also known as Loudoun Heights – that rose south of Harpers Ferry is the entrance to this Great Black Way.

Du Bois relates: 'the plan without doubt was, first to collect men and arms on the Maryland side of the Potomac River; second, to attack the arsenal suddenly and capture it; third, to bring up the arms and ammunition and, together with those captured, to cross the Shenandoah to Loudoun Heights and hide in the mountain wilderness; fourth, thence to descend at intervals to release slaves and get food, and so retreat southward.' Brown's plan was to be a 'spectacular' on an almost epic scale in terms of its goals. His plan failed because stage three failed: the arms were not brought up quickly enough to meet the vanguard at Harpers Ferry, where the arsenal had been successfully taken and held.

As Du Bois points out, Brown's intention was not to retreat back across the Potomac river to Maryland as assumed by many historians but, instead, to penetrate deep into the South and the so called Black Belt (originally the term referred to the fertile black soil but came to be used as a description of that geographical region of the South that included the highest proportion of African-Americans) 'where there were massed in 1859 at least three million of the four million slaves', using the mountains as a base to strike from. It was a plan twenty years in the making that was astute both tactically and strategically: hardly the work of a mad man as his tormenters in the Virginia court tried to claim. In fact so fearful of the import of Brown's plan were the slaveholders that all his maps were destroyed after his death.

What was it that inspired and guided John Brown to prosecute this plan to strike his intended mortal blow against slavery that shook America to its foundations, North and South? John Brown was a Puritan in religious outlook, descended from a long line of Calvinists. His family could be traced back to the first of the settlers in the English colonies of North America. The Bible was his favourite book, although he had also studied the life of the regicide Oliver Cromwell from the English revolution of the seventeenth century along with the French revolution, judging by the few other books he was known to have possessed. As was common in his time, but less so than in previous centuries, political ideas could still be couched and framed inside a religious perspective. The two most important tenets of Brown's Puritanism were the centrality of the individual's relationship with God and the concept of predestination. The godly did not require a priesthood to be near to God, merely faith. Add to that the Calvinist idea of providence - the notion that everything followed God's design and purpose and that each person was predestined to fulfil a specific part in that plan, and we have the essential outlines of the powerful ideology that drove Brown on. It all helps to explain Brown's tenacity and certainty in what he was doing, although this was something that developed over many years. The fervent religious inspiration that underscored Brown's abolitionism set him apart from many of his fellow abolitionists. For Brown racism was un-Christian. One of his sons related the story of how free black people and fugitive slaves were made to stand at the back door of a church he worshiped at: 'Father noticed this, and when the next meeting (which was at evening) had fairly opened, he arose and called attention to the fact that, in seating the colored portion of the audience, a discrimination had been made, and said that he did not believe God "is a respecter of persons"' [i.e. God did not recognise any fundamental differences between one human and another] He then invited the colored people to occupy his slip.'

Nevertheless, his religious zeal does not suffice by itself to explain his abolitionism and leadership skills. These were related to his upbringing; to his own particular family traditions. His father owned a tannery business and this social status perhaps gave him some of the confidence clearly shown in his ability to lead and get others to follow. Add to this the good fortune to have been born into a family of abolitionists. Du Bois explains:

It was natural, then, for Brown to see slavery as an affront to Christianity. From as early as 1825 when he was only five-years-old he remembers his father helping a fugitive slave to escape slave catchers. Later, in 1839 'when a Negro preacher named Fayette was visiting Brown, and bringing his story of persecution and injustice', Brown, now forty years old, told his wife and three eldest boys 'of his purpose to make active war on slavery, and bound his family in solemn and secret compact to labour for emancipation. And then instead of standing to pray, as was his wont, he fell upon his knees and implored God's blessing on his enterprise.' This was the turning point in his life. From now on it dominated his thoughts.

Brown 'sought and gained the acquaintance of Negro leaders like Garnet, Loguen, Gloucester and McCune Smith' because he saw black people as the agents of their own liberation not as victims to be lifted up by some external force – an attitude prevalent among many abolitionists, although it should be said that Brown did see freeing the slaves as akin to God leading the Israelites out of bondage in Egypt.

It was oft remarked that Brown's long white beard and piercing eyes projected an Old Testament aura, which alongside the intensity of his religious beliefs allowed others to see him as somewhat unhinged. We must remember that until the Civil War broke out, and up until 1863 when emancipation became a central aim of the North, abolitionism was very much a minority opinion. It was easy for the mainstream to write-off minority opinions as extremist fundamentalism, especially where slavery and the social position of African-Americans was concerned.

Racism was not built into the DNA of white people but it had most definitely been carefully seeded and cultivated over time by those who needed labour for their plantations after the Native Americans and white indentured servants proved unreliable and in short supply. The turn to Africa as a source for slaves as a solution provided what Marxists would call 'the material basis' of the ideas we now call racism. (It should be noted here that Du Bois was a self-avowed Marxist for much of his most productive years). The founding fathers of the American republic assumed slavery would die out, but Eli Whitney's invention of the cotton gin changed all that. Slavery exploded in step with the fabulous wealth to be made from cotton cultivation, and the products of this human chattel provided the economic underpinning for the fantastic growth in the wealth and power of the United States, and also of Great Britain.

The economic dominance of slavery was reflected in the political system. The US constitution allowed slaveholders to count each slave as being worth three-fifths of a human being for the purposes of state representation in Congress, thereby giving the slaveholders a disproportionate influence over the government. As the US grew and new states were admitted to the Union the question of whether those states should be free or slave arose.

The issue became more and more fraught as millions of immigrants from Europe came to the US to farm the land stolen from the Native Americans. If a territory or state permitted slavery it would squeeze out free labour and free soil settlers. Furthermore, the slave system and cotton cultivation in particular was such that it degraded the soil and therefore had a voracious appetite for more and more land. This fight over what sort of country the US would ultimately become – one based on 'free labour' where each individual was promised advancement through their own hard work or a slave society ruled over by a lordly minority and degraded labour – was the basis for the battle of ideas between abolitionists and slavers, between North and South. Most Northerners denied they had any designs on interfering with the institution of slavery itself. They just wanted to stop it spreading to new territories and states.

A number of events focused attention on the problem presented by slavery and began to alienate Northern opinion from the Southern-dominated US government – the Supreme Court ruling on Dred Scott which decided that black people 'had no rights that a white man need respect' and the Fugitive Slave Law of 1850 that affirmed the legality of slave catchers operating in Northern states, to allow Southern slave masters to retrieve their 'property'.

The cauldron of the slavery controversy came to the boil in Kansas where matters turned violent. Bloody confrontations took place after the Kansas-Nebraska Act of 1854 was passed which allowed slavery to enter the territory. Clashes ensued between free soil settlers and the supporters of the slaveocracy. For two years the violence was one-sided with the slavers doing the attacking and killing. In two of the worst of those one-sided battles, in Osawatomie and Lawrence, both anti-slavery towns, settlers were attacked and murdered. The pro-slavery 'border ruffians', supported in their endeavours by the US President of the day Franklin Pierce, considered the farmers a push-over until one John Brown, radicalised by the atrocities in the territory, fought back in dramatic fashion. He had gone to Kansas with the express purpose of fighting the 'slave power' and brought with him around thirty supporters, or up to 100 as Du Bois claims, all sworn to secrecy to take on the slaveholders. A *New York Tribune* reporter happened upon his band and reported: 'the old man said to me, it's a mistake, sir that our people make, when they think that bullies are the best fighters...Give me men of good principles; God-fearing men; men who respect themselves; and, with a dozen of them, I will oppose any hundred such as these Buford ruffians'.

Brown understood that to win a revolutionary war required a revolutionary spirit and ardour; a belief in what you were fighting for. Brown's band, seven in all, struck back at Osawatomie, killing five of the pro-slavery element, among them the pro-slavery district attorney Allen Wilkinson and prominent activist James Doyle. Doyle and his two sons were led into the woods and hacked to death. The killing of five pro-slavers in total changed how the arrogant and violent Southerners saw the abolitionists - they were now considered a clear and present danger.

Captain Brown, as he was known to his followers, came to national prominence in these engagements. He became known, and respected among many abolitionists, as someone willing to turn talk into action, who would take the fight to the slavers, even going so far as to launch raids across the Kansas border into Missouri to liberate slaves. A warrant was issued for Brown's arrest and he had to flee to Canada.

Most Southerners did not own slaves but because of the all-pervasive nature of the system, all had a stake in it. The slaveholders operated much like the aristocracy of old. They socially dominated their states to such an extent that poor whites often didn't have the vote because they failed to meet property qualifications drawn up by the slaveocracy. There were no public schools to speak of and the small-holding farmers were confined to the worst land and often resented the plantation owners. None of this however, led them to any identification with the slaves. On the contrary, black people were despised as inferiors and the slaveholders made sure the poor whites were well aware of the 'psychological wage' – Du Bois's famous phrase – that the slave economy bestowed upon them; their white skin made them superior even if they often lived in abject poverty. In this environment then, 'white privilege' on the surface seemed to reflect a lived reality. If you were white you could not be owned by another human being, but compared to the plantocracy of the South, all other whites in the Southern states were in inferior positions. This characteristic of the 'Southern way of life', if not an affront to Christianity, was certainly at odds with the US Constitution that insisted on the supposedly universal 'inalienable' rights and equality before the law.

This thoroughly racist society, in the South but also in the North, where there were a relatively small number of free black people, was able to gestate, on the margins, a handful of abolitionists who identified the primary contradiction that plagued the republic – a land of the free built on slavery. They sought to nullify it and to instead embrace the fundamental equality of African-Americans with their white 'superiors'. These were exceptional Americans such as John Brown but others too such as the congressional abolitionist leaders Thaddeus Stevens and Charles Sumner. White privilege theory cannot explain how such persons came to be except to say, unconvincingly, that they were the exception that proved the rule. If you are ignorant of the full panorama of US history then this may seem a valid stance. But the Civil War and the period of radical reconstruction that came two years after its end and lasted for ten years, saw thousands of African-Americans take political office at both state and national level for the first time, with Congressmen and senators among them. This revolution, which we don't have space to fully consider here, did see African-Americans and a minority of Southern whites make common cause in the Republican parties of the South, in addition to the many thousands of white Northerners who headed south, men and women, to help in the work of the Freedmen's Bureau and to build the new reconstructed governments. It was not until the early 1880s that the gains of reconstruction were fully defeated and racial discrimination and terror institutionalised in the Jim Crow regimes of the South.

The news of the raid on the federal armoury at Harpers Ferry and the ultimate defeat of Brown's ambitious plan, including its more utopian aspect that envisaged a new constitution being proclaimed in the newly liberated zones, struck America like a thunderbolt – but it wasn't exactly out of the blue. Despite many citizens maintaining a state of denial on the import of the slavery question, Brown's attack succeeded in forcing the whole society to face up to the salient fact that slavery threatened to destroy the Union; slavery was the critical and intractable issue of the day. Brown's action demanded that the American public confront this reality.

Many in the abolitionist movement distanced themselves from Brown when the news of the raid spread, while others disowned him entirely, although many of the same people had provided money for his plan without knowing it involved an attack on US government facilities. The slaveholders, predictably, labelled Brown not just a madman but a terrorist too. Key players in the Southern war effort feature in the raid and its aftermath. It was future confederate general Robert E Lee who led the counter-attack on the abolitionist raiders. Jefferson Davis, future president of the Confederacy was on the investigating committee of the court. The conduct of the court was nothing less than a show trial and summary justice. Brown was denied the chance to appoint his own lawyers, subpoenas were not sent to those who he had hoped would testify on his behalf, money was stolen from him so he couldn't pay for his legal defence. And as the trial of sorts unfolded it was the courage, bravery, humanitarian countenance, principled integrity and generosity of John Brown that meant by the end of it he had won millions of admirers in the North and even the grudging acceptance of some in the South that he had indeed shown both bravery and compassion (toward the prisoners/hostages that they had taken but not killed).

When the sentence of death by hanging was delivered on 2 November 1859, John Brown delivered one of the most memorable and well-known speeches of American history. It was a speech that touched on and answered many of those questions we asked at the beginning:

> The New Testament teaches me that all things whatsoever I would that men should do to me, I should do even so to them.... I have endeavoured to act on that instruction. I am yet too young to understand that God is any respecter of persons. I believe that to have interfered, as I have done,...in behalf of His despised poor, is no wrong, but right. Now, if it is deemed necessary that I should forfeit my life for the furtherance of the ends of justice, and mingle my blood farther with the blood of my children and the blood of millions in this slave country whose rights are disregarded by wicked, cruel, and unjust enactments, I say let it be done.

Such was the fear that Brown engendered in the South that 3,000 soldiers were brought up by Lee to guard the execution site. All outsiders were barred from attending the execution, with the exception of a handful of reporters. Cannon were trained on the prison – there was talk in abolitionist circles of plans to free Brown but they came to nothing and besides, Brown had long ago decided it would be better for the cause that he died a martyr. He had spent his time in court lain on his back because of his injuries, often with his eyes closed and a blanket over his head – he was hardly likely to be able to affect his own escape even if he had wanted to.

The Virginian authorities were putting on a show of force to reassure the slaveholders that there would be no slave insurrection and if there was it would be crushed with the utmost exemplary violence, as the South was in the habit of doing with all matters related to the 'insubordination' and discipline of slaves. Obviously the slavers were not against violence per se as the slave system was built on it, rather they were against violence that challenged their rule. Like the rulers of all states before and since, they held a monopoly on violence and it was this that bestowed 'legitimacy' on their whips, shackles and, in the case of John Brown, hangman's noose.

A month after the trial ended the day of execution arrived. The previous night John Brown wrote his last words. They were prophetic: 'I, John Brown, am quite certain that the crimes of this guilty land will never be purged away but with blood. I had, as I now think vainly, flattered myself that without very much bloodshed it might be done.'

Du Bois provides a handy summation of the philosophy and meaning of John Brown, the eternal truth of his universal message of fighting oppression and that it was God's work:

John Brown loved his neighbour as himself. He could not endure therefore to see his neighbour, poor, unfortunate or oppressed. This natural sympathy was strengthened by a saturation in Hebrew religion which stressed the personal responsibility of every human soul to a just God. To this religion of equality and sympathy with misfortune, was added the strong influence of the social doctrines of the French Revolution with its emphasis on freedom and power in political life. And on all this was built John Brown's own inchoate but growing belief in a more just and more equal distribution of property. From this he concluded – and acted on that conclusion – that all men are created free and equal, and that the cost of liberty is less than the price of repression.

This passage brings to the fore another as yet unconsidered lesson of Brown's legacy. He sought to join up the dots, to draw out the links between one injustice and another. It was no accident that many abolitionists also supported other key struggles of the mid-nineteenth century reform movement in America, such as free public schools, an end to property qualifications for voting, ending imprisonment of debtors, and the right of women to vote.

Among the troops 'defending' the scaffolds from would-be attackers was one John Wilkes Booth – the assassinator of Abraham Lincoln. He admitted freely to his 'undeniable contempt... for the traitor and terroriser' Brown. A terroriser of slaveholders he certainly was; and that is what made him a fighter for the liberation of oppressed men and women, a fight that continues today in Ferguson in that old slave state of Missouri and beyond.

IBN ARABI AND HOW TO BE HUMAN

Sa'diyya Shaikh

As human beings we continue to grapple with the perennial existential questions. Why are we here? What is the purpose of human existence? What is the ultimate end of human life? What is human nature? How do we live with integrity and beauty as human beings? How do we discern and enact virtue? How do human beings live in harmony with each other and with other forms of existence? What is the relationship between social ethics and spiritual transformation? What is the nature of connections between the individual and the social, or the realms of the personal and those of the political?

These questions invariably lead us to issues of diversity and difference. When it comes to diversity, issues of race are not all that different from concerns about gender. As Samia Rahman noted in her article on misogyny in Islam, Muslim scholars have often seen the other half of humanity as 'the race of women'. Today some people (more often men), tend to think about gender as a separate question from being human; some see it as one of 'those women's issues' and consider it as secondary or incidental to the deeper human pursuits of spiritual transformation. In fact, it should actually be a less significant question since many of us agree that men and women have access to the same spiritual realities. So gender ideally should be simply one more manifestation of divine grace and plenitude. However in reality, spirituality is always also lived, experienced and engaged within interpersonal and social spaces which are saturated by gender-biased and hierarchical norms. So, many women seeking a life of spiritual growth and social engagement often encounter a gender barricade at some point or other in their lives. This is true for women in a variety of religious traditions.

Gender hierarchies within and outside religions most often intersect with a number of other prevailing forms of injustice. Despite staggering diversity, our world continues to be characterised by global socio-economic and gendered structures that benefit a relatively small elite group of people. These insidious global hegemonies are accompanied by social norms that prize aggressive individualism and self-interest, and which are thoroughly enmeshed in intersecting axes of gendered/raced/classed power. In many contexts, political, economic, family, and religious institutions serve to reproduce the privilege of elite groups. Specialised studies in the social sciences might analyse the impact of globalising capital markets on specific local political economies or ways in which invisible structural relations reinforce forms of racism, sexism, heterosexism, or class privilege in particular societies. However, from a religious perspective another set of questions might arise: do these external inequalities, or social injustices and ecological imbalances have a spiritual dimension? Is there an underlying human spiritual deficit responsible for social hierarchies and discriminatory ideologies? What might be some of the principle deficits in human nature that support sexist, racist, classist narratives? Why is there seemingly such a short supply of human sociality and ethics characterised by values of generosity, compassion, empathy, and collective care and social concern? How do we foster alternatives to the prevalent hierarchical and masculinist ways of being human, practices that continue to deliver a harvest of war, destruction, suffering, and death? What models of human nature might produce different ways of being and social possibilities?

In struggling with sexist religious practices and teachings in my own context, I have realised that most justifications for gender inequality were based on an underlying problematic: a biased and discriminatory religious conception of human nature. In religious studies jargon we describe such an essential shortcoming to be part of a deficiency in 'gendered religious anthropology'. In other words, patriarchal behaviour and social ethics are often built on religious ideas of the human person. And religious ideas are in turn gendered in distinct and exclusivist ways. In my search for alternative and more egalitarian foundational narratives of the human person, I discovered the works of a prolific and original thinker, the thirteenth century Sufi, Muhyi al-Din ibn al-Arabi.

In ibn Arabi's works, I found that issues of gender and related ethical norms were embedded within an Islamic cosmology that deeply engaged the questions of what it means to be a human being. Here, politics and spirituality informed each other in a genuinely integrated manner and speak directly to contemporary Muslim concerns. Ibn Arabi's thought could be applied not only to critique patriarchy and sexism but is equally valuable for the conceptions of self and power, aspects that animate and inform social hierarchies such as racism and classism.

Ibn Arabi and His Critics

Abd Allah Muhammad al-ʿArabi was born in Murcia, southern Spain, in 1165 and as a young man reportedly experienced mystical visions of God. He travelled extensively in search of learned and wise teachers. His continuing mystical visions became the basis of his numerous writings, and he began to write his magnum opus, *The Meccan Openings (Al-Futuhat al-Makkiyya)* in 1201, during his first visit to Mecca. Here, he met a Persian Sufi, a woman only known as Nizam, who came to represent for him the embodiment of divine love and beauty. In fact, ibn Arabi appears to have had pervasive and rich interactions with women, not only among his spiritual teachers but also within his family and among his disciples. Ibn Arabi also reported having encountered the ever living spiritual figure of Khidr, the prophet who initiates people directly into spiritual life from the unseen realms without the regular initiation into a traditional Sufi path (*tariqa*). He finally settled in Damascus where he died in 1240 at the age of seventy-five.

There is no exact record of the number of books ibn Arabi wrote. He mentions 300, a significant number of which are extant, with copies in various libraries in the Muslim world and in Europe. *The Meccan Openings* is the largest of his works, comprising 560 chapters dealing with a great variety of topics, ranging from highly abstract principles of metaphysics, to discussions on law and ethics, to ibn Arabi's personal spiritual experiences. This work took him close to thirty years to complete. The contemporary scholar of Sufism, Seyyed Hossein Nasr, remarks that this compendium of esoteric sciences in Islam surpasses in scope and depth anything of its kind composed previously or since. Ibn Arabi states that the *Futuhat* was the product of unveilings given to him by God rather than a product of personal reflection. This work has been studied and commented on by generations of Sufis and scholars of Islam.

Perhaps the most popular of ibn Arabi's works is the *The Bezels of Wisdom (Fusus al-Hikam),* which was written in 1229. Ibn Arabi reported that this

work was inspired by a vision of the Prophet Muhammad who commanded
him to take a book from the Prophet's hand and transmit it to the world for
the benefit of humankind. In this text, each 'bezel' symbolises a facet of
divine wisdom respectively revealed to each of the Abrahamic prophets
recognised in Islam. The human and spiritual nature of each prophet was a
vehicle for communicating and manifesting particular facets of the divine.
Ibn Arabi's chapter on the Prophet Muhammad is linked to a profound
reflection on human nature and origin through revisiting the mythic origins
of humanity in Adam and Eve. Thus ibn Arabi's culminating chapter of the
Bezels is simultaneously devoted to the single-most-important figure in the
Muslim tradition, the Prophet Muhammad.

In this meditation on the Prophet Muhammad's spiritual nature, ibn Arabi
offers extensive discussion on gender and male-female relationships. For ibn
Arabi, the Prophet Muhammad is not only the final messenger and seal of
the prophets but also the ultimate model of human spiritual realisation,
embodying some of the deepest existential dimensions of divine oneness or
monotheism (*tawhid*); what ibn Arabi describes in this chapter as the divine
wisdom of singularity (*fardiyya*). This masterful discussion presents the
reader with one of ibn Arabi's most compelling explanations of the nature
of identity and intimacy between God and humanity and of human
knowledge of God. Gender is integrally woven into ibn Arabi's cosmological
fabric of ultimate value and existential significance. In his view, gender is
linked to the archetypal model of complete spiritual refinement, the
Prophet Muhammad. For ibn Arabi, 'singularity' also signifies the
ontological relationship between men and men, and men and women,
thereby providing them with a sign to apprehend their oneness with God.
Given that the Prophet Muhammad symbolises such crucial dimensions of
ibn Arabi's worldview, it is enormously significant that some of ibn Arabi's
central teachings on the nature of gender, men, and women are found in the
chapter on Muhammad in the *Bezels*. *The Bezels of Wisdom* and *The Meccan
Openings* are considered ibn Arabi's two most significant works.

Ibn Arabi's corpus also includes works ranging from topics of theology,
mysticism, philosophy, jurisprudence and Qur'anic exegesis to poetry,
biography, and mythology. He constantly challenged normative boundaries
in his substantive teachings. His style of presentation often involved
antinomies, paradoxes, and unusual allegories to convey spiritual insights or

esoteric exegeses of the Qur'an—methods that were commonly employed in works of mystical expression. Ibn Arabi's utilisation of this vast, varying range of expressions and discursive windows makes for a hermeneutically rich body of spiritual insights.

Alexander Knysh, Professor of Islamic Studies at University of Michigan, marvels at ibn Arabi's adept and extraordinary style, wherein even the recurring motifs he used escaped being mundane or repetitive. According to Knysh, the variety of different discursive expressions flowing from ibn Arabi's expert hand 'colours the very visions and experiences he endeavours to convey, making it difficult to neatly separate content from form'. the 'new verbal shells transform the very meaning of these motifs'. The diversity of disciplinary and linguistic expressions that ibn Arabi employs to present his ideas adds a textured fluidity to his thought. Ibn Arabi has been heralded as one of the most sophisticated theoreticians of Sufi metaphysics and as a distinguished practical master in his time, and contemporary scholars have illustrated the pervasive impact of his legacy in both popular and intellectual Sufi discourses.

Ibn Arabi is also perhaps one of the most contested figures in Muslim intellectual history. In a detailed study on polemical literature surrounding ibn Arabi, Alexander Knysh notes that from the thirteenth century onwards, practically every significant Muslim thinker found it necessary to comment on this controversial Sufi thinker. In Muslim literature, refutations of his work are interlaced with accusations of dangerous heresy – a heresy that many of his accusers saw as the combination of a riotous mystical imagination with a pantheistic philosophy that threatened to destroy the foundations of Islam. However, some of his supporters revere him as one of the most erudite intellectuals and spiritual savants within the Islamic tradition.

The iconic position and stature that he enjoys among his disciples and admirers are reflected in the epithet accorded him as 'the Greatest Master' (*Shaykh al-Akbar*). Among religious scholars, opinions of ibn Arabi ranged from claims that he was an infidel to arguments that he was the reigning axial saint of the time (*qutb*). One of the most strident and consequential critics of ibn Arabi was the fourteenth-century ibn Taymiyya. Incensed by what followers of ibn Arabi described as the doctrine of *wahdat al-wujud* (unity of being), ibn Taymiyya launched a frontal attack on the unifying tendencies of ibn Arabi's metaphysics. In ibn Taymiyya's sombre view, such a metaphysical system disturbingly ruptured the clear boundaries between God and humanity, between human freedom and predestination, between good and evil. The intractable jurist argued that the goal of true Sufism was to serve God more perfectly, not to delve into the impregnable mysteries of God's being or desire intimacy with the divine.

Underlying much of the controversies about ibn Arabi's metaphysical system were contestations of God's relationship to humanity. Particularly threatening to ibn Taymiyya and his ilk was the fact that ibn Arabi's metaphysics blurred the clear-cut hierarchy between God and humanity, thus leading to a type of immanentist approach, which was not regarded as properly observant of God's transcendence. For ibn Taymiyya, a view that human beings, through love, could know and cultivate an existential intimacy with God was heretical, bordering on Christian doctrines of incarnation (*hulul*) and union (*ittihad*).

Patriarchal theologies often excessively focus on elements of God's distance, majesty and transcendence. In my view, it is not entirely coincidental that distant autocratic images of God are paralleled by social and personal norms that foreground hierarchal modes of power between men and men and men and women. Within a patriarchal imaginary, relationships between the Divine and the human are commonly conceptualised through vertical modes of dominion and sovereign control, rather than horizontal modes of mutual engagement and intimate reciprocity. Proponents of such patriarchal approaches may also denigrate materiality and the body and, by extension, women, whom they primarily identify with the bodily principle. In my view traces of these types of religious anthropologies often underlie contemporary Muslim positions that do not cater for women in mosque spaces, demand segregated social spaces or argue that women cannot hold positions of social or ritual leadership.

It is not surprising that ibn Arabi's worldview, which equally foregrounded humanity's intimacy with God, viewing all creation as spheres of divine manifestation, provided a map of God-human relationships that is also portrayed as loving, reciprocal, intimate and mutually informing. More especially, ibn Arabi's religious anthropology is characterised by positive evaluations of materiality, embodiment and women, while also expressing alternative gender norms based on reciprocity and mutual enhancement between men and women. There appears to be a noteworthy correspondence between theological imagination and gendered social models. Ibn Arabi's particular assimilation of the notion of God's immanence and intimacy with human beings was found to be too bold in its theological assertions on human nature and too dangerous in terms of its social consequences. At the same time, ibn Arabi's insistence on both the transcendence and immanence of God pointed to the paradox of the divine nature that could never be contained by the fetters of human reason.

Yet other Muslim thinkers were known personally to have admired ibn Arabi's ideas while denouncing him publicly. Some religious scholars believed that ibn Arabi's teachings should be restricted to an elite group of qualified adept Sufis able to understand the complexities and intricacies of his metaphysics. In this view, the deep esoteric nature of his insights, with their nuanced constellation of ideas, would not be accessible to the general Muslim population, which would invariably misunderstand and distort. Adherents of this perspective saw ibn Arabi's ideas as perilous only when they were exposed to the limitations of spiritually unrefined human beings who could not understand the subtlety of his ideas.

Other advocates of ibn Arabi reject depictions of him as an anarchist unconcerned with social order and as a metaphysician tearing away the shield of divine transcendence. On the contrary, they argue, his ideas reflect invaluable insights into the heart of the Qur'an and *sunnah*. Based on these primary sources and inspired by mystical unveilings, proponents of this view assert that ibn Arabi's cosmological panoply superbly integrated both divine immanence and transcendence into his theological schema. They astutely point to the glaring absence of peer opposition to ibn Arabi during his lifetime, indicating that his contemporaries recognised his personal piety and impeccable adherence to Islamic rites.

Debates regarding ibn Arabi have not been limited to religious scholars. Rulers and politicians have also instrumentalised the enduring ibn Arabi controversy. The Ottoman rulers were particularly enamored with the *Shaykh al-Akbar*. Kemal Pashazade, a sixteenth-century Ottoman statesman and scholar, issued an official ban on public defamations of ibn Arabi, while Sultan Selim I commissioned an official defence for ibn Arabi's ideas. Conversely, as recently as 1979, some members of the People's Assembly, the lower house of the Egyptian bicameral parliament, unsuccessfully attempted to enact an official ban on ibn Arabi's teachings. The American scholar of religion, Thomas Emil Homerin points out how the Egyptian government attempted to use this religious controversy to gain political leverage. Conflicting images of ibn Arabi have thus been utilised for centuries to enable and disable varying ideological agendas.

God and Human Nature

Ibn Arabi's writings on human spirituality present us with compelling perspectives of God, self and human relationships. In reflecting on human origins, ibn Arabi draws on narratives from the Qur'an and the traditions of the Prophet (hadith), focusing on the idea that 'God taught Adam all of the names', (Q2:30) and that God created the human being in God's own form. In this context, Adam represents the archetypal human being; he is neither merely a prophet nor simply a male human being. In this creation narrative, human origins are linked to knowledge of the divine 'names' or attributes described in the Qur'an as 'the beautiful names' (al-asma al-husna). For ibn Arabi then, an understanding of the divine names is indispensable to genuinely comprehending human nature and purpose.

God is seen to have ninety-nine names, qualities, or attributes that together exist in a state of unity (tawhid). Like many other Muslim thinkers, ibn Arabi separates the divine names into two groups which have several sets of corresponding relationships with one another. These are broadly categorised into names of beauty (jamal) and majesty (jalal). Names of beauty (jamal) include the Most Generous, The Forgiver, The All-Compassionate, The Merciful, The Loving, The Subtle; whilst names of majesty (jalal) include The Powerful, The Compeller, The Firm, The Overwhelming, The All-High, The Great, Possessor of Majesty and Honour. Within God, all of these manifold attributes exist in harmony together.

In this narrative of creation, from the original state of Divine Oneness all things come into existence through these varied qualities or attributes. Emerging from the unified One, the divine attributes or names are birthed into the cosmos, taking multiple created forms echoed in God's utterance: 'I was a Hidden treasure and I loved to be known so I created the world in order that I might be known'. This is a hadith qudsi, where the Prophet utters the words of God. It has been discussed extensively by many Sufis including ibn Arabi; it presents us with an image of a God whose reason for creation emerges from a deep longing for intimacy. For human beings it suggests that our origin and existential purpose is to reflect the Divine and only in so doing is a person able to gain deepest self-knowledge. Also underlying this tale is a central teaching about the relationship between Oneness and multiplicity, between universality and diversity, between identity and difference. Underlying all the manifold and diverse forms of creation is a pulsating unity of being and of origin.

In this imaginary, human beings are portrayed as unique having the potential to comprehensively reflect all the divine attributes, attributes scattered more diffusely in the rest of the cosmos. This archetypal capacity is described by Sufis as *al-Insan al-Kamil* (the complete human) where the human being constitutes a polished and complete mirror to the Divine Treasure seeking to be known. The term, *al-Insan al-Kamil* does not refer to all actual individuals but rather refers to human capacities realised in some people and not others. As such, *al-Insan al-Kamil* represents the ultimate and universal map of human purpose which illustrates a spiritually and ethically refined human being.

Such a complete human being embodies the full range of divine attributes, harmoniously integrating qualities of beauty with those of majesty. At the collective level, one might view the Muslim ethical and legal traditions as endeavours to create broad parameters for the development of precisely such balances both at social and individual levels. In addition, *tasawuf* or the mystical traditions have facilitated these processes of human balance through intimate and individual teaching relationships. A novice may be guided by an advanced spiritual teacher through the critical and sensitive issue of recognising the specific limits and proportions of the different divine attributes, and about the best ways to combine and synchronise these qualities. Here ibn Arabi advises the student that love, compassion, sincerity, receptivity and surrender, all derived from *jamali* names, are the starting and returning point of all spiritual work. As such the constant cultivation of *jamali* attributes creates an inner ripeness for the correct form of receptivity to the powerful and more volatile *jalali* attributes of majesty. That ibn Arabi grants a practical precedence to *jamali* attributes for the human being is consistent with a broader existential priority of the *jamali* dimensions within the God reflected in the latter's statement 'My mercy embraces everything' (Qur'an 7:156) and the *hadith qudsi*, where God states 'My mercy precedes my wrath.' For a person who desires spiritual development and would like to embody the perfect balance of divine attributes, ibn Arabi, like many other Sufis, highlights the foundational importance of *jamali* qualities.

Simultaneously, ibn Arabi cautions the seeker against assuming the more risky and potentially treacherous *jalali* attributes at the outset. An imbalance or misalignment of these majestic qualities renders a person particularly vulnerable to spiritual danger. In particular ibn Arabi warns people in positions of social authority to be vigilant against the false impression that they have any innate or natural superiority – a misconception that ultimately results in what he describes as a state of ignorance and spiritual negligence. This insight is particularly helpful in highlighting the fact that male or racial privilege in patriarchal and neo-colonial societies are products of social power relations rather than a natural status quo. While for many of us the latter may be a self-evident sociological observation in our societies, ibn Arabi additionally informs us that such social power imbalances are spiritually damaging to all people in a society.

Within Sufi psychology, unrefined *jalali* qualities not sufficiently distilled through the filters of *jamali* qualities are more easily manipulated by the egotistical insinuations of the lower self or the 'self that commands to evil' (*nafs al-ammara*). The state of the *nafs al-ammara* is one dominated by base instincts and cravings, an uncanny parallel to modern Freudian notions of the Id. When in the clutches of the *nafs al-ammara* a person is blind to the real nature of reality and may be characterised by, amongst other things, being self-absorbed, falsely acquisitive, arrogant, and constantly seeking more prestige and authority. Within Islam, the dangers of this type of spiritual deficiency are captured in the wretched narrative of Iblis or Satan who epitomised an unrefined *jalal* in his refusal to obey God's command to prostrate before Adam. Satan's arrogant belief in his own superiority veiled him from receptivity to God, and ultimately resulted in his exclusion from the realm of divine intimacy.

So too with human beings the wiles of the lower self may prompt them to unjustly assert divine attributes of power, and in so doing obstruct their spiritual progress. These insights are particularly productive when applied to a contemporary analysis of gender power relations. Accordingly male claims

of authority and control on the basis of gender can be seen to reflect a lack
of spiritual refinement and receptivity to the purifying impact of the divine
jamal. Here ibn Arabi's prioritisation of *jamali* attributes and more cautious
approach to the *jalali* qualities echo earlier Sufi ideas. An early Sufi story
recorded by Farid al-Din Attar beautifully captures such a critique. The
renowned female mystic Rabia al-Adawiyya (d. 801) was visited by a group
of religious men who goadingly declared, 'All the virtues have been scattered
on the heads of men. The crown of prophethood has been placed on men's
heads. The belt of nobility has been fastened around men's waists. No woman
has ever been a prophet.' Without skipping a beat, Rabia evenly replied, 'All
that is true, but egoism and self-worship and 'I am your Lord' have never
sprung from a woman's breast. ... All these things have been the speciality
of men.' Here Rabia's response effectively constitutes a piercing spiritual
critique of male claims to superiority, linking such claims to the depraved
state of Pharaoh. The Qur'an depicts Pharaoh as the archetypal disbeliever
whose spiritual blindness is captured in his delusionary statement 'I am your
Lord' (Q.79:24). In Rabia's story assertions of privilege on the basis of
gender reflect the victory of the *nafs al-ammara* which has shrewdly
misguided these men from the true nature of power and reality. Notably,
Rabia also refocuses on the key Sufi principles: it is a human being's inner
state and receptivity to God that constitute the genuine yardsticks for value
and truth. Socially constructed hierarchies, including gender privilege, that
deflect and detract from the true source of reality are spiritually harmful to
all, including the supposed beneficiaries of such biases.

   This story also cautions the believer that patriarchal power cultivates
arrogance among men which in turn veils them to the nature of their
receptive relationship to God. At the same time, women's relatively more
tenuous social locations may serve to be spiritually advantageous in that it
facilitates a clearer awareness of one's dependency on God. As such,
perceived social weakness when appropriately spiritually aligned, may grant
easier access to spiritual discernment. While this insight is spiritually
significant it might also have potentially dangerous political implications.
Many Sufis are conscious and wary of the internal impact of social power,
recognition and praise as part of their practice. An important aspect of Sufi
cultivation is thus a constant remembrance of a human being's utter
indigence and dependence on God's grace. This abiding awareness of one's

deep existential need for God requires a spiritual state of receptivity captured well in the Sufi description of the seeker as the *faqir* (the poor one). In this regard, Sufism reflects an inversion of dominant social norms, where the starting point for the Sufi path places greater value on weakness and dependency rather than on strength and independence. Such priorities present a glaring contrast to the images of manhood acclaimed in many patriarchies. For Sufis, the awareness of existential weakness and dependency constitutes a spiritual strength. From this lens, men in patriarchies are spiritually disadvantaged by the trappings of male power, an insight that is potentially transformative.

Nonetheless, there is also an underside to this perspective: the grave danger that women's social powerlessness in patriarchal societies might be framed as a spiritual 'advantage,' and hence good for women. Such a view ends up providing a spiritualised and apologetic legitimisation of inequality. Detrimentally such a limited view ignores the crucial point that women's position of social weakness is the product of damaging political and structural inequalities. Sufism has historically existed and continues to do so in many patriarchal contexts, sometimes even complicitly with patriarchy and a subtle but distinctive assumption in Sufism stubbornly flouts a patriarchal logic. While many forms of patriarchal power have only allowed for limited types of female subjectivity, often negating central human possibilities for women's selves, Sufism is potentially premised on a different process. For most Sufis, the curbing of the ego is not about the negation of self as much as it is about a process of self-mastery, discipline and detachment from the usual forms of social power, which in turn facilitates increasing forms of receptivity to the Divine. For many contemporary Muslims it becomes clear that these spiritual processes are better aided by the creation of social spaces that support the formation of authentic female and male selves, based on equality between the sexes and mutual respect, even while differences are valued.

In deepening the exploration of power from a Sufi perspective, it is helpful to refer to another well-known Sufi narrative of Rabia, this time involving a celebrated early Sufi man Hasan al-Basri (d.728). Purportedly Hasan, seeking to impress the illustrious Rabia, threw his prayer rug onto the surface of the lake, walked on water to his prayer rug calling Rabia to join him in prayer. Her response to this spectacle of supernatural power was to caution Hasan that if he wanted to flaunt his 'spiritual goods in the worldly market' he should do things that his peers could not match. And as she said this she threw her own prayer mat into the air, flew up to it, and asked Hasan to join her. Since Hasan's spiritual powers did not extend to such a station, he was awkwardly silenced. But Rabia was not interested in immature gloating or simply showing him up; instead she used this as a valuable teaching moment telling him: 'Hasan, what you did, fish also do, and what I did, flies also do. The real work transcends both these tricks. One must apply oneself to the real work.'

Paradoxically this story in fact reveals Rabia's 'spiritual goods' to be superior to Hasan's, who was among the most prominent early male Sufis. More significantly however, Rabia exposes the fruitless nature of spiritual conceit and sensationalist miracles. Her wisdom and abilities suggest a spiritually refined individual who harmoniously integrates a fine balance of both *jamali* and *jalali* attributes, the birthright of men and women alike. The story reflects core Sufi teachings that spiritual growth involves eliminating conceit and spiritual arrogance, that egotistical need for public recognition can insidiously infiltrate spiritual life, and that the sincere seeker is to protect against such instincts constantly, maintaining a singular focus on God.

The narrative also prudently informs us that wisdom, insight and spiritual abilities are not contingent on gender. As it happens, men in both these stories exhibit the baser spiritual vices of arrogance, vanity, and self-importance. Rabia emerges as witty, wise, and spiritually advanced, displaying superior insights into mystical realities – her powerful *jalali* attributes appear to emerge from a full surrender and immersion in the divine *jamal*. Through diminishing the desire of her *nafs al-ammara* she is able to discern and reflect back to the divine source unencumbered. The men in these stories on the other hand, are represented as conceited, with the desire to impress others or assert authority – characteristics and behaviour which are spiritual traps set by the lower self or the *nafs al-ammara*. Gender hierarchies resulting from these illusionary, and transient sources of power blind people from perceiving the true nature of reality and dominion which alone belongs to God. As such, claims of superiority by men reflect on their spiritual inadequacies, and are confronted by the uncompromising Rabia. These stories, exemplifying central Sufi principles, also present compelling challenges to the basis of gender discrimination. Interpreted in this manner, progress on the spiritual path may imply direct challenges to arbitrary hierarchical impulses as they arise.

In addition to portraying women as amongst the earliest Muslim teachers of wisdom, Sufi sources also present us with historical portraits of women who were recognised as having attained the highest spiritual stations amidst their male and female cohort. Ibn Arabi presents us with rich accounts of his female teachers whose spiritual mastery he describes in intricate detail and with deep admiration. During the formative period of his life, he met, studied with, and served as a disciple to two women saints, Fatima ibn al-Muthanna and Yasmina Umm al-Fuqara and he discusses his relationship to these spiritual savants in both his *The Spirit of Holiness in the Counselling of the Soul (Ruh al-Quds fi Munasahat al-Nafs)* and *The Precious Pearl (Al-Durrat al-Fakhira)*.

About Yasmina, or 'Shams,' a woman in her eighties who lived at Marchena of the Olives, ibn Arabi tells us that he visited her frequently and expresses tremendous admiration for her:

> Among people of our kind I have never met one like her with respect to the control she had over her soul. In her spiritual activities and communications, she was among the greatest. She had a strong and pure heart, a noble spiritual power, and a fine discrimination... She was endowed with many graces. I had considerable experience of her intuition and found her to be a master in this sphere. Her spiritual state was characterised chiefly by her fear of God and his good pleasure in her, the combination of the two at the same time in one person being extremely rare among us.

He goes on to describe some of her supernatural abilities, including her ability to perceive things and communicate at great distances as well as the power to voice other people's thoughts. Ibn Arabi marvels at the accuracy of her mystical insights and her miraculous acts.

Here, as elsewhere, ibn Arabi accords full recognition to the spiritual mastery of a woman mystic, depicting her as superior in ability and attainment to many of her male contemporaries. She is depicted as an ideal spiritual aspirant and a role model for her fellow Sufis. There is nothing exclusively or traditionally female in his description of her spirituality; she embodies not only gracious and merciful qualities but also mastery, strength, nobility, fine discrimination, and control of her soul. She epitomises a balance of *jamali* and *jalali* qualities. Among Sufi masters, she is one among equals and is in fact distinctive in virtue and excellence. Ibn

Arabi tells us that he frequently visited her and he felt extremely privileged that Shams privately revealed to him the secrets of her spiritual state. This comment reflects not only his respect and admiration for her but also signals the intense interpersonal interaction among individual Sufi men and women in that context.

Ibn Arabi's admiration of Sufi women was not restricted to his teachers; he also describes a number of his female cohorts. *The Spirit of Holiness* contains an entry about a peer of his, an anonymous slave girl who ibn Arabi describes as unique in the time, gifted with supernatural abilities to commune with mountains and trees and able to travel great distances quickly. He admired her because her 'spiritual state was strong' and because she adhered to the Sufi path with 'unswerving sincerity.' She was rigorous in self-discipline and frequently fasted through the day and night, earning ibn Arabi's highest praise: 'I have never seen one more spiritually chivalrous in our time.'

Of another prominent Sufi woman, Zainab al-Qal'iyya, ibn Arabi tells us that despite being gifted with beauty and wealth, she had freely renounced the world, and he describes her as the 'foremost ascetic of her day,' and 'one of the most intelligent people of her time.' Ibn Arabi accompanied this great spiritual savant on a journey from Mecca to Jerusalem, observing that he had never seen anyone more meticulous in heeding the times of prayer than her. In some historical Muslim contexts, therefore, it appears that unrelated Sufi men and women interacted freely in social spaces, even travelling great distances together.

Ibn Arabi also mentions a significant number of female disciples. In a series of short poems at the beginning of his work, *The Diwan*, ibn Arabi names fourteen students that he had invested with the *khirqa* (Sufi cloak); thirteen of whom were women. Investiture of the *khirqa* signified a binding initiatory relationship, which enabled the process of inner transformation of the student, linking him or her to a chain of spiritual transmission (*silsila*) that originated with the Prophet Muhammad. While he undoubtedly transferred the *khirqa* to many male disciples, it is noteworthy that the majority of named disciples are women. With the notable exception of one, all the other women are approvingly described as genuine and accomplished disciples, including his generous praise for those distinguished by outstanding spiritual realisations on the path.

In addition to the numerous references to accomplished women Sufis in ibn Arabi's writings, one also finds his clear conceptual and religious positions on human nature that are explicitly gender-inclusive. He repeatedly points out that the station of *al-Insan al-Kamil*, the most comprehensive standard for human realisation, is ungendered, makes identical demands on men and women, and is attainable equally by both. In a profound commentary on the Qur'anic verse 33:35, he expands on the spiritual treasures delineated in that verse to describe forty-nine types of sainthood and their related forms of attainment, noting the inclusion of both men and women. Explicitly adding the phrase 'from among men and women' after his discussion of each saintly categories, ibn Arabi effectively echoes 33:35 which also describes the various virtues of believers in both masculine and feminine terms. He concludes this discussion by stating there is not a spiritual quality conferred on men that is denied to women.

Elsewhere ibn Arabi clearly states that a woman may occupy the highest rank in the spiritual hierarchy, namely, that of the reigning and axial saint (*Qutb*) of a period. In Sufi cosmology, the *Qutb* is the spiritual pivot or the axis of the universe in the invisible realm around which the welfare, needs and governance of the world revolve, and which pervades every other dimension of reality. In this discussion ibn Arabi reiterates an all-embracing approach by stating that 'everything that a man can attain – spiritual stations, levels, or qualities – can be attained by women if God wills, just as they can be attained by men if God so wills.'

Given ibn Arabi's commitment to an integrated and unified worldview, he further presents nuanced discussions of how spiritual equality between men and women translate into the area of sociality and law. Addressing a number of juristic discussions on issues like women's leadership of communal ritual prayers (*salaat*) or women's capacity to set legal precedents for the entire community of believers, ibn Arabi presents compelling arguments for egalitarian positions. His approach is distinguished by a process of careful arguments that links the full social and legal capacity of women to the foundational view of humanity's spiritual and ontological equality. One example of ibn Arabi's integral connection between spiritual and social realms is lucidly demonstrated in his discussion on women's leadership of communal ritual prayers:

Some people allow the imamate of women absolutely before a congregation of men and women. I agree with this. Some forbid her imamate absolutely. Others permit her imamate in a congregation exclusively of women. How to evaluate this? The prophet has testified about the spiritual perfection [*kamal*] of some women just as he witnessed of some men, even though there may be more men than women in such perfection. This perfection is prophethood. And being a prophet involves taking on the role of a leader. Thus, women's imamate is sound. The basic principle is allowing women's imamate. Thus, whoever asserts that it is forbidden without proof, he should be ignored. The one who forbids this has no explicit text [*nass*]. His only proof in forbidding this is a shared [negative] opinion of her. This proof is insubstantial and the basic principle remains, which is allowing women's imamate.

Ibn Arabi presents an organic connection between spiritual equality and social and legal capacities. This approach has been described by American scholar Eric Winkel as 'spiritual legal discourse….that illuminates the crossover from outward ritual to inward truth'. For many Muslims a cohesive religious worldview needs precisely such a link between the inner spiritual life and the outer public sphere. Often religious rationalisations for social and sexist hierarchies are premised on underlying notions of fixed, naturalised and mutually exclusive differences between men and women. In resisting injustice, it is thus crucial to critically interrogate the gendered mappings of human nature underlying dominant narratives of hierarchy and discrimination.

Ibn Arabi's approach offers an illuminating perspective to contemporary Muslims engaged with processes of reform and rethinking in their contexts. It presents a way to critically examine social practices, community norms and prevailing religious laws by focusing on the underlying assumptions of human nature or the gendered religious anthropology. The method of 'the Greatest Master' allows us to enhance the search for integrity between on the one hand, the core theological understandings of human nature and spirituality, and on the other hand, the practical, social, ritual and legal realities. Such an approach will facilitate a more finely-honed scepticism amongst Muslims when they confront assertions that Islam is about a spiritual equality between men and women which is not accompanied by the necessary social transformations that also reflect such equality. Ibn Arabi's logic in the above argument presents a sharp counterpoint to Muslim approaches that present abstract notions of spiritual equality between men and women while accepting particular forms of gender hierarchies in the social and legal realms. His perspective in fact enables one to clearly discern the imbalance and spiritual dangers inherent in a masculinist worldview. Instead of seeking freedom and liberty only in an ineffable spiritual realm, ibn Arabi's worldview encourages us to seek a continuity and congruence between theological and spiritual perspectives on human nature, and practical demands for social equality.

Ibn Arabi is a teacher for our times who illumines a path for individual and social transformation. His mystical insights on the nature of God and humanity present Muslims with a view of reality that inspires human interactions based on values of compassion, generosity, love, care and justice – modes of human relationality and sociality that emerge from deep-rooted spiritual prerogatives. In this unified view of reality, personal cultivation and justice-based social activism both emerge as a spiritually-alive ethics of care that foregrounds Divine Mercy (*Jamal*). Moreover from this model we also know that a spiritual deficit occurs when human beings do *not* adhere to this sublime balance – qualities of greed, arrogance, deception, insincerity, covetousness, prejudice and injustice are socially malignant and personally destructive. Prejudicial models of social hierarchy – racism, sexism, classism, neo-colonialism – result from such spiritual imbalance. Conversely, a person's cultivation of spiritual attributes in terms of ibn Arabi's model, with its primacy on qualities of love and mercy, animate forms of communal relations that enhance human flourishing.

ESSAYS

ON PRE-ISLAMIC HAJJ

Barnaby Rogerson

The Hajj has always been a source of wonder to me. At first, I must confess out of sheer travel wanderlust. For central Arabia, like the mountains of Tibet, is one of those historical testing grounds for heroic British scholar travellers. That roll call includes Burkhardt, Burton, Doughty, Palgrave, St John-Philby, Lawrence, Thesiger – not to mention women of such remarkable character as Lady Cobbold and Rosita Forbes. Later I became fascinated by its vital, lodestone-like role for the Maghreb; how for the last fourteen hundred years, generation upon generation of North African scholars would be drawn to Mecca and Medina, as an act of piety – but would often return as little incubi of revolution in their homeland. The founder-preachers of the Almoravide and Almohad Empires for example, were both returning Hajjis. Whilst the Fatimid Caliphate, the Ommayad Caliphate of Cordoba, Idrissid Morocco, and such later dynasties as the Saadian and the current ruling Alauoite dynasty were all established by exiles and refugees from Mecca – a sort of reverse Hajj. The rapidity of connections within Islam was always hinged on this annual meeting of minds at Mecca.

So much so, that I knew the broad outline of what happened: the seven circles of the Kaaba, the running between the two hills (again seven times) the camp at Mina, the march out to Arafat, the stoning of three Satans (again in units of seven), leading to the sacrifice and the joyful return to the Kaaba. I never looked in detail at the origin of the Hajj rituals. It was one of those subjects you put to one side, presuming that your understanding of what exactly is happening to whom will eventually ripen once you get hold of the right book or the right teacher. In the meantime I listened to a lot of fascinating tales about Adam and Eve, Abraham, his Arabian concubine Hagar, (the five cuts of vengeance performed on her by vengeful Sarah) and their son Ishmael, the half-brother of Isaac. A rich and ever expanding store of oral tales, such as Abraham, performing that first circumcision on himself with an axe – but then he appears to have been a mountain of a man, and perhaps acquired fine skill with a blade working beside his sculptor father. At the back of my mind, was the expectation that sooner or later, I would understand how all this also fitted into the details of the Prophet Muhammad's life and most importantly, the revelation of the Qur'an. For that surely was the point of a Hajj pilgrimage? Like the Buddhist pilgrims going to see where the Lord Buddha received his revelation, or the Christians looking to find spots of Jesus's teaching, death and resurrection, or Jews looking for some fabric of the Temple of Solomon at Jerusalem in which to lodge their prayers – that was the point of the Hajj, surely? It took a long, long time, for the penny to drop.

I can remember the instance to this day. For I was once again quizzing a Muslim friend about their Hajj and their journey to Mecca, asking about the mountain of Light, Jebel Nur, where that first famous revelation came upon the forty-year-old Prophet. An incident in historical time that lies at the very heart of Islam for me. I was amazed to hear that not only was there no shrine or mosque there, but that there was some rather messy graffiti, some old quarry workings and that visitors were actually discouraged from ascending the mountain....Then it came to me. I finally realised that little about the Hajj rituals was based upon either the revelation of the Qur'an or the life of the Prophet.

So let's go over the history very briefly. After twelve years of Qur'anic revelation and preaching, Muhammad leaves the hostile environment of pagan Mecca, just before his attempted assassination, in 620. For the last six years his followers had been isolated, placed under a social and trade boycott, if not actively persecuted. They were excluded from any public rituals and naturally preferred to pray at home. They were a powerless minority of under a hundred people. Muhammad then led a ten-year struggle against the pagan aristocrats of Mecca. During year six of this war, he rather recklessly risked all his winnings in an attempt to join in the pilgrimage (a traditional period of truce) but was halted by his enemies. It was a moment of crisis. His followers were unarmed, and were so clearly attached to the sacred geography of Mecca, that they were reluctant to perform the rituals in another landscape. This event, at Hudabaiyah, is the only reported incidence of hesitancy amongst his followers. But they eventually did perform a version of the pilgrimage and out of this crisis, came a negotiated truce with the pagan enemy. This allowed Muhammad to lead his followers, the following year, into the landscape of Mecca and perform the traditional pilgrimage.

Muhammad and 2,000 followers were once again unarmed and clad in white linen, not naked like their pagan hosts, but were given just three days to rush through the rituals in empty Mecca, all the time observed by their pagan enemies from the hills. It was clearly not the right time to experiment with anything drastically revisionist, indeed the order, discipline and respect with which the Muslims treat the Kaaba (which would have still been filled with pagan statues and surrounded with bloody altars) went a very long way to ending the war, especially the enduring image of the Muslims, lining up peacefully shoulder to shoulder, making the Kaaba the central direction of their prayer rituals. Defections from the pagan leadership ranks started almost immediately – such key pagan warrior-commanders as Khalid ibn al Walid and Amr ibn Al As.

Indeed next year, eight years since he left it, Mecca submitted with hardly a hand raised in resistance to the Muslim army of 10,000. The Kaaba was cleansed, and the adjacent temples of the Arabian goddesses suppressed. In all other matters, the Prophet went out of his way to forgive the Meccans and include them in his rapidly expanding egalitarian community. However he was too busy campaigning, preaching and peace-making in northern Arabia to make the pilgrimage that calendar year, which was instead commanded by his trusty confidant Abu Bakr. This was the last year that pagan Arabians were allowed to perform the pilgrimage – so it must have been a rather bizarre mixture of the old pagan pilgrims, performing their ancient rights naked, side by side with the Muslim contingent deep in prayer and meditation. Clearly this again was not a year when any sort of reformation of the old rituals was possible.

The next year was the decisive year. The pagans had been warned not to come; Muhammad was now in sole command of all Arabia, and he alone had the authority to make any changes to the ancient pilgrimage rituals of Mecca – but he also seemed to know this was the last year of his life. Indeed on the way back he made a sort of oral will at the campsite of Ghadir Koum. I imagine his energies were directed on keeping the unity of his followers, rehearsing his key followers in the completed Qur'an (unwritten but chanted through the night vigils in unison), accepting the submission of the last pockets of pagan Arabia, making truces with Christians and Jews and all the while planning to reverse a recent military defeat in Byzantine Syria, where his adopted son, commander Zayd, was killed. There were also domestic problems due to complicated mosque-household arrangements, and fuelled by the difference of opinion between Aisha, his youngest wife, and his daughter Fatimah and cousin-son-in-law Ali, made even more intense by the arrival of two healthy, happy male grandchildren.

One feels the last of his abundant life energy being poured into the celebrated Last Sermon, believed to have been delivered at the emotional height of the pilgrimage during the standing at Arafat. He was emphatic that the Kaaba was being returned to its old monotheistic purity, the long pagan centuries washed away, returning it back to the altar established by the well regarded ancestor of the Arabs: Ishmael, the son of Abraham. As an unlettered Prophet, to whom the texts of the Jews and the Christians were a closed book, this was for once found to be in pleasing agreement with their scriptures. He also struck decisively, but very gently, at the seasonal nature of pagan rituals, by disconnecting the old solar, seasonal calendar, from the new religious, lunar calendar of Islam. So unlike Christianity, which after 2,000 years is still stuck with pagan symbols of spring at Easter, and the pagan symbols of mid-winter at Christmas, Islam got itself free of eggs, rabbits, binge feasts and Christmas trees right from the start. And to those who know their Qur'an, there was always truth to be learned beneath the outer haze of the Hajj rituals: 'Their flesh and their blood do not reach Allah, but it is the devotion from you that reaches him' (22:37).

When Muhammad finally returned from this Hajj (which in a way was his first and his last, truly Muslim pilgrimage) to his house in Medina, he had just two months left to live. After his death, the example of his life, was preserved as an unbreakable heritage. His actions the foundation of sharia, reinforced by the hadith, the body of his remembered sayings, which fixed the Hajj ritual for eternity.

To my outsider viewpoint, it seems clear however, that some of his closest followers thought he could have been a bit tougher with the old pagan rituals and chopped off some bits. Some remembered trying to skip the running between Safa and Marwa (remembering the time of pagan lewdness when the hills were capped with representations of male and female sexuality) before a Qur'anic verse specifically instructed them, 'verily Safa and Marwa, are among the symbols of God. So it is not harmful for those performing pilgrimage to walk between them'. Omar was famously remembered to have addressed the black stone, 'Verily I know that thou art a stone, thou dost no good or harm in the world, and if it was not that I saw the Prophet kiss thee, I would not kiss thee'.

So we have seen how the old rituals of the pre-Islamic Hajj passed gradually into the body of Muslim practice. What can one make of them? Nothing can be certain, but for those who enjoy speculation there are some intriguing clues to help us imagine the reality of pagan Mecca.

There are very few traces in the Qur'an of the old pagan ways but we get to hear the names of the three Goddesses that were worshipped at Mecca: Allat, Al-Uzzah and Al Manah. We know that the pagan pilgrimage was also fixed on the spring, which was in the middle of the three-month period of truce. We also know that the Kaaba was roughly as it stands today, a rectangular cube with a flat roof, surrounded by a sacred space set apart from the trading town that included a sacred spring and a holy stone. From early Muslim historians, as well as classical and Babylonian sources, we also learn that the sanctuary of Mecca was renowned for being sacred to the moon and that at some point it was furnished with a statue of the Syrian God Hubal. This odd obsession with seven was also present, seven circuits of the Kaaba, seven runnings, and batches of seven stones being hurled at the representation of Satan.

Over the last hundred years the excavations at Palmyra have given us a lot to go on, for the great extant sanctuary of Bel is uncannily similar to pagan Mecca, something that was only revealed once the ancient village was cleared away in the 1920s. A rectangular sanctuary in a great sacred-space beside a sacred spring. It was once equipped with a pool for sacred ablutions, a place for sacrifices, a tunnel for animals and open air altars. It is dedicated to three gods, the inter-related trinity of Bel, Aglibol and Malakbel. Roughly speaking the supreme male sky and sun-god, the male moon-god and a sacrificial male fertility god (with the tell-tale emblems of a pomegranate and a cypress tree). So at a running guess we can imagine the pagan Meccans addressing a roughly similar male trinity at the Kaaba, with the Syrian derived name of Hubal as the storm, fertility war-god, Sin as the moon-god and some form of Baal, or Bel as 'our supreme Lord and

Master'. This Arabian trinity would be recognisably different from the rest of the ancient world, as desert dwellers had a contrasting take on the pantheon of male gods. The power, and the essential role of the Moon is always stronger to those accustomed to making use of the cool of the night to enable travel in the desert, not to mention the night dews and welcome shade. To further express this, the Moon god was often credited to be the father of the sun (*Shams ibn Sin*). The sun was also customarily split into two identities: the good lord of the dawn and dusk, often credited with watching over the vital oasis springs of the desert. For instance in Palmyra the vital oasis spring (which disgorges 80 litres of water a second) is known as Afqa, 'dawn or sunrise spring watched over by Yahribal whose name is blessed forever, the most gracious, the most merciful, presented for thanks giving'. The midday sun was execrated as an almost Satan-like figure, or compared to the deities of the underworld or the Arab war-god, Nergal. Some have seen the noon-tide stoning of the three Satan stones of the Hajj as a memory of this, for noon was the time when travellers were forced to stop, pitch camp and take shelter from the destructive sun.

The three names of the Meccan Goddesses are a great help for fixing the nature of pre-Islamic Mecca. For from texts and inscriptions elsewhere, we know Al-Lat rather well – she is one of the many names of the great Syrian Goddess, Astarte, addressed by the Babylonians as Ishtar and the Sumerians as Inanna, Astoreth and Attartu. The temple associated with her at Palmyra was built over, after the sack of the city in the third century AD, by a Roman army camp, but was once considered to be of comparable size to the temple of Bel, connected together by the great processional avenue of Palmyra – still one of the wonders of the ancient world. There is nothing quite like the Syrian Goddess in all the spiritual imagination and myths of the classical world, so no wonder she was addressed and given statues (even at Palmyra) as Athena, Artemis and Venus and furnished with a symbolic creature, the Lion. And at Mecca she was also given three identities. Al-Uzza was Ishtar's Venus-like softer identity, just as al-Manah, 'fate' saw in one of her implacable, all-powerful faces.

Allat/Ishtar was a mother goddess, presiding over the fertility of crops and herds and reproduction, the Great Mother who bestowed power to kings, but she was also the goddess of sexual love – fickle, insatiable and cruel. There is a celebrated description in the Gilgamesh epic of how she has bewitched every creature in the world through love and her irresistible sensuality, before tiring of them, and turning them into her slaves.

In Syria, the great annual passion of Astarte for her lover-brother-son, Tammuz (who, like the crops, must be planted, cherished but finally cut down in the sacrifice of harvest and yet reborn next spring) fed the whole agricultural year with its seasonal rituals, its laments, its forty day Lent-like/Ramadan-like fasts, its songs (authentic echoes of which can be heard in The Biblical Song of Songs). Tammuz, was the adored young Adonis-deity, fated to die and be reborn with an annual operatic intensity. At times Astarte is both a Juliet in love with her Romeo, and a heroine-magician, like Isis, putting the dead Osiris back together and nursing the new-born, redeemer god Horus for mankind. But that was not all.

The Great Goddess in Arabia and Mesopotamia was also much more. Recent translations of Babylonian and the even more ancient texts of Sumerian Inanna have revealed the complexity of her nature and how her cult was strongly associated with the number seven. She dominated the events of the spring festival, which year after year remembered her first terrifying descent into the underworld of death; the all-powerful Great Goddess, gradually being stripped of her powers, her beauty and her vestments, as she progressively passed through the seven gates of Hell. Then naked, vulnerable and weak, she entered the portals of the underworld and was condemned to die. She ran between the seven judges, begging for mercy, before being left to perish slowly on a stake: a sort of crucifixion-like moment (probably mimed at the pagan equivalent of the standing at Arafat). Without her presence the earth was deprived of sex, and so nothing grew, the universe was full of mourning and sadness, and eventually the great distant all-powerful sky god consented to aid his capricious daughter. There are many versions of how she escaped hell, (such as the tale of the gad-flies at the gates of hell) and how bit by bit she gathered up her vestments and beauty at the seven gateways. Her return was a triumphant procession, with feasting and sacrifices, that led to the return of fertility and sensuality to the land. Men and women, having been kept apart, were then permitted to sleep together. The returning goddess was married to her male partner by processions that took the statues of the two gods to each other's temple, and/or a sacred wood. In the past these actions were also physically acted out by the reigning king and queen, high priest and high priestess.

There is also an even darker twist to the tale in the Sumerian telling, for she finds her husband Tammuz, insufficiently delighted at her return, and tricks him into the underworld, for she had promised the deities of hell to send someone to take her place....

It is this powerful, capricious Goddess, served by sacred prostitutes, song, drunken feasts, blood sacrifices, which upheld and inspired the cruel old society of pagan Mecca, where the powerful, the strong and the rich, could do as they wished, and the poor, the old, the unwanted or inconvenient children, widows and elderly waited for a preacher-prophet to bring the good news of a Merciful God who could be worshipped through prayer and the creation of a just society.

LONDONISTAN'S OTHER BIG BANG

Abdelwahab El-Affendi

In the summer of 2010, I drove Abdulilah Benkirane and another friend to the Islamic Cultural Centre in East London. Benkirane, leader of Morocco's Justice and Development Party (PJD), had just finished his speech at a conference I helped organise, but was not very happy with the way the event proceeded. When we met at the coffee break, he was still fuming after a heated exchange with a participant. I informed him that I was on my way to another function in Whitechapel and offered to take him along. It would be an opportunity to meet some leaders of the British Muslim community, I suggested. He welcomed the break. That was my first meeting with Benkirane, a jovial and extremely modest man, with a salt and pepper beard and a disarming smile. A couple of years earlier, I had hosted his leaner and taller predecessor as PJD leader, Saadeddine Othmani, at a conference organised at the Centre for the Study of Democracy at the University of Westminster. The topic of the December 2008 conference was 'Islamism, democracy and Arab intellectuals: the missing dimension in democracy promotion.' But more of that later.

The trip to Whitechapel took much longer than we had anticipated, even though it was a Sunday. Our dear friends in the English Defence League had chosen that of all days to mount an anti-Muslim demonstration close to East London Mosque. A large police contingent was deployed to prevent clashes with angry Muslim youths, and traffic around the centre almost came to a standstill. It was not the best way to introduce our guest to our usually hospitable city, but it gave us an opportunity to talk at length and for me get to know him better.

I was slightly taken aback by his ardent monarchism. He really believed that the monarchy was a vital institution for unity and stability in Morocco. This was a rare stance for the leader of an Islamist party. But then PJD was not just any Islamist party. It had acquired its name in 1998, a full four years before its more famous Turkish namesake emerged. But the party has deeper roots going back to the 1950s, when its founding leader Abdelkarim al-Khatib, a veteran of the independence struggle, became a leading figure in a pro-palace party, the Popular Movement, opposed to the dominant Istiqlal Party. (This explains the monarchism; Al-Khatib was King Muhammad V's personal physician). However, al-Khatib, who was the Speaker of Parliament at the time, dissented after King Hassan II declared a state of emergency in 1965. In 1967, he split from the Popular Movement to form the Democratic and Constitutional Popular Movement (MPDC), which campaigned on a platform of 'Islamic constitutionalism'; hence the pro-democracy and Islamist leanings of the party.

Benkirane, meanwhile, was a veteran of a number of clandestine Islamist movements, including Al-Chabiba Al-Islamiya (Islamic Youth), which he joined as a university student in 1976, but left later because of its radicalism. In 1982, he formed the Jama'a al-Islamiyya (The Islamist Group), which was described by one observer as 'more anti-Marxist than anti-monarchist'. No wonder, then, that it was tolerated by the authorities and even permitted to publish a magazine. In 1992, the group was granted legal status under a new name: Al-Islah Wa Attajdid (Reform and Renewal). In 1996, it changed its name again, this time to Attawhid Wal-Islah (Monotheism and Reform). Clearly this lot were quite restless. That same year, the group merged with the MPDC and fought the 1997 parliamentary elections under its banner, winning fourteen seats. The following year, the name was changed to PJD.

Significantly, the group became the first Islamist party to officially adopt a 'secular' organisational arrangement. The religious functions of the group were assigned exclusively to Attawhid Wal-Islah, which had its own leadership structure separate from the party, while the latter was transformed into a purely political organisation, with no religious functions at all. That dispensation became the topic of intense debate among Islamists.

After the event at East London Mosque, I treated my guests to lunch at a shabby East London joint, and then drove them back to their hotel in the heart of Arab London in Bayswater, where we had coffee and talked some more. Little did any of us know that we were having an audience with Morocco's first ever freely elected prime minister: in November 2011, Benkirane was named Prime Minister after the PJD won the most seats in the first parliamentary elections since constitutional reforms had been instituted earlier that year. The Arab Spring had arrived in Morocco, and Benkirane was one of its first beneficiaries.

In London, you often bump into some very pertinent people. In recent years, however, the city has acquired notoriety as 'Londonistan', the world capital of violent jihadists. The reputation is not totally undeserved, as the city appeared at one point the locus of disturbing manifestations of bigotry, even insanity, among some sections of the Muslim community. However, the impact of these relatively isolated groups was greatly exaggerated by the likes of right-wing *Daily Mail* columnist, Melanie Phillips, and the recently departed militant atheist Christopher Hitchens. This designation of London was first coined and promoted by disgruntled French officials and authors dismayed with the UK's relatively liberal policy towards immigrants, and its lack of enthusiasm for France's 1990s proxy war in Algeria. (But then the French had been equally unhappy about London harbouring fleeing Huguenots in the seventeenth century, and fugitives from the revolution the following century).

True to its long tradition of hospitality, London has also offered a breathing space and an arena for reflection, rethinking and re-organisation for myriad groups of political exiles, victims of repression and idealists dreaming of reshaping their societies along more humane and just lines. None of these exiles dreamt of blowing up London buses, and most were not concerned in the least about British politics, except when it tended to compound their misery. They resented the fact that Britain was too friendly with the regimes that hounded them from their homes, but they were grateful for the safe haven. Given that their exile appeared interminable, many developed affection for the place, even if the hardiest optimists were not yet ready to call it home.

But, in particular for Arab exiles, London was much more than a safe haven and a surrogate home. From the late 1970s, London has won the toss against Paris and Larnaca to become the Arab media capital. This title had been Cairo's to keep since the late nineteenth century. However, with the stifling of press freedoms under Nasser from 1952 onwards, Cairo began to lose that role. It remained a cultural power house and a media giant, if only because of Nasser's unrivalled propaganda machine and his popularity in the Arab world. However, Beirut surreptitiously moved in to acquire the status of the most vibrant media centre in the Arab world. Political exiles escaping the rising number of Arab tyrannies flocked to Beirut and frequented its cafes and dingy newspaper offices. Even the tyrants, including Jamal Abdel Nasser, the second President of Egypt, began to grudgingly admit Beirut's primacy, and sought to win over its newspapers, or buy themselves some influence on them. When all failed, intimidation became a last resort (or first for some). A number of journalists deemed too dangerous were not infrequently assassinated.

However, when Beirut succumbed to its troubles after the eruption of the civil war of 1975, soon to be followed by a Syrian occupation, another exodus began. A few newspapers relocated to Larnaca, Cyprus, for what they thought would be a temporary exile. Others chose Paris, always close to the hearts of many Lebanese. A few chose London. In the end, London won. As a cosmopolitan city with a strong and long-standing connection to Arab countries, London remained by far the top holiday destination for the Arab elite and middle classes of the Arab East, a status which was enhanced following the oil boom of the mid-1970s. This in turn created a vibrant industry (in catering, restaurants and real estate) which blossomed to serve the rising numbers of Arab visitors, in turn providing jobs from immigrants and exiles.

The definitive sign that London has won came in 1977, when the Saudis decided to set up a publishing house at the heart of Fleet Street, producing the first pan-Arab daily newspaper, and a host of other publications. This was a radical move in itself, since the Saudis were extremely cautious, even shy, and had up to then preferred to fight their media battles by proxy: never enter into a confrontation when cash could do all the talking. The fact that they had decided to 'come out' was significant in itself.

Following the Saudi example, every self-respecting Arab publisher and regime tried to get a foothold in London. Even established newspapers, such as the Egyptian *Al Ahram* and the Kuwaiti *Al Qabas* began to produce 'London editions'. In the early 1990s, official Britain accepted this new reality, and decided to enter the fray. Given the fact that the Arab world had become, after Desert Storm, an area of vital interest, this appeared inevitable. Following the lead of the Saudis who set up the first Arabic satellite TV station in London in 1990, the BBC set up its first Arabic satellite television service in 1993.

There was a twist to this story. The exodus of Arab media to London was motivated by the imperative to escape tyranny and intimidation. However, that proved to be in some sense a mirage. In the pre-internet era, publishing from London did not guarantee automatic access to readers back home. Since the raison d'être of London-based publications was to avoid the clutch of Arab regimes, the latter could not be expected to welcome the fruits of freedom which they fought at home. So the only readers a publication was guaranteed were the official censors.

More significantly, the logic of the market gave the Gulf countries an unassailable advantage vis-à-vis the hapless editors and publishers. In this regard, the Saudis found themselves in a very comfortable position. Having contributed to the high costs of publishing by offering lucrative salaries to their staff, they realised they need not pay a penny to ensure that the 'free' Arab press in London toed the line, with not even a whisper of criticism of the House of Saud. All they needed to do was to promise access to the Saudi market. In the end, all the 'exiled' Arab press in London and elsewhere came under virtual Saudi control. There were a few exceptions, such as the PLO-backed *Al-Quds Al-Arabi* and a few radical papers. But the logic of the market meant that any Arab publication would not survive in this market without generous subsidies.

The culmination of this was the supreme irony that, when the BBC launched its Arabic TV service in 1993, it also resorted to Saudi funding. A Saudi company, Orbit Communications, provided all the funding for the channel. So much so that when, two years later, in April 1996, the company decided to pull the plug in protest at a Panorama interview with the leading exiled Saudi dissident (who had also chosen London as a base) the channel was immediately closed. The staff was not even able to get access to the equipment, which was all owned by Orbit, and were all sacked with an hour's notice anyway.

But then something extraordinary happened. The tiny Gulf state of Qatar took all the BBC staff and gave them a new station to work in, in Doha. They called it Al Jazeera (The Peninsular, short for Arab Peninsular). It started broadcasting on 1 November 1996, barely six months after BBC Arabic was shut down. That moment was seen by some as the real starting date for the Arab Spring. The new channel broke all the taboos and started discussing the subjects about which silence was enforced in the Saudi-dominated and official Arab media. The 'Kingdom of Silence' lost its stranglehold on the media, and things would never be the same again.

Regardless of intentions, Al Jazeera had the same impact as the desperate act of protest of the Tunisian fruit vendor Mohamed Bouazizi fifteen years later, and for the same reason: it was a spark in a tinder box. It gave the Arab masses a voice they had been denied for decades, and forced the world to sit up and listen. Suddenly, everyone discovered, as the title of the first issue of *Critical Muslim* had it, that the 'Arabs are alive!' They existed beyond the façade of the sclerotic leaders who wanted to be the only Arabs to speak. And suddenly, everyone wanted to speak Arabic: Britain revived its Arabic television service. America set up one for the first time, so did France. Even Russia created its own Arabic service. The Saudis, now panting to catch up, started Al Arabiyya, which became the news arm of their pioneering satellite station, MBC, (set up in London in 1991 and now relocated to Dubai). But Al Jazeera still remains the leader of the pack. And it was, let us not forget, a London transplant.

London Redux

The rise of Al Jazeera shifted the balance of power, media-wise, in the direction of the Gulf. However, London still maintained its privileged status. For even if the silence has been broken, it was still a very risky business for dissidents in countries such as Syria, Libya, Tunisia or the Gulf to speak to reporters. Even for Al Jazeera, it was in offices abroad, mainly in London, that the interviews which made waves were being conducted. So it was back to London.

The Arab regimes did not sit back, but used London as a battleground in many arenas. The funding war raged unabated. The Saudis and the Iranians were the main protagonists in the battle which had raged since the 1980s. But the Libyans, Iraqis, Kuwaitis and even the Yemenis and the PLO, entered the fray. Bribery and corruption were, however, the least worry of exiled Arab journalists as there was a rather sinister side to these contests.

In April 1980, Muhammad Mustafa Ramadan, a respected Libyan journalist working at the Arabic service of BBC radio, was gunned down as he emerged from Friday prayers at the Central London Mosque near Regents Park. His killers were never apprehended, but there are no prizes for guessing who had sent them. Two months earlier, another London-based Lebanese publisher and journalist, Salim El Lozy, one of the Arab world's most influential media personalities, was killed in Beirut. El Lozy, a critic of the Syrian regime who had earlier relocated his *El Hawadess* publishing operation to London, travelled to Beirut to attend the funeral of his mother. He was kidnapped while on his way to the airport on 25 February. His severely tortured and mutilated body was found nine days later, with a bullet in the back of the head. His fingers had been burnt and the flesh had been torn off his right hand. A number of pens were stuck in parts of his body. This is a pointer towards the respected Syrian cartoonist Ali Farzat, who was abducted in Damascus in August 2011, severely beaten and had his fingers and arms broken. But luckily, he was left alive after being told that this was just a warning. Not so lucky was the singer Ibrahim Qashus, who compiled a song asking Assad to leave. His larynx was torn off before his mutilated body was dumped in a river in his home city of Hama. Since the Syrian uprising started in March 2011, hundreds of local and foreign journalists have been killed, abducted, imprisoned or made to 'disappear'.

Journalists targeted in London included the Palestinian cartoonist, Naji al-Ali, a vociferous critic of the PLO leadership and other Arab regimes, who was gunned down in August 1987, near the London office of the newspaper where he worked. Paris has also been the site of the assassination of journalists, most prominent among being the seventy-eight-year old Salah al-Bitar, editor of a dissident magazine, shot dead in July 1980. Al-Bitar was a co-founder of the Baath party and a former Syrian prime minister who broke away from the Assad regime. In 1982, a car bomb exploded near the offices of another Paris-based anti-Iraqi newspaper.

However, the most belligerent warrior against freedom of expression, the Tunisian regime of President Zine El-Abidine Ben Ali, did not use any guns. Its armoury incorporated a combination of diplomacy, bribery, intimidation and misinformation campaigns. Ben Ali's regime was obsessed with its media image, and its insistence on silencing the most trivial criticism, were legendary. Any newspaper editor who reported criticism of a human rights watch dog, or any mildly negative coverage in his/ her paper, could expect a phone call, or even a visit, from the ambassador himself. The Tunisian pressure was so intimidating that even Al Jazeera refrained for many years from hosting Tunisian dissidents on its programmes. Once it timidly permitted Rachid Ghannoushi, the then leader of the banned Islamist Ennahda party, to take part in one of its programmes via telephone from

London but the call was abruptly cut off minutes later. Sources close to Al Jazeera revealed that President Ben Ali himself telephoned Qatar officials to protest. Later, when Al Jazeera became more daring, hosting the then leading dissident and human rights activist, Dr Moncef Marzouki on one of its programmes in 2006, Tunisia closed its embassy in Doha and launched a fierce campaign of vilification against Al Jazeera and Qatar.

The Tunisians were also known to go on the offensive with their own kit of dirty tricks. In November 1993, a London Sunday paper published an article accusing Ghannoushi of masterminding the bombing of hotels in Tunis in 1987, in which British tourists were injured. It just happened that Ghannoushi was in jail at that time, being tried for his political views. The alleged perpetrators were arrested, tried and executed shortly after, and none of them had links to him. Such scurrilous attacks through 'leaking' defamatory stories to the media became a 'nice little earner' for Ghannoushi, who sued the paper and received an apology and a handsome out of court settlement in 1996. He also successfully sued London-based Saudi publications which carried similar stories, so it was not all bad news for dissidents.

I met Ghannoushi for the first time in Tunis in the summer of 1986, where I had gone to interview PLO chief Yasir Arafat for a London-based magazine. A friend, who was the correspondent for another London magazine, arranged for me to see the man few outside Tunisia had heard of at the time. He was in hiding then, fearing impending arrest as the ageing autocrat, Habib Bourguiba, had expressed a determination to 'eradicate' the budding Islamist movement. So we had to resort to elaborate precautions to evade the ubiquitous security services. I walked for quite a distance from the hotel before meeting my friend, and we then took a taxi before taking another walk to a waiting car, which drove at a snail's pace to flush out any possible tail. It was like Hollywood movies. We then drove to the house of one of Ghannoushi's associates and waited there for a good while before the man turned up. We sat there talking all night.

What impressed me then was the man's open-mindedness and his almost dogmatic commitment to democracy. Not long after our visit, and the series of interviews with him we published, Ghannoushi decided to come out of hiding, and was immediately arrested. In August 1987, a state security court sentenced him and a number of his followers to death for allegedly plotting to topple the government. When the sentence was commuted to life imprisonment by another court, President Bourguiba ordered a retrial, insisting on a death sentence. But the defendants were saved by a real plot to topple the regime, this time hatched and implemented on 7 November by Bourguiba's own prime minister and chief of security, a certain Ben Ali. Ghannoushi and hundreds of his supporters were released from prison, and the new regime promised a new democratic dawn. However, when Islamist-supported candidates (Ennahda party was still outlawed) made an impressive show in the April 1989 elections, Ben Ali had second thoughts, and Ghannoushi was again on the run.

I met him again in London in the early 1990s. A friend of mine, Julian Crandall Hollick, a British broadcaster based in the US, was making a radio series called *Living Islam*, for which he was profiling Ghannoushi. He enlisted my support as an interviewer and translator. We spent several months on and off on that project, and I got to know probably all there is to know about the man. I was impressed even more.

Academically Speaking

It was around that time (in June 1993, to be precise), that I was invited to take part in a symposium organised by the Council on Foreign Relation in New York on US policy towards Islamist parties. The debate had already been framed by two articles published in the spring 1993 issue of *Foreign Affairs*. The first was written by another friend of mine, the *New York Times* journalist, Judith Miller, entitled 'The Challenge of Radical Islam'. Maybe fewer people call Miller a friend these days, and she has come under some vociferous criticism for her closeness to senior figures in the Bush administration and some of the darker episodes associated with the Bush-Cheney White House. But I have a lot of affection for Miller, and I believe the feeling is mutual, as I received a flattering dedication in one of her books, which angered many of my other friends. Shortly before that, I had arranged for her to meet Ghannoushi at my North London home. She recounted an encounter with the Tunisian foreign minister, who told her they would never permit the Islamists to operate legally for a simple reason: they would win. 'If the Pope ran for elections in your country,' he said to Miller, 'would he not win hands down?' (Apparently, His Excellency had no idea how unpopular the Pope was in America!) She was amazed both at his naiveté and bad faith.

However, between our meeting in London and our New York encounter, Miller had moved perilously close to the position of the Tunisian minister, and now argued vehemently that there was no such thing as a moderate Islamist. All Islamists, she argued in her article, were against women's rights, against Western interests and against Israel. And given that they were likely to win elections, the US should desist from promoting democracy and insist merely on respect for human rights. (That position was given a more cogent expression in another *Foreign Affairs* article, published in 1997 by Fareed Zakaria, advocating the promotion of liberalism, rather than democracy). On the other side in the debate, Leon T. Hadar's article in the same issue of *Foreign Affairs*, under the title 'What Green Peril?', argued that fanning the fear of Islam was both irrational and counterproductive. I supported this stance, and summarised my position in one question to Miller: Let us suppose you are right; what policy are you going to recommend? For the amount of repression demanded by your prescriptions would dwarf any benefits you hope to bring about. And in any case, it is going to be futile, judging by the fact that seventy years of Stalinist eradications in Central Asia and the Caucasus and 130 years of French cultural enforcement in Algeria did not preclude the rise of Islamism in those areas. What more could anyone do?

However, as one of the participants told me privately, our debate was 'academic' in the worst sense of the word. For the policy issue had been resolved by the fact that all America's key allies in the region (Israel, Egypt, Saudi Arabia, Tunisia, Algeria, Jordan) were unanimous on one thing: they all came to warn President Bill Clinton of the threat that disturbs and unites them all – Islamism. That makes it impossible for the US administration to contemplate any accommodation with Islamism, even if it wanted to.

This did not deter me from pursuing the academic debate. In 1998, the Democracy and Islam Programme was set up at the Centre for the Study of Democracy (CSD) at the University of Westminster, and I was put in charge of it. CSD, founded in 1990 by the inimitable political scientist John Keane, its first director, was a unique outfit that has brought together some of the best talents and minds into an innovative enterprise for the study of the most pressing issues in modern politics and international relations. After one year of exciting work in the company of such intellectual giants as Chantal Mouffe, Barry Buzan and many others, the Programme came into being.

Our objective was summed up at the time by a phrase which formed the project: 'the Muslim world was a frontline for democratisation and a frontier for democratic theory'. In this vision, democratisation in the Muslim world was inextricably linked to challenging and critically re-evaluating the unexamined assumption of democratic theory. By the same token, if and when democratisation becomes the norm in Muslim regions, it would inevitably deconstruct many of the founding myths of modern political and democratic theory.

It did not take long for us to be mugged by reality. We were not in denial about this reality to start with, and one of the points we continued to emphasise was that the Muslim world did have a problem with democracy, and this problem had to do mainly with its complex internal dynamics. The way Islam was being practised and interpreted, and the way Islamist and other groups conducted themselves, was a major factor. However, what we rejected was that these problems were inherent in the culture. We were very sceptical, to put it mildly, about the claim that the victims of tyranny were somehow the ones to blame for their own plight. For this reason, it was vital for our argument to showcase a Muslim model where democracy had done reasonably well, if not flourished.

That was not an easy task. Turkey, which Bernard Lewis described in 1994 as 'the only Muslim democracy', did not qualify in our judgement. In fact, we perceived Turkey at that time as a marginally milder version of Iran. I did visit Turkey in the summer of 1997, where we were hosted by the mayor of Istanbul, a certain Recep Tayib Erdogan. I spent many hours signing copies of the Turkish translation of my 1991 book, *Who Needs an Islamic State?*, which argued that modern Islamic thought should prioritise democracy over all other considerations. A short while after that, the mayor was asked what books he was reading, and he gave that title, which was good news for my Turkish publishers. Up to this day, they use a framed copy of that interview to boost sales.

A large portion of the rest of my time in Istanbul was spent fielding questions from the Turkish media. Most of the interviewers were worried that Islamists were going to take over Turkey eventually, and seeking reassurances from me (I had no idea why) about this matter. One journalist predicted that Islamists could take over within twenty years. She was rather optimistic, it turned out. It took less than five years.

Commenting on a dinner held in our honour at a historical Ottoman palace, I remarked in an article published in a Council of Foreign Relations publication later that year, that Erdogan was keen to impress us with Turkey's past, but he also wanted to subtly convey the perception that he was also Turkey's future. Within a couple of months of that article appearing, Erdogan was hauled in front of the courts on charges of trying to undermine the Turkish secular order. The evidence? Reading a well-known poem at a political rally. He was given a stiff prison sentence and banned from holding political office. It was an irony that when his Justice and Development party (AKP) won two thirds of the seats in parliament in 2002, he was unable to take up his seat in parliament or the office of prime minister straight away.

So Turkey certainly did not qualify at the time. But thank God for Malaysia. That country may not have been the perfect democracy, and in fact Freedom House, the independent watchdog, does not accord it the rating of a free country. However, that remains a gross misjudgement. What is neglected by most observers is that Malaysia remains the only Muslim majority country which has never witnessed a military coup or a collapse of the democratic order established since independence in 1957. It is also one of the few Muslim countries, perhaps the only one, where the main Islamist party (PAS) has never been outlawed and was in fact in control of a couple of states. (Jordan and Kuwait have also tolerated their Islamists, but they did not consistently recognise political parties. Kuwait still does not). Malaysia had also developed a successful model of consensus based democracy, ensuring the peaceful co-existence between its main communities, including the large and extremely wealthy Chinese community and the less sizeable Indian minority. In the 1990s, Malaysia was probably also the only Muslim country that appeared on the threshold of a real economic take-off, becoming one of the most vibrant South East Asian 'Tiger' economies. So here was a genuine Muslim success model to showcase.

In addition, the Deputy Prime Minister and Finance Minister, Anwar Ibrahim, was an old friend. As soon as we informed him of the Programme and invited him to deliver the inaugural lecture, he accepted with enthusiasm. We agreed initially on tentative dates in October 1998.

However, as I kept exchanging messages with his aides during the summer to finalise arrangements, the messages from Kuala Lumpur suddenly became hesitant and erratic. At times my emails went unanswered for weeks. I ascribed this to the demands of the financial crisis which hit the region during that period. Malaysia's Finance Minister would have a lot on his plate at a time like that. Some of my Malaysian friends, and some friends in London who were in the know, began to make some cryptic remarks when I enlisted their help, but I did not pay much attention to at the time.

However, in early September, everything became clear. Anwar was sacked from the government and immediately sent to jail, where he was beaten up and tortured. He was then charged with sexual indecency and given two sentences of six and nine years in prison, a bit excessive even by North Korean standards. We had to get someone else to deliver the inaugural lecture, several months later. It was one goal for the opposition. The evidence that Muslims could not handle democracy was mounting.

Big Bang in London

If I were the superstitious kind, I would say that I was bad news for my friends. Leaders I sought to promote, from Erdogan to Ibrahim, somehow ended up suffering one misfortune or another. However, things were not all moving in the same direction. The term 'spring' began to be bandied around in association with Arab politics at around 2000. There was a 'Damascus Spring' (a very brief one) in Syria in 2000, and at around the same time the even more promising 'Manama spring', ushered in by accession of another youthful heir to an Arab throne, Shaikh Hamad bin Isa Al Khalifa (King Hamad since 2002) of Bahrain following the death of his father in 1999. Political prisoners were released, a new constitution was passed in 2002 and the opposition was legalised. In the same year, King Mohammed VI also succeeded his father to the throne in Morocco, and also instituted some political and human rights reforms. Similar developments took place in Jordan, also in 1999, when King Abdalla succeeded his father to the throne. Even in Libya, Saif al-Islam Gaddafi, who emerged as heir-apparent in the late 1990s, began to toy with human rights reforms.

Then 9/11 came, and the whole world was engulfed in turmoil. But when the dust settled, Washington made it clear that it was going to tolerate despotism in the Arab world no more. The ideas were given a coherent formulation in the proposal adopted by the 2004 G-8 Summit in Georgia, proposing to promote democracy in the region.

All these developments had an impact on London as the capital of Arab opposition. In fact, it was the beginning of a 'Big Bang' centred on London, scattering Arab opposition all over the place. After years of London acting as a centre of attraction for dissidents escaping persecution in Arab countries, now an exodus started in the other direction. A few Libyan exiles found it safe to return home, though not many decided to stay. Leaders of the Bahraini opposition also returned home, and one former student at CSD became the leader of the largest bloc in the new parliament. Many of our Iraqi friends also went home and occupied key positions in the new government. But not all were fortunate. A prominent Londoner, Sayyid Abd al-Majid El-Khoei, was one of the first to return to Iraq, long before that famous scene of the Saddam statue in Baghdad. But he was murdered by a budding Iraqi militia, an ominous sign of things to come.

Talk of the 'Arab Spring' started again in 2005, following the apparent 'success' of Iraqi parliamentary elections and the eruption of the 'Cedar Revolution' in Lebanon. In most Arab capitals, talk about reform became the order of the day, especially to forestall whatever plans the Bush administration may have had to influence political development of the region.

At around the same time as the US plans for democratisation were being announced under a project called the Greater Middle East Initiative (later changed to the Broader Middle East and North Africa Initiative), the UNDP-sponsored *Arab Human Development Report* was in an advanced state of preparation, and the two projects immediately came into conflict with one another. The Bush administration angered the authors of the report by quoting liberally from its pages in the preamble to its paper on democratisation in the Arab region, which the authors protested unfairly linked their project to its 'imperialist' designs in Iraq and elsewhere. When the final report strongly criticised US policies in Iraq and Palestine, American threats caused the UNDP to delay the publication of the report by over six months.

In 2006, one year after the publication of the report, we had encounters with US and German diplomats who agreed to co-sponsor a conference we were planning later that year on the political role of Islamists in Arab politics. The Norwegians were happy to back it as well. As a concession to our American friends, we invited the outgoing Iraqi Prime Minister, Ibrahim al-Jaafari, another friend and former London exile, to take part. The theme of the conference was 'Electing Islamism: Islamist politics and the prospects for Arab democracy', and its focus was to evaluate the impact of recent electoral successes of Islamist parties on the democratisation process. The conference was envisaged before the landslide Hamas victory in the January 2006 Palestinian elections, but the trend was already clear from elections results in Egypt, Morocco, Iraq, Kuwait and even Saudi Arabia (where municipal elections were held in 2005). And of course there was Turkey. The conference was thus well-attended, with senior diplomats from Europe (but a low-key representation from the US) and Islamist leaders from all major Arab countries. Scholars from Europe, US, the Arab world as well as Turkey and Iran, also joined the debate.

The discussion was lively, frank and direct. Speaking for Western policy makers, Ambassador Hans-Gunther Gnodtke from the German foreign ministry, welcomed the marked shift in Islamist discourse towards espousing democratic values, but pointed to serious doubts (shared by many in the region) over whether Islamists could be trusted. 'To rephrase this question polemically: will Islamists, once in power, drift in the directions of the Taliban or of Erdogan? Obviously, if the Europeans had a say in this, they would strongly favour a Turkish model for the rest of the region', Ambassador Gnodtke said. He added: 'Western governments have constituencies too, and I would argue that especially gender equality and religious freedom will be the litmus test for Western appreciation or disapproval of emerging political agendas... What matters is the general direction. Should it be backtracking from what has already been achieved in these crucial areas, then doubt will prevail.'

In response, Rachid al-Ghannoushi argued that while some Islamists may not believe in democracy, the majority want it. 'The problem,' he said, 'is in convincing the rulers of the merits of democracy, since the shortest way to prison and the gallows in the Arab world is to win elections.' However, and this is the crux of the matter, the regimes which obstruct democracy are being rewarded by the West, while the people who elect freely are repaid with sanctions.

In my own intervention, I argued that the problem with Islamists was that they were not ambitious enough, which meant that they have not prepared themselves for government. Their formula for reassuring their critics was to refrain from seeking to gain a majority. The Brotherhood in Egypt won two thirds of the seats it contested, in spite of the blatant rigging by the ruling party. So they are very likely to win any fair elections outright, which would be more of a predicament than a triumph. Thus Islamists needed to confront the realities, including that they might win elections, in spite of themselves.

In my opening remarks at the conference I said: 'I have been telling the media that this was the first conference of its kind. I also have a strong apprehension that it is going to be the last. So let us make the most of this unique opportunity.' In a sense, I was right. We did hold a series of conferences on related themes in subsequent years, but the Western diplomatic presence continued to be low-key and rather timid. Western capitals have again bowed to pressure from Arab despots and decided to bury their heads in the sand, pretending that Islamists did not exist, and hoping and praying they could be wished away. In this, Robert Satloff, writer and director of Washington Institute for Near Eastern Policy, who is wrong about a lot of things, was right on the Islamism debate being a serious threat to political and diplomatic careers.

We at CSD, however, kept the pressure on the Islamist parties. The following year, in October 2007, we held another well-attended conference, this time on 'Islamism, Democracy, and Political Violence in the Arab world: The Hamas Challenge'. The challenge in question was that of commitment to democracy. Earlier that year, Hamas undertook what amounted to a military coup, taking power in Gaza and driving Fatah and the Palestinian Authority's troops out. This appeared to confirm the worst fears of critics of Islamists, who continued to argue that their commitment to democracy remained tenuous. In addition, claims by groups like Hamas and Hezbollah that acquiring a capability for violence was directed only at external threats was no longer sustainable. So Islamists needed to give water-tight guarantees about a commitment to keeping violence out of politics, and on accepting democratic outcomes, no ifs or buts.

In December 2008, we organised yet another conference, this time on the theme: 'Islamism, democratisation and Arab intellectuals: the missing dimension in democracy promotion'. This time, we presented a dual challenge to Arab intellectuals in general and to Islamists in particular. For the intellectuals, the challenge was to conceptualise the obstacles for Arab democracy, and for Islamists the challenge was not to become one. We revisited the findings and impact of the *Arab Human Development Report*, but we also looked at the results of another study (in which I also took part), led by Institute of Financial Economics American University of Beirut. That study brought together economists and political scientists, working collaboratively on selected Arab case studies to determine what variables affect democratisation or justify lack of it. We warned that Islamists are risking becoming an obstacle to democratisation precisely because they happened to be the most powerful opposition groups, but continue to be reluctant to shoulder the ensuing responsibility for leading the democratisation drive. To avoid this, they would have to take one of three options. They could move out of the way and leave it to others to get on with it. This would entail them getting out of politics altogether, and concentrate on preaching and social activities. Alternatively, they could try to build democratic coalitions and join with others in the fight for democracy. Or, finally, they could modify their programmes radically and adopt something akin to the Turkish model. This would enable them to assume the leading role in the democratic process. What they, and the Arab world, could not afford, was the status quo of stagnation and despair.

That meeting was significant for an additional reason. It marked the tenth anniversary of the launch of the Democracy and Islam Programme, and was a reminder that this had been a long slog, an uphill task undertaken in difficult circumstances and adverse conditions. But someone had to do it. On that occasion, we made an attempt to get Anwar Ibrahim to address the conference and compensate for his earlier enforced absence, but he could not make it. He was released from prison in 2004, and had assumed a new political role, this time as opposition leader.

Twilight in Suburbia

In June 2011, we held another conference, and it was as if we were back again in 2006. The Islamists looked once more on the verge of sweeping elections, and this appeared again to be a challenge, if not a problem. But even in our wildest guesses we could not have predicted the clean sweep they would make in Tunisia, Morocco and later in Egypt. But we had a sense of what was going on. So we again pressed the point about the need for

Islamists to play the most constructive role in order to safeguard democracy. This meant they needed to take options two and three together: build coalitions (something which they have managed to do during the revolutions), but also radically change their programmes to prioritise democracy and reassure their compatriots.

Meanwhile, a lot had changed in the intervening years: the Arab Spring took place. The majority of Libyan and Tunisian exiles, like Iraqis and Bahrainis before them, had either returned home or were planning to do so. Ghannoushi had to travel to the conference from Tunis, where he was able to go back for the first time in over twenty years. 'It must be a lonely place now,' Ghannoushi joked, as I greeted him.

Yes, London looked distinctly deserted, a twilight zone of haunting memories. It was the end of an era, and things will never be the same again. In one sense, it looked as if Britain was re-colonising the Arab world. A large number of ministers and top officials in the new regimes from Iraq to Tripoli happen to be British citizens. At least a couple, including the new Tunisian Foreign Minister, happen to be CSD graduates. But something had changed fundamentally. Never will London regain that status as the lung through which a gasping Arab world could breathe. From now on, if things go bad, as they have in Libya, Egypt and Iraq, London will not be the destination of choice for those fleeing persecution. Already we have seen signs of things to come during the Arab Spring. The bulk of Libyan activists flocked to Doha, with many London residents joining that exodus. There, they received not just a welcoming sanctuary, but generous funding for their media and political activism. The same happened for Syrians. Istanbul became the favourite haunt for Syrian dissidents after the uprising there. Again, Turkey was much more welcoming and much more generous than London could ever be.

In future crises, Doha and Istanbul would have competitors in Tripoli, Tunis, Cairo, and Casablanca. The new Arab revolutionary orders have every sympathy for those fighting oppression, and gone now is the era where sensitivities and caution would preclude offering asylum for the victims of tyranny. Even now, Syrian dissidents are being accommodated, in addition to Istanbul and Doha, also in Cairo, Amman, Tunis and even old Beirut. This is already happening. Very few came to Europe. Things have really changed, in a very radical way, for the Arab world, and for London. Perhaps, London would still retain a special status as a residual media capital and, more importantly, as a most desirable locus of academic excellence. And no doubt, we will have those conferences again.

Meanwhile, things have not turned so bad for some of my friends. Ghannoushi, the one-time fugitive, is now the most powerful man in Tunisia. Erdogan won three elections handsomely, served as prime minister and is now the President of Turkey. And in spite of some troubles, he is one of the most powerful men in the world today, and without a serious rival at home. During his reign, Turkey has not only become more genuinely democratic than ever, but also an economic power house and the foremost regional and world power.

And yes, Anwar Ibrahim did finally make that lecture engagement, in July 2011, thirteen years too late. Even after his sentence was quashed and he was released from prison, he was still disqualified from running for political office until 2008. The ruling party took precautions, calling early general elections in March 2008, one month before his ban was due to expire. This did not prevent him from masterminding a grand opposition coalition which deprived the ruling National Front from its absolute parliamentary majority for the first time in Malaysia's independent history. As if by way of response, new allegations of sexual misconduct were again brought against Anwar. Nevertheless he ran successfully for parliament in August 2008, becoming the most formidable leader of opposition Malaysia had known. And we managed finally to get him to Westminster to give his long awaited lecture. His topic? 'The Arab Spring and Democratic Transitions in the Muslim World'. What else is there to talk about?

***

At the time of going to press, Anwar is back in court facing the same old charges of which he had previously been acquitted. The countries of the Arab Spring are in a mess, and the headline news from our region are dominated by reports of murder and mayhem, either committed in the name of Islam or to silence those invoking it. Are the Orientalists right after all?

AMONG THE RUINS

SYRIA PAST AND PRESENT

CHRISTIAN C. SAHNER

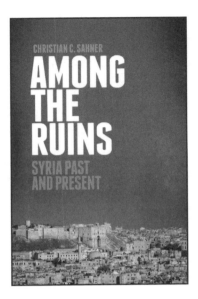

ISBN: 9781849044004
£20.00 / Hardback / 240pp

As a civil war shatters a country and consumes its people, historian Christian Sahner offers a poignant account of Syria, where the past profoundly shapes its dreadful present.

Among the Ruins blends history, memoir and reportage, drawing on the author's extensive knowledge of Syria in ancient, medieval, and modern times, as well as his experiences living in the Levant on the eve of the war and in the midst of the 'Arab Spring'. These plotlines converge in a rich narrative of a country in constant flux — a place renewed by the very shifts that, in the near term, are proving so destructive.

Sahner focuses on five themes of interest to anyone intrigued and dismayed by Syria's fragmentation since 2011: the role of Christianity in society; the arrival of Islam; the rise of sectarianism and competing minorities; the emergence of the Ba'ath Party; and the current pitiless civil war.

Among the Ruins is a brisk and illuminating read, an accessible introduction to a country with an enormously rich past and a tragic present. For anyone seeking to understand Syria, this book should be their starting point.

'*Among the Ruins* is a uniquely vivid evocation of the past of Syria and a prescient record of its present state. Deeply humane and drawing on subjects from all walks of life, Sahner has a gift for presenting them against a past that is as varied and as ancient as the country itself. We are brought to the edge of the precipice over which, alas, a magnificently diverse society appears to have stumbled. We will be both better informed and wiser for reading it.' — Peter Brown, Rollins Professor Emeritus of History at Princeton University

WWW.HURSTPUBLISHERS.COM/BOOK/AMONG-THE-RUINS

41 GREAT RUSSELL ST, LONDON WC1B 3
WWW.HURSTPUBLISHERS.COM
WWW.FBOOK.COM/HURSTPUBLISHERS
020 7255 2201

ARTS AND LETTERS

IN CAMERA: BOSNIA

Ruth Waterman

Stay crouched on the earth,
come closer to our disintegrating bones.
You are so far away.

COUNTRYSIDE

'I feel that everything I touch turns to sand.'

'I'm very tired. I'm impatient with everyone, just want to be alone, go to the village and sleep and work in a garden and not be with anybody, not even my husband. I'm tired of stress, tired of everything.'

'I feel worthless – sometimes I don't want to live anymore.'

'I think there will be another war.'

Many Bosnians are despondent and suffering from the late emergence of symptoms of trauma.

'I am so angry. About the war. Yes, it's finished almost twenty years, but my brother escape and now he lives in Australia, so how can I see him? I visited him last year, and it was wonderful to be with him and his family, but when it's time for leaving, it was very hard. I cried, you know. And I still crying. Families are scattered in the world. All because of the war. I am so angry.'

During the Bosnian War of 1992–95, over 100,000 people were killed, and two million were displaced.

'My marriage is broken. My trust is gone, and I feel so differently. I have a good job, but there's bad atmosphere at work and our salaries go down each year.'

Divorces have soared and unemployment has been over 40 per cent for many years.

'There's one war criminal, convicted nearly twenty years ago, and he's served many many years in prison. And now he being released, and those stupid people, they welcoming him! Like he's a hero! Those people are very stupid, they don't understand anything.'

War crimes are being tried not only in The Hague, but also in national and local courts. Many people complain about the lengthy delays of the trials and the low numbers of war criminals apprehended.

'It was Europe's fault. The war. I mean, Europe let it happen, and then waited over three years before it bombing and ending it. Three years!'

The Bosnian War ended after NATO bombed the Serbian positions besieging Sarajevo. Many Bosnians felt abandoned by the outside world and still feel resentment.

Bosnia is unhappy. I've not been there for five years and now that I've returned, I am rocked by its onslaught of despair, fatigue and pessimism. For Bosnians, the future seems to offer a fearsome spectre of poverty, unemployment, injustice, corruption, division and, for some, even a renewal of war. But mainly an intolerable continuation of the present, hopeless status quo.

This is bleeding into the personal lives of my friends, in the form of divorce, depression, suicidal impulses, and suspicious death. But fortunately the nightmare seems to spare some of the younger generation, who are marrying, starting families, and beginning to make their way as anything from teachers to tourist guides.

There has been much rebuilding, not all of it tasteful, and some of it rather puzzling – for instance, a huge modern shopping centre in Sarajevo containing luxury goods that hardly anyone can afford, and a rash of mosques although people say that existing mosques are not at all over-subscribed. But there are fewer abandoned ruins, and tourists now crowd the narrow streets, so the towns feel more normal, if one can ignore the common spattering of bullet holes in the walls.

For me the saving grace of this visit is the unfailing warmth of its people. My friends, acquaintances and former students welcome me with open arms and an immediate offer of deliciously strong Bosnian coffee. As we settle down to our conversations, they take me into their confidence and lay out for me the details of their lives, fears and dilemmas with touching bravery and honesty. And it does take courage to endure all this, on top of the ghastly memories of the war itself which, of course, still hang in the air. It's been twenty years now, but it will take many more years before its effects start to fade.

I have my own personal disappointments. I was looking forward to hearing the wonderfully romantic folk-music of the region, called *sevdah*, but no-one can tell me of any bars or clubs where it is played anymore. And the famous bridge in Mostar is no longer white and pristine as it was when it was first rebuilt and unveiled in 2004. It has lost its sheen, and somehow this embodies my sense of Bosnia itself.

Despite all this, I have to admit that I'm very glad to be back. Yes, it's incredibly stressful to see how my friends suffer, and to listen carefully to their distressing tales for hours on end. But the young people are grasping at enjoyment where they find it, and there is an intensity and rawness to life here that I know I will miss when I return to London next week. I'm lucky to be able to come and go, and I bless my lucky stars every day that I'm here.

GRAVES ON THE HILLSIDE

Speed is all, you said.
Sunlight hurts my eyes. I'm speeding now –
along its tracks the train is carrying me to.

We'll go together, you said.
You said, it's not so far, see,
just across the street,
two big breaths will do it. Ready?
Onetwothree, you said.
We ran.

Often. Every week.
Sniper Alley.
Onetwothree, you said.
We ran.
But you.

Grass and weeds grow over.
Sunlight hurts my eyes.
Speed is all, you said.

During the war, snipers positioned themselves in tall buildings and fired on civilians – men, women and children – as they ran to pick up water and food. The main street in Sarajevo became so dangerous that it was renamed 'Sniper Alley'.

THE NEW STARI MOST

'It's not at all the same – it's our bridge, but it's not our bridge.'

The hill catapults fire
throughout the night. A choir
of missiles calls us from our beds,
from dreams of ordinary times
before they conjured crimes,
split our town, crazed our heads.

We run to broken windows.
Does the Bridge stand? Shadows
of stone flicker into the river.
Emptiness is hard
to see. The air is jarred
to flow so free. Oaks shiver.

Mostar's iconic bridge, built by the Ottomans in 1566, was destroyed by days of shelling in November 1993. Its reconstruction was meticulously carried out by an international consortium, to the exact specifications of the original. When the new Stari Most was unveiled in 2004, its stone was a brilliant white, and it seemed to float and shimmer high above the green river. But now it has lost its sheen, its surface is already greying and stained, and it no longer seems capable of reflecting the light of the sun.

A SMALL ALLEYWAY IN MOSTAR

Playing music – not an option, while
outside my window, 'that' is going on.

My violin stays unbidden, mute, packed
inside its case, no glorious melting sounds

to soothe and make a pillow for my shattered
trust. What music keeps us true to our

burning, coruscating anguish? holds us
inconsolable? Music, choking,

falters into silence, while they fall,
dying, on the lane outside my window.

MOSTAR, THE MOST DESTROYED CITY IN BOSNIA, LIES IN A BEAUTIFUL VALLEY, WITH ITS PRETTY HOUSES REBUILT WITH ITS ORIGINAL LIGHT-COLOURED STONE.

Darkness oozes from my pores,
blackens my thoughts,
fills my days with night.

Fault-lines in my skin slowly
widen, tear, split;
debris from those three mad years,
now fermented, ripe,
push towards the light.

I can no longer hold myself together.
Cover the sun, and I will sleep,
before my heart scatters like shrapnel in the field.

OLD AND NEW

After that, I didn't go out.
Stayed inside my two dark rooms.
They brought me food, my friends.
I wasn't going out. Ever. Never –
my body smothered in terror –
until this is over.

It won't be over.
Every day a month.
Every minute a year.
I read my books, slowly.
Centuries pass.

And then, one morning,
I opened my door,
walked down the concrete stairs and out
into the autumn air.
They can't make my home a prison. And
they can't make me run. I'm not
going to run. Ever. Never.

So I walked, a crazy young woman, head held high.
I walked in my town and smiled at the sky. And
wherever I went, they held their fire.
They saw me coming, normal and easy, and
all of them held their fire.

To Be To Be. Shakespeare's existential conundrum is altered to become a double affirmative. In Sarajevo, there is no question.

Maybe they are right.
Their thoughts, unspoken,
stare out of their eyes:

'She has no right
to be sad'
because
there was
no bullet
no sniper
no grenade
no mortar
no explosion

no fire
no dying from starvation

only a car, an everyday car,
an everyday
car accident.

It shouldn't be allowed in the middle of war –
accidents –
pitifully low in the hierarchy of deaths.

So I have to slaughter my grief
smother it
strangle it
starve it
push it deep where its pulse can't be felt.
Mourning is postponed until further notice.

Today, and today, and today, I estrange myself from myself.
I make myself unnatural, a living ghost.
Until tomorrow.

ELABORATE DOORWAY. SARAJEVO STILL BEARS SIGNS OF ITS COSMOPOLITAN CULTURE.

Sevdah! Sevdah! How I long for you!
A bride in white waits for her faithless groom,
and many a girl sighs as fruit is picked.

Sevdah! Sevdah! Where are your sweet tones?
Magicked on the bare karst mountain slopes,
flavoured with green valleys, stone-clad towns,
where are your plaintive harmonies? your swaying
rhythms? sad, accepting melodies?

Sevdah of my soul, of all our souls,
keep us in your embrace, together, whole,
sevdah, my love, we are too much divided.

Sevdah loosely means a longing of the soul, melancholic love. The lyrics are
mainly romantic outpourings used in courtship. The performance of *sevdah* is
becoming less frequent as popular music takes over.

TWO DOORS IN SARAJEVO

Sometimes you have to forget.
Because forgiving is impossible.
And even if forgiving were possible,
You'd have to forget.

If you succeed in forgetting,
You won't know what you should be forgiving.

HYBRID IDENTITY

Tasnim Baghdadi

Tasnim Baghdadi works in multimedia: graphic design, digital illustration, and photography. She is of Moroccan heritage but was born and raised in Cologne, Germany. She see herself not just as someone residing in two cultures, but also as someone who is deeply connected to the Moroccan culture, religion and ancestry of her parents and grandparents. For her, art is a symbolical mirror to our own sub-consciousness. When making art, she says, 'we first and foremost find ourselves in them'.

These illustrations are character designs for a graphic novel called *la bédouine obscure*, a fictional version of her journey of hybrid identity. 'I want my love for different cultural traditions and their art forms to manifest itself in this story, using contrasts to bring all of it together. Rural meets urban; traditions encounter modern ideas and science fiction; spirituality mingles with different religious traditions. In all of that there is a girl and her life's journey'.

THE LADIES' BEACH

Aiysha Jahan

The sand was different here. Sana wondered if it could be called sand. It looked like someone had taken a truckload of rocks and shells and steamrolled them into billions of multi-coloured grains. That's exactly what it is, silly, except, the waves pounded them so. Don't you remember any Geography from school, chided the half of Sana who, while being a responsible mother of two, still seemed to hold quadratic equations, electrolysis and weathering patterns in her bit of brain. The other Sana, the dynamic multifaceted one, cupped a handful of sand and let it stream between her fingers as she splayed them. Much grainier than Dubai sand. Maybe I can market it as a scrub, the entrepreneur piped up as she pinched a little sand and rubbed it on the back of her other hand. She'd once walked past a stall at Mirdif City Centre that sold Dead Sea beauty products. If someone promoted a local sand that's bursting with minerals and polishes away dead skin cells, they could make a lot of money. But rational Sana cut short the thought by reminding herself that the sand belonged to the government, not a housewife who dreamed up a new business idea every week.

'What're you doing, Mama?'

Sana looked up at her sixteen-year-old daughter and noticed again the T-shirt that wasn't long enough and the jeans that were far too tight. It was her fault, and, if she were to assign blame elsewhere, the fault of the girls who used to bully her when she was at school. To be more like them, Sana had once cut herself a fringe, but she hadn't realised two things: because her hair was curly it looked much shorter than she'd cut it; and because she had no way of straightening her hair, a fringe, even the right size, would never look good on her. Although Sana couldn't remember what the girls had said, she knew it made her pin up the fringe every day until it grew out. She'd wanted Maya to be confident. Sana always told her she was beautiful, something her own parents had never done – not because they thought she wasn't, but because it just wasn't done – and she encouraged Maya until she did whatever she pleased and there was little Sana could do to stop her that didn't involve an argument.

'You know we could sell this as a scrub,' she said to stop herself from mentioning the shirt again and ruining any chances of a pleasant day out. It had taken weeks to convince Maya and Hamza, her fourteen-year-old son, that a family outing to the east coast of the UAE was more enjoyable than spending yet another Friday in front of the TV or on their various internet enabled devices.

'That's silly, Mama. No one wants to rub that stuff on their faces. Abbu wants to know where you packed the matches.'

Feeling sufficiently vindicated, sensible Sana turned away from the pounding waves to help her husband unpack the car.

'This is a good spot, isn't it?' Although it had felt unnatural at first, she and Sameer spoke mostly in Urdu to each other. In the first few years the couple switched between English and Urdu, but when the children opted to respond to their parents exclusively in English, they began to champion Urdu in a bid to preserve it in the home.

'Yes, baba, much better than the beach in the city.' Sameer had wanted to stop at Khor Fakkan corniche, but it was crowded and techy Sana had whipped out her phone to find a beach further up the coast. The new phone Sameer had bought her came with a free trial of Etisalat's 1GB monthly data package and she'd made good use of it, watching the little blue dot on Google maps follow the coastline. For the first ten minutes there was nothing but a low wall with rocky breakwaters on the other side. When she'd become sufficiently worried that she was mistaken or that they'd missed it somehow, the breakwaters gave way to a beach.

'Aha, this is the one! This is the one,' she'd called and Sameer had pulled into the unpaved shoulder which was wide enough to serve as a car park and impromptu campground.

Natural Dubai was a sandy place but the east of the country yielded hills and mountains and Sana had always found its wilder beaches more exciting. From the car park, paths had been worn into the rock down to the beach, which was a playground of boulders and pools that led to a craggy outcrop. There were people here too, but it was much quieter than the city. This is the perfect family beach, all of Sana agreed. Although she was pleased with herself, she realised that playing the role of the adventurer had meant that she couldn't ask Sameer to make a toilet stop. She tried to ignore it now as she busied herself by carrying the bag full of marinated meats down to where Sameer had already set up the first load of barbecue paraphernalia.

Hands on hips, Sana beamed as she waited for Sameer to join her with the two foldable chairs she'd bought last night in preparation for the outing. 'Just look at all the families enjoying themselves. Look at that one, Sameer. They're camping,' she said pointing to a white A-frame tent set up to the left of where the cars were parked, a few metres from a short but steep drop to the beach. 'Maybe we can stay the night sometime.'

'No way, Mama! There are no toilets here! Look at their tent, anyway. It looks like the tents on TV. Those Afghanis must have brought it with them when they left their refugee camp,' Maya said, setting down a bag full of bottles of cold drink.

'Maya! That's not nice,' responsible Sana said, even as she agreed with her daughter about the tent. It definitely didn't look like anything you could buy at Carrefour. Despite feeling annoyed at her daughter's lack of respect for others, she couldn't help but be impressed by her. She'd been trying to decide if the group were of Pashtun extraction and now she felt sure they were. 'They're so many of them, aren't there? They don't look like the sort to camp,' she said, switching to Urdu.

'Come, let's stop worrying about them and enjoy ourselves. I'm going to start the fire. The children are already hungry,' Sameer responded.

'There are lots of snacks in those bags,' Sana said, her eyes still on the family. There were women in and around the tent, some with babies on their hips, others with young children running about them. Their men were sitting on white lawn chairs set out in a semicircle around the open boot of a saloon car. Both men and women were dressed in shalwar kameez. Incongruous popped into her head and responsible Sana, who read newspapers every day so that she could discuss them with her children and who encouraged them to buy books from Kinokuniya regularly, felt quite pleased that she knew and could apply the word. Both she and Sameer often wore traditional clothes, but not to the beach. Sameer wore them on Eid and at weddings, and Sana much more often in the hope that Maya might be inspired to don any of the number of pretty outfits that were confined to her daughter's wardrobe. Sana wondered why a group of Pathans – all

Afghanis and northern Pakistanis were labelled Pathans by others from the subcontinent, not because the latter knew that's who they were, but because their pale skin must mean they are – would be inclined to camp. Although she wanted to talk about the family, she knew Sameer wouldn't be interested in matters he considered trivial.

Sameer was a good man, of course. Her parents had made a sensible choice, and she knew that exciting conversation was usually beyond the scope of a seventeen year old marriage. What's so thrilling about a group of Pathans camping, anyway? It's just different, the Sana who wondered if there was more to life at thirty-eight wanted to respond, but let the thought simmer for a moment before burying it. They had a stable life. Sameer earned enough money as a doctor to rent a neat three bedroom flat in one of the new-builds in Karama which was only ten minutes from work, and although he rarely saw his last patient before nine, he was always home in the afternoon between one and four and had Fridays and Wednesdays off so she couldn't complain. They had sex a couple of times a month or so now that the children were older – Maya stayed up most nights and Sana was always worried she'd walk in on them one day – but she didn't think having more sex would make their lives exciting so it didn't bother her too much. If only they talked about things other than the children and their everyday routines. About things that intrigued her, like the family that were camping.

She'd always considered camping a very Western institution. Unless they're staying at a hotel, people from the subcontinent don't sleep away from the comforts and conveniences of home. In the West, they live outdoors for pleasure; in the East, they live outdoors if their homes are destroyed in a flood or an earthquake or the war on terror. A friend of Sana's was married to an officer in the Pakistani Army and when her husband was posted to the border with Afghanistan, her friend talked about how the people of the region lived in mud and stone houses and could survive on next to nothing. Perhaps it's in their blood. They want to experience that life by camping on a beach and going to the toilet outdoors. There isn't much water out there, her friend had said, so they wipe themselves with stones afterwards. That's why the men sometimes walk around with their hands down the front of their trousers, to clean the drip. Sana had been disgusted then, but now the thought of urinating men reminded her of her own need to empty her bladder.

'Where's Hamza?' Sana asked as she turned away from the family and looked in the direction of her husband's pointing finger. Hamza was sitting at the edge of an empty rock pool, staring into his iPad. An Arab father, probably Egyptian, and his toddling son were by the pool as well. The boy, licking the contents of his runny nose from his lips, walked tentatively towards Hamza. His eyes were on the iPad. Sana smiled at the child and spoke to her son, 'Are you reading something, Hamza?'

'Nah, there's too much light out here to do anything.' Hamza moved the iPad out of the little boy's reach.

'Come look at this pool. Have you seen the creatures?' Sana was pointing at the dozens of limpets that studded the pool's walls, but she couldn't remember what they were called.

'What are they? They look dead,' Hamza replied. Struggling to keep the boy from his iPad, he got up and stood next to his mother.

'I've seen them on TV before. There's no water in the pool right now because the tide is low so they look dead, but later they'll move around on the rock,' Sana said, hoping he would be satisfied with an answer that didn't give him their name and annoyed at herself for not remembering it.

When Hamza sighed, she thought her son had caught her out, but she found him looking helplessly at the boy who had followed him. The father was still by the pool, but he did nothing to stop him. Typical Arabs. Never control their children. My children might trouble me, but they never bother others. Feeling fiercely protective of her son, Sana gave the little boy a stern look which he ignored.

'I think the shells are empty,' Hamza said, shrugging his shoulders and handing the iPad to his mother.

'No, no, they're like tortoises,' she replied, making sure to say tor-tis not tor-toise. Ever since her children had made fun of her a few years ago, she was always careful to pronounce it correctly. She hadn't believed them at first. All the teachers at school pronounced it like that. Oh, Mama, your teachers were wrong. We study at a British school, we should know. But I studied at a British school, too, Sana said, putting her foot in it. She knew what they'd say: Yes, Mama, but your teachers were all Indian, ours are British. She wanted to say the exams were the same and that back then they were tougher, but she didn't. Her teachers hadn't taught her how to pronounce tortoise correctly – or sword, which she and everyone she'd known before her children went to school pronounced as it's written – and that counted more than tougher exams. 'They're just waiting in their shells for the tide. We can look at some of the other pools with water in them. You know that hilly area at the end of the beach still has waves hitting it.'

Hamza's eyes travelled to the outcrop. 'It's miles away, Mama.'

'Come on! It's not far away. We could race there,' Sana said, hopeful, yet aware that neither of her children had inherited her love for athletics. She was grateful, though, that Maya played netball at school and Hamza a little cricket some weekends with his father, and although they spent the rest of their time on the sofa or in their bedrooms, the inactive lifestyle hadn't resulted in fat children. They are naturally lean, like me and Sameer. Have you looked at your tyres lately? nasty Sana asked in response, but the rest of her ignored it.

'I'll wait for the tide to come in. Anyway, Abba needs help with the barbecue,' he said and taking the iPad from his mother, he headed towards Sameer. The little boy started after him, but his father picked him up and took him away.

Sana allowed herself to feel a little satisfaction at the boy's tears and the father's annoyance.

A photo someone had posted on Facebook read that daughters love their fathers and sons their mothers, but Sana knew both her children preferred Sameer. It wasn't that he loved them more, it was because he never tried as hard. He never had to. It's easy when you're barely there, rose to the surface in a jealous bubble that Sana burst right away. He loved the children and worked hard to put them in a good school. She wondered sometimes what their lives would have been like if there hadn't been any children. Would they travel more because they'd have so much more money or would Sameer work shorter hours because he wouldn't need to make as much? Perhaps they'd talk more. She always felt guilty after such musings.

Sameer was kneeling behind the portable barbecue with the children on either side of him, Hamza handing his father a pair of tongs and Maya sitting cross-legged eating cheese Doritos and listening to something on her phone. Sana realised she wasn't feeling guilty today. She felt an irritation born of discomfort. The sound of the waves pushed their way into her thoughts and she realised both with relief and a renewed urgency that it wasn't the children that were the cause of her discomfort but her bladder.

If she asked Sameer to take her back into town, the children would never let her hear the end of it. Stupid fool for not stopping when there was a chance. She'd have to try to keep busy.

Back at the picnic, she unpacked the chicken kebabs and beef Behari kebabs she'd marinated overnight in the spice mix her mother had taught her. Local calls were free so her mother would spend hours talking Sana through recipes when she first got married. And once the children arrived, Nani was always there to take care of them. Unlike Sana and Sameer, whose grandparents had always been hundreds of miles away in India, Maya and Hamza had grown up with theirs only a short car ride away. Reluctant to leave, and frequently with no homes to return to, so many of Sana's parents' generation were still in Dubai. In order to stay, they worked for as long as they were allowed, with many trying to dodge forced retirement at sixty for expatriates. Sana didn't want the same for them. She often tried to convince Sameer to emigrate to the West, but he didn't want to leave his parents behind. Not yet, Sana, he'd always say, and after the first few years, she gave up pestering. Now that they'd both spent their entire lives in Dubai she understood why so many never left, preferring to die at home abroad, rather than returning to a foreign place that was called home.

The flame had died back now and Sameer covered every free inch of the small aluminium barbecue with meat.

'It's not coating the meat with silver paint this time, is it?'

'No, I don't think so,' Sameer replied, lifting first one and then another skewer to check. When they'd first cooked on the barbecue last year, they found silver grid marks all over the meat when they turned the skewers. Should we eat them? Sana had asked, and Sameer had said it was fine and that they could avoid giving them to the children if she was worried. They tasted no different to any of the other kebabs. They just look funky, hip Sana had said and Maya had laughed at her for using the word. 'The paint got burned off last time, anyway.'

'I'll go for a walk,' Sana said, shaking the sand out of her trainers and putting them on again.

'What about lunch? The meat's going to be ready soon.'

'I'll be back before it's ready. It's only a short walk.' If I move around I'll be fine, Sana reasoned, as the pressure in her bladder increased. She set off for the outcrop, curious to investigate it and see more of the beach at the same time. As she neared the stretch of beach below the camping family, one of the women, with a blue chadar draped over her shoulders and head, threw a bag of rubbish over the edge. It landed a few metres from Sana's feet. She huffed. Typical Asians, always making a mess and expecting others to clean up after them, she thought, surveying the area the family had been using as a tip. Indian cities were decorated with plastic bags. Long after the food inside them had rotted or had been scavenged, the bags floated in the wind like coloured balloons until they got stuck in trees and bushes or pulverised into rubble underfoot, along with all the other artefacts of decades of human consumption. Sana knew that Dubai would look no different if the workers that the municipality employed didn't clean up after people 24/7. She'd been to Europe with Sameer and the children. Once to Switzerland and another time to Paris and London. Every street, house and mountain in Switzerland looked like it belonged in a postcard and even Paris and London were clean compared to Indian cities, except in places where the foreigners lived, she'd observed. When they ended up in Whitechapel with one of Sameer's friends who wanted to treat them to the best curry in London, she thought it felt like she was back in Calcutta with the Bengalis everywhere, garbage littering the streets and even a man with his trousers down in an alleyway, emptying his bowels onto the street. You can even take them to a palace, but they'll never change, Sameer's friend had said.

Sana tried to catch the woman's eye so she could give her a disapproving look, but found her watching the water. Sana followed her gaze to a group of girls who were waist deep, fully dressed. The younger ones were wearing jeans and t-shirts, which practical Sana thought must feel like they'd lined their clothes with lead weights. The older ones were dressed like their mothers, except that they had arranged their dupattas on one shoulder and tied the ends together on the opposite hip so that they hung like sashes. Only one of the girls, a particularly rosy cheeked one, wore hers as a headscarf. This was one of the reasons why Sana loved the UAE. It's the one place in the world where a woman is free to swim in both a bikini and an abaya. I'm sure the abaya-clad ladies disapprove of the women who swim in their underwear, and those in bikinis must find the fully dressed absurd, but everyone gets along and everyone has a good time. Sana felt a surge of pride for the place where she'd grown up and which, she recalled, had given her a safe and comfortable home for all of her thirty-eight years. Now if only they'd provided a toilet at this beach.

As she went past the girls in the water, she noticed that closer to the outcrop the beach was mostly empty. A couple of young children, a boy and a girl, both with soft caramel curls and naked from the waist up, were digging in the sand. Their mother, in a paisley sundress, was sitting a few metres away. They must be twins, Sana thought. She'd always wanted twins but no one in her family or Sameer's had ever had any. Sometimes when she saw young children she considered having another baby, but she knew how her children would react. When one of her cousins in India had a son twelve years after the first one, Maya had responded with, Ewww, that's disgusting. Is she crazy? and even Hamza, who didn't usually listen to conversations about family back home, said, That's embarrassing. Sana knew they were talking about parents having sex. It was one thing to do it secretly, but for teenage children to see a product of their parents' activities was too much. Sana reminded herself that her babies would never look like these twins, anyway. Her children were beautiful, of course – Maya has her father's straight dark hair and large eyes and Hamza my soft curls and his father's picture perfect smile – but there weren't any eyes other than brown ones anywhere in their families, and none of her children would have the pale skin of Pathan children or white ones. At least Maya will never have to resort to Fair and Lovely. She, like Sana, had what Indians described as a wheatish complexion, which was on the right side of the fairness scale. Maybe it won't even matter in a few years' time. Women might be judged on their intelligence and education by the time Maya gets to marriageable age. But she doubted that. If she had to admit it to herself, she'd have to say that she'd never want a dark-skinned daughter-in-law. There's nothing wrong with dark skin, of course. If Sana were to settle on the answer that made her the least uncomfortable, she'd have to say that it was just too different. Not like us. But if someone were to ask her how she'd react if her son brought home a white wife, she knew her objections would be cultural, not racial.

'It's a castle! Wonderful!' the mother of the twins said in French. Sana smiled. The basics she'd learnt at school over twenty years ago proved useful every once in a while. She couldn't understand the people in Paris, though, because they spoke too quickly and in colloquialisms. Luckily, because neither Maya nor Hamza could understand anything either, they didn't make fun of her. If I could turn time back to when the children were that young, I could do things differently. Perhaps she'd tell them off a little more. But I can't turn back time, can I? Not even long enough to stop at a petrol station in Khor Fakkan.

I need to pee, Sana said, the way her children had learned to say from their friends at school. Voicing the need made it stronger. For a moment she had to stand very still and press her thighs together to stop the urine from escaping. She was desperate now and had to find somewhere suitable before she ended up doing something far more embarrassing than urinating behind a rock as a grown woman. When she was a child and Dubai didn't have many public toilets, her parents sometimes had to stop the car in a sandy lot between buildings for the children, but now malls, parks and even the Gold Souk had toilets. Surely the Afghani family must need to go to. They must use the rocks, Sana thought. As she neared the outcrop, she tripped over a taut fishing line that someone had tied to a peg wedged in the sand and unreeled all the way out to the sea. A little urine leaked from her as she righted herself and rushed forward.

As she clambered onto the rocks, she heard a commotion behind her. Fearing it had something to do with her, she glanced back to find one of the Afghani women in the car park shouting and gesticulating at the girls in the water who were all huddling together, the older ones rounding the others up. If her need wasn't urgent, Sana would have waited to see what was going on, but she had to keep moving to stop nature from taking its course. Realising the boulders were slick with moss, she tried to keep to the more jagged rocks. The sea was much louder here and fearing she wouldn't be able to hold it in any longer, she turned off into a gap to the left that led up the outcrop a short way until it dead-ended. It would have to do. She hastily unbuckled her belt, pulled down her jeans and squatted, letting the urine run noisily onto the rocks.

To Sana's despair, it seemed like her bladder, finally allowed to relax, was going to empty every drop of its contents. It was like those times at the cinema when she'd drunk too much Coke. She'd hold it in until she just couldn't any longer and then the quicker she wanted to be done so she wouldn't miss anything interesting, the longer it took. Embarrassed, she tracked the stream that flowed from between her trainers down the slope of the rock. That's when she noticed that there was a gap in the rocks in front of her. Her instinct was to pull up her jeans, but she realised that although she could see the beach she'd walked on, someone would have to be looking at exactly where she was sitting to see her, and even then, they would only get a glimpse of colour between the rocks and nothing more. Looking down at the beach she realised what the commotion was about. A white man was walking towards the outcrop – she had to hurry up – and the Afghani mother, annoyed that he might see one of the girls with her top sticking to her wet body or that he might go into the water and be near them, had been warning them about him. Sana saw the man speed up as he got closer to the rocks. She pulled her trousers up, disgusted that she had nothing with which to wipe herself, but the disgust was overridden by the need to get away from the place. Sana descended quickly and emerged from the gap as the man arrived there. She jumped back.

'Oh! Oh, so sorry! I didn't mean to. I was just....' He raised what looked like a pickaxe for a moment, then quickly lowered it again mumbling, 'Oh, you idiot!'

This is surely a joke. 'What?' Sana asked, her eyes following the instrument in his hand.

'I'm so sorry. I was just going to look for fossils. It's a Geology pick,' he said, pretending to wedge something out of the rock face.

Sana relaxed a little. Witty Sana wanted to say something like *And here I thought you were a serial murderer, the way they did in the movies,* but all she managed was a small laugh. She noticed that he was younger than her and taller than her husband. She also noticed that he had mousy brown hair and a nose that dominated his face. *He isn't handsome, but he has a kind smile.* 'It's okay. Don't worry,' she added, perhaps in order to look less ill at ease. Dubai was a city classified by nationality and although Sana and Sameer visited the same malls and shopped at most of the same stores as Westerners – which was the catch-all term for any white people who either spoke English or didn't speak English but weren't from the Eastern Bloc – they lived in separate worlds. Sameer, his father and hers worked with them, but always in subordinate roles and there was never any meaningful social interaction outside office parties. When she was growing up, most Westerners lived in Jumeira and she and her family lived in Ghusais. Her parents still lived there. Once an Australian couple had moved into the flat next door to everyone's surprise, but it soon became apparent it was because the husband's workplace had not provided the accommodation he had been promised. Within a year he had changed jobs and they'd moved to an area that suited them better. Although she knew there was nothing wrong with her English, because she'd never had any Western friends Sana tended to get tongue-tied whenever she spoke to them. Maya always preferred to take Sameer with her for parents' evenings.

'I'll go back,' the man said, and turned to leave.

'They won't like it,' Sana said before she could really measure her words. She wanted to help him. He'd already blundered his way into an awkward situation.

'Are you with them? The ladies.'

'No. Why?' Sana asked, although she realised she probably had a much better idea of what was wrong than he did.

'Well, a woman started yelling in the car park. I looked up at the ridge and saw her gesturing wildly at this gaggle of girls who'd been bathing in the sea. They got really agitated and started flapping about like they were trying to get away from a shark. I wanted to mind my own business so I kept walking, but as I got closer to where the girls were, instead of coming out of the water like they were doing before, they retreated again. I realised that it was me they were trying to get away from at exactly the same time when the woman on the ridge threw a stone in my direction. Her aim was pretty good because it landed by my feet. She was staring right at me. That's when I ran for it. I almost tripped on a fishing line on the way.'

Sana wanted to laugh, but she didn't.

'I just wanted to dig up some rocks,' the man said, holding up his pick again.

He had long fingers and beautiful fingernails. They were like the hands of a boy she'd liked when she was in Grade ten. She'd sit next to the aisle on the school bus and when he walked past to get to the back of the bus, his left hand would rest for just a moment on the seat in front of hers. The man looked at Sana with blue eyes that squinted uncomfortably in the sun. For a moment daring Sana's thoughts strayed to what it would be like to be with another man. She did not contemplate sex. Just touching someone else was a thought scandalous enough to make the rest of her shut it down.

'They just don't want you near their girls, that's all. That's why they were swimming off to one side. There was no one else there, you know, like a ladies' beach.'

'Oh, I didn't know there were any in the country. I'm new.'

'There aren't. Well, there are some beach parks with ladies' days, but that's all. I think they just didn't expect a man to turn up by himself. They thought that if a man saw all those girls together, he'd know he shouldn't go that way.'

The man looked confused. Sana sympathised with him. 'It's a cultural thing,' she added to make him feel better.

'I'll just wait here until they leave the water.'

Sana considered this response. Sameer wouldn't mind if she told him she was just helping the man out. They'd laugh about it afterwards. 'I have to go that way. You could walk with me. They won't feel threatened then.'

'Are you sure that's all right?'

She thought about what they'd look like to those who'd see them walking together. 'Yes, it's fine.' For a couple of hundred metres it would be absolutely fine, all of Sana agreed.

BILAL

Dorothea Smartt

From a sequence of poems that excavate the missing history of Samboo –
renamed Bilal – an African who died within days of his arrival in eighteenth-
century Lancaster, and is presumed buried at Sunderland Point.

On Sunderland Point of the Lune Estuary

Samboo of River Lune estuary
cut off and submerged
under waning facts,
buried in Lancaster's memory
the myth of Sunderland Point
muddied with trade and profits
human sales
relentless waves of merchandise;
its shipping tides cut off and flood
far and near lives.

Locals say he came
off a ship, a faithful slave
to a captain gone to town.
Abandoned by this master
Samboo, stupefied, dies
and christian sailors with goodness
bury this poor heathen soul
on the shore where Sunderland
points to the highways of the open seas,
to ships returning from triangular trading.

Samboo's Elegy: no Rhyme or Reason

If I don't sing you
who are you?
Does not the word make the man?

Maryse Conde, *Segu*

Lying at the site of Samboo's grave,
waiting for full earth to speak to me,
waiting for buried bones to whisper
as a flow of fears floods through me.

I'm held here at Lune River's estuary,
caught in fear, not daring to go down
again into the ship's deep belly –
the slaving schooner, moored off the coast,
its cargo-hold gasping with bodies
unable to stretch out. Heaving, I
breathe out; each heady in-breath a dream-
catcher, shipping me into the craft's
dark stench, weighted with irons, smelling
of vomit, sickly death of shit-piss
fear. The surging, billowing, rolling
never stops, and I bang! Holler! Cry out!
Moaning in my body *Let me out!*
Let me go! Sweating, as I reach up
in the black recess, I search for God.
Grip tight to that faith, like a light-shaft,
a slippery life-raft. *Merciful*
Aaa-llah, hold me! Merciful Aaa-llah
avenge me! Invoking old forces,
pagan ways, my ancestors, my expiring
neighbour! Anyone! Anything sacred –
Please spare me from this. Trial of
hopelessness, faithlessness, for months
no sight of land, only the world of
self-contained lashing brine, the ship on
foaming sea; men become beasts, bloodied

brutally beaten, raped, spewed on deck.

Lying at the sight of Samboo's grave,
waiting for full earth to speak to me,
waiting for buried bones to whisper,
as a flow of tears floods through me,

poet, reluctant to reconnect, I
reach out, switch on my bedside light,
waking with terrors that will not leave me.

99 Names of the Samboo

Bilal
ibn
beloved
son
brother
husband
father
grandfather
kin
elder
ancestor

sold
livestock
cargo
chattel
property
guinea-bird
savage
enslaved
captive
servant
worker

heathen
cannibal
beast
blackamoor
darkie
nigger
uncivilised
wog
fuzzy-wuzzy
coon
negro

tamed
eunuch
pet
uncle tom
minstrel
golliwog
survivor
mirror
mask
chameleon
creole

signified
dehumanised
damned
vilified
debased
silenced
invisible
camouflaged
trickster
caliban
signifier
threat
animal
oversexed
terrorizer

buck
bull
breeder
raper
lynched
rhygin
rebel

warrior
bussa
cudjoe
leader
toussaint
revolutionary
guerilla
cimarron
subversive
cuffy
duppy-conqueror

outsider
illegal
other
criminal
refugee
foreigner
exile
uprooted
immigrant
sojourner
hyphenated

prodigal son
garveyite
rasta
nubian
kushite
nation
fulani

blood
progeny
family
Bilal

Lancaster Keys: the Brew Room

Sunderland points to West Indies plantations.
A Samboo, like Gillows' crafted mahogany,
is farmed and forested, torn from root
systems to harden or die,
to be shaped into something new
and of use to Lancaster Town.

Sunderland points to a new home
for a Fulani, Bilal, called Boy (no matter
his age) by his owners,
their primrose path paved with mahogany
bodies. Fallen nature. Hardness
of heart, shameless water courses.

The ship's crew gave their cabin boy
a name: Samboo. Like he didn't have
his own old father's family line,
names respecting Allah, the
One, Allah the beneficent, the
merciful, names that speak of a
way paved with his ancestors, each
name an elegy, a praise song.

A Samboo – a converted life,
fed just enough to confiscate its labour,
and disposable as an animal past its use;
Lancaster keeping the harvest, fermenting
a homesick bitter brew – a Samboo
kicked from his calabash pot.

A desolate breed lashed from

the shaft of his life-source,
trapped by distance and isolation,
their Samboo pines for his master, mythical
imagined key and centrepiece of his world.

I see this Samboo, this boy Bilal
in the Brewery room – outpost
of a West Indian estate – away from the boiling
reek of molasses for rum,
pining for the familiar, where rooms are many,
in one dwelling, in one
compound, in one village, in one
land, in one kingdom, in one
empire, in one continent.

A fermenting homesick brew, he drains out,
kicked from his split calabash pot.

These poems originally appeared in
Ship Shape by Dorothea Smartt,
published by Peepal Tree Press, Leeds

THREE POEMS

Elmi Ali

Pirates and Co.

Can you swim?
Do you sometimes wear skirt-like wraps?
Do you have pitch-black skin and good hair?
Do the words,
Waryaa, Nayaa and American dollar,
Mean anything to you?

The Somali pirate's society wants you.

We have Saudi oil tankers,
Rich holiday makers,
And resident Korean tuna trawlers,

Register now at your local offices,
And we'll even throw in a free motorized dinghy.

The Somali pirate's society,
Making water profitable.

A study in memory

I ran out of the city,
my lovers name
a thorn in my mouth, gaging on the truth,
Wardhiigley smouldering behind me –
the fat settling

in the cul-de-sac where I left our house.

I became a contortionist,
folding my body
into self-pity,
turned religion into a bunker,
squatted
in the interviewer's office
holding on to God
like a key.

I pulled my tongue out
stretched it over
a new language, learnt
to bend over a toilet bowl,
took pills
for the heart burn, became British
without
memorising my lovers face.

Headland

My mother is an adolescent girl
with the soul of a widow still in mourning.
Her voice is unsure and her mouth an open window,
the rubble of her past successes
lodged in her throat.

On a good day she crosses her hands
over her distended breasts – each nipple
heavy with generosity – sits at the edge of an entire continent
her left foot in the sea,
her right touching the ocean
and looks at the world
like a sharp thorn entering a heel.

REVIEWS

HOME IS THE JOURNEY

Declan Ryan

Ruth Padel's *The Mara Crossing* might easily be termed *sui generis*, if it didn't helpfully explain its roots in the mediaeval *prosimetrum* in its opening chapter. Even knowing that it's rooted in a rich tradition where prose and poetry are bound together, however, doesn't bring us closer to explaining its scale, ambition or achievement. A study of migration, Padel's interest ranges from the cells of the body to the flight patterns of wild geese, from dispelling the myth of mass lemming suicide to chatting to her daughter on Skype. Under a catch-all investigation of what it is to migrate, including the etymology of the terms involved, she explores rootlessness, asylum, displacement and many of the other most pressing political concerns of our time in clear-sighted, lucid prose. Interestingly, for Padel the prose which makes up the majority of the collection is figured more as preamble than overpowering or pushy neighbour to the poems: 'the prose interludes are not essays but introductions to each run of poems – as in a live reading poets introduce poems with a little information, so the audience knows something about them when they listen.'

Ruth Padel, *The Mara Crossing* and *Learning to Make an Oud Nazareth*, Chatto and Windus, London, 2012 and 2014, respectively.

We can certainly read the prose chapters in this sense, many of the poems in the collection are ones which would require a fair bit of setting up at a reading given their often complex scientific interest and terminology – 'Cytoskeleton, little net/of peel and fibrous scaffolding/within the cytoplasm' – and therefore the prose which precedes each run acts as a generous guide, at times making the chapter feel like notes and research building to the handful of poems which close it. Padel's deep interest in and reading of, among other things, conservation, biology and semantics, however, means that the prose does more than act as mere prop or stage-setter, and as much as the poems are the driving force behind the book, the prose builds in its own right a rhythm and authority thanks to Padel's ability to handle masses of material across a sweep of time and deliver it unfussily, cogently and with a great deal of diligent sensitivity.

The Mara Crossing of the collection's title acts as a sort of anchoring metaphor, derived from the perilous journey undertaken by gazelle, wildebeest and zebra in order to get at the phosphorous-rich land waiting for them on the other side of crocodile-packed waters. As Padel reminds us, nature is profligate, and for the many that die attempting to make it to their own version of the promised land, more survive this crossing. The book is an investigation into why almost every species, including our own, make their equivalent journeys, taking such calculated and often desperate risks. In one of the most bracingly impassioned sections of the book, Padel exposes the 'bitter' and 'deceptive' connotations of 'Mara', before – via the comments pages of a newspaper – stating that it is hope which drives migration and issuing a plea for compassion and empathy. This is an important piece of writing, and it feels both achieved and earned when it comes – the effect of its contrast with the run of poems that follow it, including 'Wetbacks' and 'Maltese Fishing Boat and Broken Net' with its closing lines 'Cut the rope! What would you do? / We lose our catch but we get home. / A hundred are drowning – / why should we six die too?' is all the more devastating for the righteous anger of their prose 'introduction'.

It's worth dwelling on both the righteous indignation of this section, and more widely on the political ambition and interest of the book, not least because it is such a rarity to find, at least with this degree of control and insight, in contemporary British poetry. The decision to include these introductory sections in prose is not, then, merely a means of allowing a gloss on otherwise difficult concepts and terms in the poems, it also – like lengthening a line or breaking metre – gives Padel scope to bring in more of the world, to develop important discussions and to clear the ground in order that her poetic gift might have access to hitherto unavailable subject matter, once it's been properly set-up for the reader. The nuance and empathy required by her discussions of asylum – its historical roots and the modern stigma of the word – require a degree of unpacking which would be impossible to do without making too many artistic compromises in a lyric poem, with its requirement of density and explosive compression. By allowing herself to use prose – always a poet's prose, if not prose poetry – Padel manages to break new ground with this ancient form, the *prosimetrum*, with each chapter displaying the concerns and swagger which have come to characterise her poems, albeit with a much broader palette. A chapter on 'Strangers', for example, flits back and forth in history, taking in Hopkins and Darwish as well as examining the Greek roots of the word for exile and Padel's own visit to Madrid in 2006 where Brueghel's paintings and TV images of Israel's invasion of Lebanon appeared to parallel one another. In short, that kind of movement – back and forth in time, literary allusion, personal insight – has often been the kind of journey Padel's poems have taken a reader on, albeit in a much shorter and more traditionally stanzaic, space.

As well as the crossing of the Masai Mara, another well-judged thread which runs through this expansive book is a series of deceptively small-scale meditations on Padel moving house, her garden, and the birds which visit it. Padel writes of her daughter, away in Bogota, and of packing up and moving on, reminding us always that the grand ideas behind migration, the movement of cells, birds or tribes is based on need, and on the attempt to establish a comfortable home in which to thrive. This rootedness, in a book about movement and searching, is perceptively done, and acts as a counterpoint to the more philosophical discussions of souls, and transmigration, assuring us that whichever route we are to be taken down there is a sense of roundedness at the back of it, and that our feet can remain planted on solid ground. Padel, towards the book's close, makes the point that poetry and exile, or displacement, are common bedfellows, and that the draw of art is that it allows one to make sense of the journeys, both physical or inner. The collection's dazzling closing poem, 'Time To Fly', with its long lines and litany of 'You go because...' is a suitably mobile and driving close to a book about flight of every kind, and its concluding phrase 'You go because you must', given everything that's gone before it is a masterstroke of resonant understatement.

Without Padel's immersion and investigation, evident in the prose of *The Mara Crossing*, the poems of that collection wouldn't have been possible, or even viable. In an interestingly analogous way, but for her fascination with the science and language of movement and migration, the poems of *Learning to Make an Oud in Nazareth* could not have emerged as the visceral and arresting declarations that they are. There is no accompanying, or supporting, prose – aside from the notes at the back – but this latest collection has built on the gains made via the freedom Padel allowed herself in her previous collection, and more than ever these poems feel able to gather into themselves a huge range of history, allusion and learning without compromising their status as achieved lyrics. Having taken the lengthened step of the *prosimetrum*, Padel appears to have found a way of bolstering an already authoritative voice into one capable of reaching for the difficult register of rhetoric, and the results are consistently captivating.

There are a number of underlying movements in this new collection, which overlap and, together, create something like an *ars poetica* which combines faith and hope with an artisanal devotion. If it was hope that emerged as the driving force behind migration in *The Mara Crossing*, it's also the keynote here, but not in a glib or saccharine sense – this is hardly poetry as self-help – but in a much more interestingly defiant, fallibly vulnerable one. 'A Guide to the Church of Nativity in Time of Siege' is a tour de force, a dramatic monologue which in its slow unfolding and subtly revealing use of inference looks back to Tennyson or Browning as much as a modern master of the genre such as Michael Donaghy. It also contains a line which resonates throughout the collection, helping to shape the philosophy of the book in its way – 'In Arabic and Hebrew/verb *to be* does not exist. No Present, only Future/and the Past.' That's not to say that this collection is one steeped in nostalgia or prediction, but – at a far more interestingly central sense – one in which the idea of present, and presence, has to be enacted and rescued, rather than taken for granted. It is a book which has both the long view of history, as alluded to in the same poem – 'even emperors bow to time'. This is also hinted at in 'The Hebrew for Egypt Means Narrow' where the loss of certainty, or easy answers, is presented as our state but the opposite is a constriction which is no more appealing, resulting in the somewhat Arnoldian statement that 'We are out in the wilderness now'.

If *The Mara Crossing*'s poems were supported by their explicatory prose, the one down-side to that level of scene-setting was that the element of surprise had to be sacrificed in order to guide the reader through otherwise difficult and dense material. No such sacrifices have been required here, and as a result the thrilling multiplicity of the range of subject on show, coupled with the boldness and confidence derived from following such a wide-ranging project as the previous collection, means that we are transported through time and space, myth and register, dance and fight, throughout. The opening, title, poem is a triumph of this sort of navigation, mixing the language of craftsmanship with that of Biblical love, shifting from the tender sensuality of the maker – 'The first day he cut rosewood for the back,/bent sycamore into ribs to make a belly' to the expressive declaration 'He shall lie all night between my breasts.' What makes this poem feel like more than a mere exercise in virtuosity, or a tethering together of past and present, is the way Padel manages to make this conflation feel inevitable, in the bones, with the old and new rituals and the old and new acts of violence chained together by a heightened version of the sort of interpersonal care and close observation on show in *The Mara Crossing*'s domestic scenes. That the wider impulse behind all this cutting, paring and sanding was that 'his banner over me was love' takes on more than a merely touching, romantic satisfaction when re-read in the light of the rest of the poems here.

   If hope is the still point in the turning mechanism of this collection, conflict and violence are absolutely central too, and it is this clash between the bloody and the resolute which provides the momentum and charge of the best poems here. Christ's final words are brought together in a stunning suite of focused snapshots, where it isn't only the spring in the rhythm that stuns, but the intensity of focus on minutiae, the sheer corporeality of the hanging man, with his 'bubble-wrap of viscid spittle' and 'wrecked lungs' fighting his desire to cry out for help, or even admit to his human thirst. The third poem of the sequence, focusing on his mother's love and the loss of his boyhood, is one of the book's high points and a masterpiece of reined-in melancholy.

   Time, also, is a presence, often with an elegiac note which brings with it not morbidity or fear but rather resolution and a desire to persist and endure. The meditative quality of the phrase 'Landscape/is your life seen in distance, when you know//for just an interval of sunlight/how to join time travelled with time still to go' is refracted in the elegy to J.G Farrell 'Mill Wheel at Bantry' with its closing lines 'There's been so much/ I haven't attended to. So much I didn't see' and colours the poems at their bloodiest or most seemingly hopeless. Picking up on the previous focus on migration, home here is still in flight, and motion, in never staying still, and this desire to attend to experience and act in a meaningful fashion is perhaps most eloquently summed up in 'The Chain's declaration that 'I'm trying to transform sin into grace.'

That idea is more than a spoken intention, and in a sense is the overarching architecture of this book, and of the poems' making. It is a collection obsessed with salvage and rescue, with empathy and the transformation of suffering into something like grace, and so even at its darkest moments, where Brueghel paints *The Triumph of Death* to give us 'the world as it is' there is hope to be found, albeit possibly only in retrospect, from his 'painstaking draughtsmanship'. At times in this often devastatingly undeceived book, light and reasons for optimism may be difficult to see, but they are unfailingly present – even on the Western Front, where 'they may have wondered why a thing with wings/would stay in such a place.' As alluded to elsewhere, we know that in Dickinson's phrase hope is just such a winged thing, and despite all the odds it is clear that it endures, just as even the act of breakage that is Kintsugi is a strange version of triumph, which adds value and allows for 'the joy/of finding and then bringing back/to the world (this is porcelain/we're talking of here, not a life)/what was, or what could have been, lost.'

The book's closing poem, 'Facing East', feels like a poem wrestled not only from experience in a worldly sense, but also in terms of the artistic strides gained over the course of the previous collection's addition of a new set of poetic tools by virtue of the *prosimetrum* form. There is no simple 'to be' to fall back on, we are a migrant, moving people but as this final poem attests in a line which echoes Larkin's earlier epiphany: 'What will survive are meanings we have found/in what the world has made'. In a poem which alone takes in Greek myth, modern warfare and classical music, the steely summation feels hard-won and has the air of something like faith and permanence in a defiantly transitory world – 'Making is our defence against the dark.' Padel's poetry, which can take us from hotel rooms watching CNN to the site of the crucifixion, is a testament to the power of making as a means of bearing witness, and at their height both books have the unquestionable sense that they have been made because they must.

COOL MUSLIM WOMEN

Samia Rahman

My university days were played out pre-Facebook and therefore documented only in photographs possessed by very few and viewed only by a chosen few. Life was certainly very social but not broadcast via any form of media. I had what was once called a 'private life', locked away for the most part in memories and nostalgic reminiscing. For this I am eternally grateful, not least because university was the setting for a formative transition from adolescence to adulthood. It was the exciting and fragile launchpad for a journey negotiating an evolving sense of self. It is here that I began to come to terms with what it meant to me to be a second-generation British-Pakistani Muslim woman. I became enamoured with postmodern concepts seductively espoused by Homi Bhabha and Gayatri Spivak, fancying myself to be the embodiment of hybridity, occupying a third space, having no home yet many homes, an outsider within. I devoured postcolonial literature and theory and made it my story. Identity and race politics offered me an enticing narrative I could call my own.

Then 9/11 happened. Identity politics became complicated by perceived religiosity. Suddenly no other aspect of my comfortably fragmented Self mattered more than my religious identity. Islamophobia was not born, it had always existed, but it was now the ultra-definition of Otherness. Race became transcended by religion but I knew a world when this had not been so ominously so. A recent conversation with a young British-Arab Muslim woman, about to begin her undergraduate studies in London, reminded me I was fortunate to remember life before my faith came to vehemently symbolise the antithesis of Western civilisation. She had been listening to a radio talk show and had been deeply upset by the anti-Muslim sentiment of the callers and the host. She confided how overwhelmed she felt by the level of antipathy towards Muslims and the media sensationalism that twisted every small news item into a diatribe against Islam. A devout and earnest eighteen-year-old, her existential struggle to reconcile the essentialising and racist stereotypes with her own reality of the Islam she grew up with – unremarkable, peaceful and beautiful – was distressing to witness.

It is such negotiations of identity and formation of self that Shabana Mir unpacks in her riveting book. She combines reportage and ethnographic analysis to bring the diverse spectrum of American Muslim female experience on college campuses in Washington DC to life. She is at pains to illustrate the heterogeneity of the Muslim women in her study. They diverge in ethnicity, religiosity and social background. They are united only by the fact that they self-identify as Muslim, were raised in the US, and are negotiating the perilous path of identity in a shared space, namely two college campuses in the capital.

Shabana Mir, *Muslim American Women on Campus: Undergraduate Social Life and Identity*, University of North Carolina Press, Chapel Hill, NC, 2014.

Mir interrogates the formation of identity at this crucial period in any young person's life by focussing on the social lives of these women. Through in-depth interviews, casual conversations and off-the-cuff remarks, we are invited to peer into the intimate thoughts of the participants as if we are 'friending' them on Facebook – viewing their comments, likes, photos and posts. The insight into lives actually lived in the shadow of 9/11 is both mesmerising and troubling. The anxieties of young adults, struggling to emerge unscathed from searing scrutiny not only by non-Muslims but also by fellow Muslims, can at times be unsettling. Mir's use of first-person excerpts from conversations and interviews provide a platform for rarely heard voices that serve to shatter reductive stereotypes and subvert mainstream preconceptions of that most fetishised subject – the Muslim woman.

What makes Mir's book unique is the blistering honesty with which the participants lay bare their lived realities. Buoyed by a tacit understanding of confidentiality, and undoubtedly secure in their trust of the writer, we become privy to the most personal of conversations. The reader is encouraged to sit back, get comfortable and witness, as if a fly on the wall, a gossipy conversation during a girls' night in, or a Facebook messenger exchange or a WhatsApp dialogue. The fiercely contested terrain of female Muslim agency is brought to life in these passages; and young Muslim women, so often discussed, analysed and upon whom so much is projected, are allowed to speak with their own voices and be heard. The sense of intimacy is compounded by Mir's decision to focus on the twenty-six participants' social lives and how they navigate the pitfalls and opportunities that characterise campus life. Muslim women have often been associated with concepts of shame and family honour, so it is perhaps intriguing that Mir should focus her research on the most private aspects of an individual's life: sex, alcohol and fashion.

No doubt some Muslims will see these as 'controversial' issues; and argue that Mir is deliberately focussing on the frivolous and titillating in a lame effort to be sensational. I would argue otherwise. These are significant social tropes that are fundamental to the construction of identity. How we navigate social dilemmas locates us in the perceptions of others. All young Muslims are faced with the choice to drink alcohol or not to drink alcohol and whether or not to occupy spaces in which alcohol is distributed and consumed. These choices reflect how we define ourselves in terms of the religious framework that underpins our lives. It is this that Mir explores tenderly, devoid of the reductionist tone of a tabloid gossip expose.

The burden of double scrutiny is one that contextualises the experiences of the American Muslim female undergraduates featured in the book, although it has to be said that empirical studies of immigrant communities often point to the same conclusion. In such cases the subject is acutely aware of the normative expectations projected upon them by fellow Muslims and non-Muslims alike. Mir is right to focus on these contested spaces because they dominate social discourse during a crucial period in a young Muslim woman's life. It is likely she is living away from home for the first time, free of parental constraints and watchful eyes of conservative relatives. Thrust into unfamiliar, perhaps thrilling situations, she is able to make choices that were previously unavailable to her. Mir resists caricaturing her in the language of the satirical 'Catholic girl' who stereotypically drinks, parties and enjoys sexual freedom to excess once she is released from her religious shackles. Instead, the participants employ varying shifts in power that inform their actions. These powers are the consequences of the double scrutiny that the participants feel keenly and are indicative of the diversity and sophistication of their approaches. Mir invokes Homi Bhabha but applies the idea of the 'third space' that he championed in a measured tone: 'this third space demonstrates the incompleteness of hegemony, as marginal individuals use the cultural resources at their disposal – including Orientalist discourse, dominant majority practices, stereotypes, and slurs – to perform and to reinvent identities, and to represent communities, ideologies and themselves.'

I was never an undergraduate in the US but such quandaries resonate with my own university adventures here in the UK. I remained resolutely teetotal but was surrounded by copious amounts of alcohol at the parties, gigs and clubs I frequented. Hence my relief that the pitfalls of Facebook were not yet invented, paving the way for inevitable misrepresentation and reputation car crash. I wore my religion on my sleeve and let it be known to anyone who was listening that I did not drink, did not have boyfriends, and definitely did not wear fashionable garments that exposed my flesh 'because I am a Muslim'. My university friends were respectful, interested and at the same time quite unfazed. I now wonder whether it was because we occupied a sub-culture of our own that defined itself outside the mainstream. We were the indie/rock kids into our own alternative music and fashion, the Other to the rugby lads and hockey-playing girls who represented bland, conformist cultural hegemony. I am definitely not cool now but back then I was a cool Muslim. I don't recall feeling the tension articulated by Heather, a white, upper-class, research participant, who 'acted drunk' yet never gave a reason for why she did not consume alcohol, eventually feeling marginal to what she perceived to be an alcohol-dominated social world. Amira also went to bars and parties where everyone around her was drinking and made a point of saying she did not drink, in as genial and non-judgemental way as possible. Yet she never explained the reason why, to such an extent that her non-Muslim peers did not even realise that she was teetotal or that she was a Muslim. Other participants made a point of steering clear of spaces where alcohol was consumed altogether. It struck me, and is noted by Mir, that the Muslim women in her study made conscious or unconscious attempts to behave as inoffensively as possible, almost in an attempt to assuage the dominant narrative of the blood-thirsty, terrorist Muslim or oppressed, submissive woman. As Mir explains:

In the social spaces of campus, my research participants commonly passed as 'normal' and covered Muslim identities. But often, too, they countered normalised discourses about Muslims and projected identities tailored to challenge common stereotypes. 'Spoiled' but not broken, they constructed identities in new combinations, keenly aware of the gaze that fixed and curbed them. My participants became objects to themselves when they met the 'Muslim Woman' in their peers' heads and internalized this image but this objectification created possibilities of agency against symbolic violence. The possibility of agency is in fact catalyzed from the mix of conflicting Orientalist stereotypes that cast Muslim women as objects of fear and objects of pity, as sexual objects and virginally chaste: this repetition and doubling, these contradictions, betray the weakness in Orientalism, and they engender the possibilities for stereotyped persons to transcend inscribed identities. Thus Muslim women become not mere victims of cultural processes but participants in them, 'active appropriators' of majority discourses and practices 'who reproduce existing structures only through struggle, contestation and a partial penetration of these structures.'

You may agree or disagree with these women, but you have to acknowledge they are anything but submissive objects of fear and pity. I see them as rather cool; and eminently sensible and aware of the wider issues. As Amber points out, 'no matter how much you try to live in this moment, we have to think about what's happened in the broader context'.

Mir's conclusions are not particularly original. But then reality too is often unsurprising. Muslim female identity, Mir says, is a construction, a negotiation of competing influences and agencies that are in constant flux. There is no essential Muslim identity that can be projected onto a homogenous swathe of people because there is no such thing as a typical Muslim. Plurality of self-identification and an individual's unique navigation through life are the only typical Muslim experience. Or in the words of Somali-born, basketball player, Intisar, being a young Muslim woman is 'not an agenda, you know, every day in the morning you wake up and say, OK, now I'm *going* to pray and I'm *going* to play basketball! It's contradictory, but it's just life, we just go through it'.

Sectarian Politics in the Persian Gulf

Edited by Lawrence G. Potter

ISBN: 9781849043380
£20.00 / Paperback / 320pp

Long a taboo topic, as well as one that has alarmed outside powers, sectarian conflict in the Middle East is on the rise. The contributors to this book examine sectarian politics in the Persian Gulf, including the GCC states, Yemen, Iran and Iraq, and consider the origins and consequences of sectarianism broadly construed, as it affects ethnic, tribal and religious groups. They also present a theoretical and comparative framework for understanding sectarianism, as well as country-specific chapters based on recent research in the area. Key issues that are scrutinised include the nature of sectarianism, how identity moves from a passive to an active state, and the mechanisms that trigger conflict. The strategies of governments such as rentier economies and the 'invention' of partisan national histories that encourage or manage sectarian differences are also highlighted, as is the role of outside powers in fostering sectarian strife. The volume also seeks to clarify whether movements such as the Islamic revival or the Arab Spring obscure the continued salience of religious and ethnic cleavages.

'A timely contribution to understanding sectarianism on both sides of the Persian Gulf. The contributors are well-established historians and social scientists who offer nuanced interpretations of a malaise, at once contemporary and ancient, which threatens to redraw the region's political map. The result is an erudite exploration of the meaning of sectarianism in the context of old nations, and in newly forged ones — weaving local political contexts with transnational connections and outside interventions — which all seem to have escalated sectarian divides against a background of negotiated and fluid identities. The book paints a compelling picture of past and present coexistence and conflict.' — Madawi Al-Rasheed, Visiting Professor at the Middle East Centre, London School of Economics and Political Science

WWW.HURSTPUBLISHERS.COM/BOOK/SECTARIAN-POLITICS-IN-THE-PERSIAN-GULF

41 GREAT RUSSELL ST, LONDON WC1B 3
WWW.HURSTPUBLISHERS.COM
WWW.FBOOK.COM/HURSTPUBLISHERS
020 7255 2201

ET CETERA

SOUTH ASIAN PRIVILEGE

Naima Khan

Remember the 1990s? The era when Saudi-influenced political Islam had a strong hold on British South Asian Muslims and black Muslim women were told, in no uncertain terms, that their headwraps were categorically not hijab? Remember when ten years later a sizeable number of Asian women donned all manner of African-influenced headwraps without bothering to acknowledge the roots of their appropriated clothing?

I remember. I, like other countless South Asians, Africans and Caribbean people across the UK, add this cultural event to the ever-growing list of incidents, attitudes and appropriations practised by South Asians, which ignore, undermine and insult other minority groups. Top of the list, when it comes to Muslim-specific behaviours, is the much-referenced story of Bilal. His resilience and triumph over adversity has, for all intents and purposes, been co-opted by non-Black Muslims to impress on others our fair treatment of those we continue to oppress. While we repeat our sound bites about 'equality in Islam' and one *ummah* of all races, we keep schtum about the trans-Saharan slave trade; we choose to ignore rampant casual racism within our own communities ; and we shrug off our indifference at the seemingly unconquerable problem of looking down on Africans. Our attitudes of indifference and disdain towards black people have aided our ascent on the racial hierarchy in Britain. Success in the UK means reaching for an integrated anglicised ideal, and that include stepping on the backs of those who sit lower down the ladder than us.

I write as an Indian Brit, aware of the intricacies and the problematic nature of pointing a finger towards South Asian privileges. Referring to 'South Asians' is a nod to the way white British ruling classes have seen us for centuries: as an amalgamated mass who, compared to criminal black men and angry black women, don't seem to be doing so badly. It does, however, put us at least one rung below the nice East Asians, the folks from China, Hong Kong and South Korea, whose low levels of crime, English first names and superlative offspring put us to shame. The term 'South Asians' lumps together a range of people whose incomes, religions and circumstances are varied. It ignores that some of us live in the most deprived, underemployed areas of the country while others rub shoulders with policy makers and politicians. It sidelines the struggles that South Asians continue to experience in this country, including the old perceptions of wheeler-dealer men, submissive women, and oppressive family structures. More importantly, it pays little attention to the powerful white people and wealthy Arabs who stoke the flames of racial divide.

Tricky terminology aside, since we know the world doesn't consist of clear cut perpetrators and victims, where has this incipient racism within our communities come from? Why do we not take a moment to recognise the advantages we have over others given that being able to ignore our privilege is a privilege itself?

This prejudice is partly a product of our perception of religion. The oil-rich Arabs who funded our mosques and religious centres also turned them into bastions of Wahhabism, which tends to look down on anyone who does not follow the true ultra-conservative and puritan path of this sect. Given that most of the Wahhabi, and their Deobandi off-shoot, mosques were controlled by South Asians, they naturally saw other Muslims, particularly the Africans, as lesser beings. Their Islam was contaminated with Sufi ideals and African folklore, their women did not 'dress properly', which made them somewhat inferior in the eyes of true believers. Through a process of osmosis, the Wahhabis also transmitted their hierarchical notions of race and racial purity to their South Asian fellow travellers.

But there are also specific historical roots to this racism. South Asians are among the beneficiaries of certain historical events, which produced favourable depictions, associations and assumptions made by non-Asians about us. These include how we are perceived by the white community as well as language and terminology associated with us, and dissociated from us like the term 'racial privilege' which is usually synonymous with white privilege. Consider, for example, the notion of the 'model immigrant', to borrow an American term. These immigrants are the ones who contribute significantly to the infrastructure of their country and make an effort to integrate in ways outlined by the host population. By doing so, they align themselves with the dominant majority, overcoming resistance to their own civil rights. As the noted American historian of race, Noel Ignatiev notes, this alignment is necessary for successful social mobility where race is a factor. It is a way immigrants can convince the establishment that they are worthy of equal treatment. The other key element of social mobility is distancing oneself from less desirable communities. For the Catholic American Irish of the 1850s, whom Ignatiev writes about, the least desirable were the black population including the free and the enslaved. You could argue that black people, particularly those who retain a visible or audible African-Caribbean identity, still occupy the lowest levels of the racial hierarchy today. These two elements are of course linked. If you can convince the dominant population that you have a common enemy, you appear pleasing to them. You have fallen in line; and removed at least some barriers to climbing up the social ladder.

South Asians have aligned themselves with the dominant white culture in modern day Britain in a similar way. Our visible social mobility since the 1950s has seen the suit-wearing members of our pack join political parties, enter into government, and grace the media. We own multi-million pound businesses, we are board members of FTSE 100 companies, we own luxury restaurant chains, and we are reliable regulars in annual rich lists. The younger generation are doing their part too by dutifully anglicising their names, developing impressive technology start-ups, and populating clubs and bars. They've not only entered into relatively new desirable professions but continue to conquer the traditional ones such as medicine, law and accountancy. These client-facing white-collar careers are one way to communicate a clear message to those who might oppose our claim to equal status in this country: when it comes to equality, we deserve it.

While this seems innocuous, and indeed it is, the foundation beneath this success is altogether murkier than we would like to admit. Our top level positions in so many fields are proof that a significant number of South Asians know how to be seen as equals. To our great advantage, we've had hundreds of years of British rule to give us a head start. And yes, I know exactly how that sounds and it makes me cringe too. I'm not suggesting we should be grateful to have been colonised. However, in terms of our status as a model minority amongst a white British majority, it's hard to deny that our historical image as obedient colonial subjects makes us more palatable in Britain today, especially in comparison to African communities in the UK.

One example of the British Empire's long standing disdain of blackness and preference for what they considered 'Asian qualities', is evident in its construction of the Uganda Railway. In 1896, when construction began, the British imported 32,000 labourers from British India to work on the railways. Although the conditions were horrendous and the work gruelling, the attitude behind the import of those Indians was centred on the idea that Indians would make a docile, diligent workforce whereas black people were too lazy, stupid and volatile to do the work. These ideas about black labourers came from years of trials in Britain's Caribbean plantations after the abolition of slavery in 1833. After the slaves were freed and given their due rights, the workforce consisted of paid, strong, black, male bodies with a freedom that made them all the more feared and loathed. Many of them left their former slave masters and the plantation owners shipped in workers from China, Europe and India to fill the labour gap. They concluded that by British standards, Indians were the better workers and so kept them on.

The British implemented a similar labour import of Indians in colonial East Africa. The Indians were entered into a new form of temporary slavery while much of the Ugandan population refused to work on such a dangerous job. The construction of the railways lasted only five years after which, the Indians stayed and fuelled the rapid growth of cities like Nairobi and Mombasa. They became shopkeepers, hotel workers and administrators. To their advantage, they could also do business with the more established Indian traders who had followed Arab trade routes to the coast of Kenya, Tanzania and Zanzibar. Though they were not allowed to own farms and were excluded from middle and senior positions in government, by the time the British began their process of decolonisation after the Second World War, Indians had a stronghold on commercial trade in the area. These Asians were to become the professional class that Idi Amin expelled from Uganda in 1972, the class who were acknowledged as 'the backbone of commercial life in Uganda'.

While the expulsion itself was a tragic episode, the discourse around it viewed Asians favourably compared to their black immigrant counterparts.

Despite facing tough legislation including the 1968 Commonwealth Immigration Act introduced specifically to curb an influx from East Africa, many Asians in Uganda held British passports and could lay claim to British citizenship. These new Asian immigrants were seen by many Brits as educated and entrepreneurial and so able to create employment opportunities for the British population. The sentiments were summed up by a white-collar worker interviewed on the BBC News in 1973: 'There's no doubt about it, Ugandan Asians coming to the North East will prove to be a very very valuable asset to the North East. In the first place, most of them are businessmen. They will offer employment opportunities to the North East, to local Geordies and of course to the local Asian population. They shouldn't be a drain on the social services, there's no evidence to suggest that...I would say that the Ugandan Asians, if they do choose to settle in this area, will not only be invaluable in providing more jobs for the North East but that they will play a lot in the work, life, culture and the society of the North East.'

But the Ugandan Asians also brought their preconceptions of blacks with them. As the writer Yasmin Alibhai-Brown points out, it was not uncommon for Asians in Uganda to hold extremely racist views about black people which mirrored the white establishment assumptions of them as stupid, dangerous, easy to fool and incapable of leading commerce the ways Indians could.

Asians arrived here from Africa on a wave of sympathy and hope, a very different story to the people who arrive from Africa today. As expected we faced predictable racism but we found we had allies. There was a sense of solidarity among Asian and black communities against their racist abusers – and we fought racism jointly and often successfully. But that solidarity has now evaporated, thanks largely to the conscious distance the Asians have placed between themselves and the black communities. The current state of affairs is neatly summed up by Lance Bunkley, one of the first black immigrants to arrive in Wolverhampton. He was asked by journalist Sarfraz Manzoor, exploring the legacy of Enoch Powell's 'Rivers of Blood' speech in Birmingham, whether he would rather be a young black man in 1968 or today. 'In those days', Bunkley replies, 'we were a community. We looked after one another; we paid each other's debts; blacks and Asians worked together. Today, there is no sense of community and everyone is an individual'.

Since 1968, there has been a fierce jostling for position in the racial pecking order that has not just separated Asian and black people but caused fault lines to form within our communities. The dissonance centres around ideas that blackness is bad and those wishing to prove they deserve acceptance in the UK will uphold the notions that black men are criminal and that black women are undesirable. We see this today in the prejudice surrounding interracial marriages between our two communities and in the preference for Asians who have European features and fair skin. We see it in the dismissive attitude we have towards young Asian boys who emulate the perceived stereotypical mannerisms of their black counterparts. We see it in the Asian shopkeepers who perpetuate ideas about beauty by supplying Indian hair extensions to black women. There is a cruel ignorance in our expectation of black people to conform to their stock characters while we consider ourselves worthy of more nuanced depiction.

The South Asians have been good students; we have internalised the lessons of our colonial masters. We have learnt that subjugating black people is in our best interests when it comes to establishing ourselves among Britons. Our success in so many fields as a single ethnic South Asian group rather than part of an amalgamation of equal, cooperative and successful multi-ethnic immigrant communities is a testament to our understanding of Ignatiev's two principles of social ascension.

And we are passing these lessons on to our children. They are being taught to abuse the next wave of immigrants. Take a walk in any area with a discernible South Asian population and hear what our young have to say about Somalis, Sudanese and Nigerians. Not to mention the Poles, Romanians and the Albanians.

ON TRINIDAD

Hassan Mahamdallie

It is Eid day. The smartly dressed congregation are flocking to morning prayers at the large Nur E Islam Mosque, in Farouk Avenue, that serves the Muslims of San Juan (pronounced saa-waa), a suburb of Port of Spain, the capital of Trinidad. Each person is eager to get a place in the shade before the sun unleashes its full splendour on the congregation. The imam, alert to the fact that he has before him his seasonal captive audience, conducts a rather lengthy but moving sermon about the need to value common humanity which ends with him breaking down in tears.

Just as he composes himself for his closing injunctions, top of the range four-by-four wagons pull up outside the masjid. Those of us stretching our legs on the pavement look on wide-eyed as each vehicle discharges an extravagantly dressed African-Trinidadian woman, dripping with jewellery and covered in elaborate niqab, with smartly dressed young children in tow. They verbally joust with the young lads hanging about on the street: '*A salaam alaykum, wa'appen bhai?*' (everyone is *bhai* in Trinidad, a small mark of the syntheses of ethnicities, cultures and languages that converge in Trinidad patois).

It's quite an entrance and contrasts sharply with the huddle of destitute and poor people nearby, who, kept in line by a muscular policeman armed with a shotgun, wait patiently for post-sermon alms. 'Who are these sisters?' I ask, not understanding why they came so late and dressed in such ostentatious opulence. 'Gangsters Molls,' whispers a fellow street loiterer. 'From Abu Bakr's Black Muslims from St James'.

And there we have it. The latticework of politicised, racial and religious distinctions that characterise post-colonial Trinidadian politics, society and culture, comes to the surface.

Abu Bakr of 'Abu Bakr's Black Muslims' is well known in the country. In 1990, he along with members of his Jamaat-al-Muslimeen organisation stormed the Trinidad and Tobago parliament, the Red House, and the national TV station in an attempted coup. The ensuing crisis lasted six days during which the prime minister and MPs were held hostage, twenty-four people died and much of Port of Spain, including the police headquarters, was reduced to rubble and burnt out properties. He was arrested, imprisoned, but later given amnesty.

Now he runs an empire from his masjid in the St James area of Port of Spain. He has amassed a great deal of wealth through various means. Clearly one of the island's great political survivors, he has far reaching influence. It is rumoured that he is behind successful bids for municipal works' contracts in areas like Laventille, the sprawling African-Trinidadian shanty town that clings to the hills overlooking Port of Spain that suffers from a fearsome reputation for murders and gang-related violence. Trinidad has one of the highest murder rates in the Western world, much of it related to drug and gun running from South America, aggravated by the mass poverty that exists in the ghettoes.

The US authorities, I am reliably told, still keep a close eye on Abu Bakr and his supporters, suspecting them of encouraging terrorism. In 2011 the government declared a state of emergency, ostensibly as a response to a violent crime wave, during which a number of arrests were made linked to a rumoured conspiracy to assassinate Prime Minister Kamla Persad-Bissessar. Those arrested were Muslims. Incredible as it seems, this tiny beautiful Caribbean island, just 50 miles long and 40 miles wide, with a population of just 1.2 million, is regarded by the US as a source of violent Islamism. The island's security services are extensive and disproportionate to its size – there are no less than six different agencies tasked to gather intelligence under the huge and costly Ministry of National Security. No doubt much of their information is sent straight to the Americans. Trinidad's politicians remain mindful of 'Operation Urgent Fury' – the 1983 full scale American military invasion of the even tinier neighbouring island of Grenada, launched to defend US 'national security'.

Abu Bakr is never far from the headlines, although it is impossible to glean the truth of the many allegations made against him. In 2005 he was arrested, but not charged, over the bombing of a night club in St James. He was then accused of incitement, sedition and extortion after his Friday sermon in which he allegedly threatened the members of his organisation with 'war' and 'bloodshed' if they did not give zakat during Eid al-Fitr.

But all this is far, far away from the consciousness of the Muslims preparing for the Eid celebrations. Everything is as it should be; and it all begins with confusion over when the first day of Eid al-Fitr falls. 'Is it Thursday or Friday?' – the question that vexes us all – is finally and definitively answered by my ten-year-old nephew: 'Somebody said they saw the moon in Guyana - but it wasn't confirmed'. End of story. So Friday it is, which is fortunate, because that means it coincides with the government of Trinidad and Tobago's designated Eid national public holiday. So it is not just the Muslims who will get the day off, everyone will.

Vast quantities of meat is bought and prepared in huge pans. Beef is plentiful, but for a month chicken has been scarce on the island for some reason, so that takes longer to track down. The right grade of vermicelli is purchased to make buckets of *sawine* (or is it *sawanyan*, as they call it on the Subcontinent), the Trinidad Eid treat of choice. To the vermicelli is added cinnamon, evaporated milk, sugar, raisins, cherries and vanilla, and is doled out piping hot in cupfuls to visitors and neighbours. I prefer the traditional Trinidad Christmas drink of choice, *sorrel*, best drunk to the accompaniment of the Parang guitar troubadours from nearby Venezuela who come across the Gulf of Paria especially for the festive season. At my family home, lunchtime approaches and local young men, Sikh and Hindu, who work at the car tyre shop across the road are invited in to partake in the Eid feast.

The island, and its smaller sister island Tobago, is today a collection of peoples pulled from across the world, swept onto its shores and pushed into its higgledy-piggeldy houses.

It is the mixture of peoples and cultures that is both Trinidad and Tobago's greatest strength and weakness. First on the island were the Amerindians, the Caribs and Arawaks, almost completely wiped out by the first colonists, the Spanish (who were later displaced by the British). The island and its sugar and cacao economy drew free and unfree labour. African slaves and free blacks, the flotsam and jetsam of Europe; slavers, plantation owners, poor whites, criminals, adventurers, administrators, pirates, mercenaries. Later came Syrian and Lebanese immigrants, and then after the abolition of slavery, indentured Chinese and Indian labourers. In recent times Trinidad has attracted more prosperous sojourners desperately seeking paradise, such as celebrated British artist Chris Ofili.

Trinidad truly is a multicultural society, and every day individuals and groups negotiate myriad encounters with each other, finding common interests and synthesising shared culture, building temporary alliances and allegiances, making compromises and getting things done, treating each other with the full spectrum of tolerance to mutual respect, all the time pushing things forward in a totally unique way. That is not to say that everything runs smoothly and without friction. The British graded this mishmash of peoples into hierarchies according to their origins, race, ethnicity and skin tone and then divided them against each other, and the island suffers from the legacy today.

The two majority groups, those of African and Indian heritage, today make up 35 and 34 per cent of the total population respectively, and remain in many ways suspicious and resentful of one another. This is even though it is clear that the circumstances of their ancestors' arrival on the island and the manner of their subsequent exploitation in the cane fields constitute a shared experience. Of course slavery is not the same as bonded labour: being owned by another human on the one hand and suffering forced labour for a period of five or ten years on the other is not equivalent, but neither is the gap that large.

The academic Eric Williams, whose ground-breaking 1944 book *Capitalism and Slavery* nailed the lie that the British abolished slavery because of some kind of humanitarian impulse and reclaimed the agency of the slaves themselves in their own emancipation, steered the island to independence in 1962. Known as 'the father of the nation', Williams can perhaps now be seen as a more successful historian than a politician. His rule ended in controversy, with accusations of dictatorial tendencies, including at one point placing his former mentor, the writer and radical CLR James, under house arrest.

Under Williams and subsequent administrations the economy was roughly divided between the two ethnic groups, with the Indians capturing the business sector and the Africans the public sector. Political parties mirrored these ethnic divisions – the Indians had their politicians, the Africans had theirs, and each grouping served their 'own kind' – doling out jobs, kickbacks and influence amongst their ethnic-based networks and supporters. Corruption became embedded, and the not insignificant riches generated by oil and gas disappeared into overseas bank accounts, over the heads of the mass of the population, who, brown or black, continued to live in poverty.

These divisions are also mirrored in the construction of religious identity on the island. Up until recent times the religious denomination 'Muslim' was seen as synonymous with the Indian ethnic identity. The 1891 colonial headcount reckoned that of the 45,800 Indians in Trinidad, 60 per cent were Hindu and 13 per cent were Muslim, the remainder being Christian, Buddhist and other faiths. Today Muslims are estimated to comprise about eight or nine per cent of population, the majority of Indian descent, but increasingly include people of African descent. However, it would be a mistake to think that the African Muslim presence is a novelty.

The first Muslims in Trinidad were not Indian indentured labourers, they were Africans. In one of those strange quirks of colonial history, 700 former black slaves of Muslim faith and their families who had fled the slave plantations of Georgia to fight for the British against the Americans in the War of 1812, were rewarded by being granted land in Trinidad. They were followed between 1817 and 1825 by other groups of black Muslims who had fought for the British in exchange for their freedom. They became known as the 'Merikins' and were recognised for practising their faith. They were settled in areas such as the coastal village of Manzanilla, away from the plantations, lest their free status caused unrest amongst the slave population.

The historian Carl Campbell has charted the life of one of these former soldiers. Muhammad Sisei was born around 1788 or 1790 in the Gambia. His father's name was Abu Bakr and his mother's Ayishah. After seeing action with the British, he was settled in Trinidad in 1816. However, instead of staying with the other 'Merikans' in Manzanilla he moved to Port of Spain and became a member of the Muslim group there led by Yunus Muhammad Bath who was involved in petitioning the British to free Muslim slaves. Sisei was described as 'quick and intelligent and a strict follower of Islam. He knew the Qur'an very well and certain parts of it he always carried with him'.

The historic influence of Islam on Trinidad manifests itself in fascinating ways. Every year, since around 1854, a 'Hosay' parade has taken place through St James. Mounted by the island's small Shi'ite community to mark *Aashura* – Husein – Hosayn – Hosay – miniature mausoleums, or *tadjahs*, are processed through the streets of the city. Crowds turn out for what has become a national cultural celebration, including other Muslims (the majority of whom are Sunni) and other Trinidadians, who add the island's staple indulgencies of rum, food and dancing to the religious ritual. Mass participation in Hosay can be traced back to colonial times when it took on for the authorities the same kind of threat of public rebelliousness and subversion that gave birth to Carnival. In 1884, against a backdrop of strikes and civil unrest, the British banned the procession. Organisers defied the order and mounted a Hosay procession in San Fernando, Trinidad's second city located in the strategically important oil and sugar belt in the south of the island. They were fired on by troops, with maybe up to twenty shot dead and many more injured. This became known as the Jahaji massacre.

But today, like elsewhere in the Muslim world, Trinidad is gripped by conflicts from within. Traditional Muslim leaders, who consider themselves guardians of moderate Trinidadian Islam, handed down through generations and gradually adapted to Caribbean culture, are raging against the growing influence of Salafi and other external influences. The Muslims of Trinidad have always seen themselves as an embattled minority, particularly in relation to the Hindus that make up the majority of the population of Indian descent. Now their leadership feel the heat of a challenge from within the Muslim ummah itself.

They say the change in attitudes and allegiances is marked by the building of new Gulf-sponsored mosques, of Salafi preachers from overseas recruiting from amongst young people, of Muslim converts being churned out of the prison system, and by the recent adoption by young women of the hijab and even the niqab. Much of this is to do with the fact that Muslims in Trinidad are becoming more globalised, are travelling more, and thus coming in contact with the prevailing Middle Eastern culture and codes that dominate Muslim societies. One can argue that these manifestations do not, and should not, be lumped together as signs of extremist influence, but without doubt the argument is out in the open. And it is unfortunately being conducted along racial lines.

In a 2011 newspaper article headed 'Afro-Trini Muslims are zealots', Iqbal Hydal, a prominent Imam, was quoted as saying 'our forefathers came from India with a very docile Islam', before adding 'you must understand that Afro-Trinis were converted into Islam, it is not that they were born into Islam and like in any other religion once you are converted you become a zealot'. Referring to the Muslimeen coup, Hydal suggested that 'they were all converts to Islam', 'they went to shed off all that they have learnt from Christianity. They want to make sure they become more zealous rather than zealots if you want to use that word'. It should be noted that Imam Hydal is a representative of the island's Ahmadiyya sect who have more than their fair share of brickbats from hostile Salafis.

Those connected to the growth of Islam amongst the African-Trinidadian population argue that they are catering for Muslims who are disenfranchised and ignored by the island's traditional religious leadership. One of those detained (and released without charge) in 2011 over the alleged assassination plot, Ashmeed Choate, gave an interview in which he said his mission was to spread the message of Islam to people 'who are less fortunate, deprived, people who are marginalised in the community'. He said he was shunned by the mainstream Muslims because, although born in Trinidad, he had studied Islam in Saudi Arabia, rather than learning it through indigenous means.

Within my own family in Trinidad, I can see the various cross-currents – 'traditional Islam', a handed-down relaxed pan-Indian religious culture, stretched to incorporate Caribbean island life, and the influence of global Islam and its austere revivalist nature. But it remains to be seen where this particular battle is going, and whether it will serve any useful purpose for the Muslims in Trinidad and their relations with their island compatriots and the wider world.

Every time I visit Trinidad I make a pilgrimage to the grave of C.L.R. James in Tunapuna. His tombstone, paid for by the Oil Workers Union, has a quote engraved from his best known work, *Beyond A Boundary*:

Times would pass, old empires would fall and new ones take their place. The relations of countries and the relations of classes had to change before I discovered that it is not the quality of goods and utility which matters, but movement, not where you are, or what you have, but where you have come from, where you are going and the rate at which you are getting there.

TEN XENOPHOBIC EUROPEAN POLITICAL PARTIES TO AVOID

A spectre is haunting Europe: the spectre of the far-right. Right across the continent, extremist political parties are attracting millions of votes. They now have solid representation in national and European parliaments. They receive strong doses of, to use the words of the late Margaret Thatcher, 'the oxygen of publicity' from the media, and their leaders are regarded as having something important to say.

Once confined to the wilder shores of conspiratorial and violent activity, the far-right are today planted firmly in the mainstream. They have succeeded, in differing degrees, in pulling the political centre to the right, with negative debates about multiculturalism, immigrants, the 'Muslim problem' and the fate of other minorities now the daily fare of newspapers, television and politicians of all stripes. Many of these parties have organic and generational roots in the fascist period of the 1930s, although most in Western Europe have sought to 'detoxify' their past and pose as modern democratic players in the political realm. In the south and east of Europe, however, there are far-right parties who revel in Nazi-style insignia and violent street confrontations. They are all against the European Union and claim to champion the 'little man' exploited and over-run by dark-skinned immigrants.

Although many of these parties have taken up a virulent anti-Muslim agenda, and agitate against the manufactured phantom of the 'Islamisation' of Europe that led terrorist Anders Behring Breivik to murder seventy-six people in Norway in 2011, their hatreds go much deeper. Anti-semitism and anti-Roma racism remain a recurring motif in their rhetoric. In the end, it is all about racial purity and supremacy.

So here, in no particularly despicable order, are our top ten to avoid. Read; and choose by playing the time honoured parlour game of the uneasy immigrant: 'if I were to move to another county in Europe it would be…'

1. Jobbik (Hungary)

Jobbik, the Movement for a Better Hungary (Jobbik Magyarországért mozgalom), is without doubt one of the nastiest ultra-nationalist parties around. Its ideological roots lie with the Nazi collaborators of the 1930s, and anti-semitism still drives its ideologues. Today there are just 120,000 Jewish people living in Hungary, compared with 850,000 before the Holocaust. Yet they are a constant target of Jobbik, with supporters seen giving out leaflets depicting an image from the film *Easy Rider* with the slogan 'Jews are the problem – it's time to step on the gas!' The party's paramilitary front like to goosestep in the streets wearing black uniforms with WWII fascist armbands.

In November 2012, Marton Gyongyosi, the party's deputy parliamentary leader, called for a security register of Hungarian Jewish legislators and ministers. Gyongyosi said: 'I think such a conflict [in Gaza] makes it timely to tally up people of Jewish ancestry who live here, especially in the Hungarian parliament and the Hungarian government, who, indeed, pose a national security risk to Hungary.' The apparently bottomless well of hatred and violence of Jobbik supporters is also directed at Hungary's Roma and Gypsy population. The European Roma Rights Centre (ERRC) reported sixty-nine violent attacks on Roma – in which nine Roma were killed – in Hungary between January 2008 and September 2012. Jobbik and its supporters hold provocative rallies in Roma neighbourhoods, its supporters attack Roma property and their election material uses the term 'gypsy crime'.

In 2011, in a sinister echo of the Nazi period, the small town of Gyongyospata was invaded by 2000 Jobbik supporters, many of them armed, claiming that one Roma family was responsible for a suicide of a 'Hungarian' resident, and that the town's Roma were responsible for all crime in the area. The town's mayor, a Jobbik supporter, subsequently started segregating the local schools, with different floors for 'Hungarians' and Roma, along with barring Roma pupils from using the school's swimming pool and toilets.

After the parliamentary elections on 6 April 2014, Jobbik became the third largest party in Hungary.

2. Golden Dawn (Greece)

Although the neo-Nazi Golden Dawn (GD) was founded in 1983 as an anti-Semitic, pro-dictatorship organisation, it only emerged as a dangerous force as a result of the economic crisis that has torn Greek society apart. Golden Dawn's ideology is a repulsive cocktail of extreme nationalist politics, white supremacy, Holocaust denial, a distorted male virility, anti-immigrant pogroms and enacting violence against the 'enemies of Greece' – lesbians and gays, black people, the left and Jews. The organisation believes that Jewish thought has 'infected' Christianity and therefore Greeks should 'reject the Old Testament and reveal the genuine Greek cultural identity [for centuries suffocating] under the layer of Jewish tradition'. Golden Dawn also agitates for the 'unification' of Greek minorities outside the borders of modern Greece, including calling for the annexation of all of Cyprus.

Golden Dawn has a track record of assassinating its opponents, most recently the leftist and anti-fascist rapper Pavlos Fyssas, who was stabbed to death by a GD member in September 2013. The popular backlash against the murder forced the Greek government, whose security forces have been accused of supporting Golden Dawn, to declare the party a criminal organisation and round up its leadership including nine MPs.

However Golden Dawn has also played a clever hand by posing as a friend of ordinary Greeks, beset by the Euro-provoked economic collapse that has resulted in a jobless rate of 27 per cent, with 3.5 million people working to support more than 4.7 million unemployed and inactive people. Golden Dawn vows to stand up for 'Greeks in danger', and distribute food parcels to poor communities (as long as they are ethnic Greeks). In the 2014 European elections over half a million Greeks voted for GD, giving it three seats in the European parliament.

3. Front National (France)

The Front National (FN) is the most successful far-right party in Europe, and has a deepening influence within French society, pulling mainstream politics towards its xenophobic and anti-Muslim agenda.

Founded by anti-communist street brawler and Foreign Legionnaire Jean Marie Le Pen in 1972, the Front National combined ex-Vichy collaborators with assorted neo-Nazis and members of the OAS, a secret paramilitary group that conducted terrorist outrages in an effort to stop Algeria becoming independent.

Le Pen is a serial Holocaust denier, notoriously describing the gas chambers as 'a mere detail in history'. In recent times he has mostly saved his racist bile for France's Muslims, a tradition continued by his daughter Marine Le Pen, who took over leadership of the FN in 2011. She compared Muslims in France as equivalent to Nazi occupation during World War Two: 'fifteen years ago there were no veils, then there were more and more veils, and then there were prayers on the public thoroughfare. For those who like to speak about the Second World War, here we can talk about occupation … Certainly there are no tanks, there are no soldiers, but it weighs heavily on local people.'

The FN's electoral breakthrough came in the late 1980s, as voters increasingly perceived the two mainstream parties of the left and the right to be virtually indistinguishable in their policies. Le Pen then morphed his anti-Semitism into anti-Muslim racism, seizing upon the Salman Rushdie affair to ignite a poisonous debate about the position of Muslims in French society. In line with other parties in Europe with Neo-Nazi roots, the FN has sought to erase its nasty past. Marine Le Pen is known as the 'de-toxifier', and has tried hard to distance herself from her father's anti-semitic statements, even going as far as sending her partner and FN deputy leader Louis Aliot to Tel Aviv to court the vote of French-Jewish expatriates.

Increasingly courted by the media, Marine Le Pen was ranked as seventy-first in 2011 as the *Time* magazine's top 100 'most influential people in the world'. The magazine praised her 'less divisive style and her oratory talents' that have made 'Le Pen France's fastest-rising politician'.

In the 2014 European elections the FN gained nearly a quarter of all votes cast in France, giving it twenty-four MEPs.

4. Sweden Democrats

Who? Very few people outside the bastion of north European social democracy had heard of the Sweden Democrats until the 2010 general election when they won twenty parliamentary seats, a figure that they more than doubled in 2014. It is now the third largest party in Sweden.

Despite its soft focus party logo of a pastel seven-petal flower, and its attempt to sanitise its past, this lot are a nasty bunch. Descended from various neo-Nazi, white supremacist and skinhead groups, the Sweden Democrats tick all the far-right boxes: xenophobic, Islamaphobic, anti-EU, anti-immigrant, anti-gay, pro 'traditional' Swedish culture, pro-nuclear family, against rights for ethnic minority groups (particularly the Sami people) and so on.

Their parliamentary representatives are a particularly unpleasant rabble. In 2012 a video surfaced showing three intoxicated Sweden Democrat MPs abusing Soran Ismail, Swedish comedian of Kurdish descent, in the street, threatening a drunken man, calling a woman a whore, and picking up iron bars. Shortly afterwards another of their number accused two immigrants of pushing him out of his wheelchair and robbing his backpack. It later transpired he had left his backpack in a restaurant and that the two 'immigrants' had in fact helped him after he had fallen out of his wheelchair of his own accord.

However the SD leadership has not only managed to ride out this buffoonery, but has succeeded in posing as an alternative to the mainstream parties who are blamed for presiding over the relative decline of this former paradigm of comfortable social democracy. Sweden now has the fastest-growing income gap of all the OECD countries, along with crash privatisation of the 'nanny state' that once provided a secure safety net for its citizens.

5. National Democratic Party (Germany)

'Africa Conquers the White House'. So ran the headline on the website of the National Democratic Party of Germany (NDP) reacting to the news of Barack Obama's accession to the White House in 2008. The NDP characterised America as being 'swept up in Obama fever which resembles an African tropical disease'.

In 2001 the German authorities tried to ban the NDP on the basis that the party was 'anti-constitutional'. The move failed after it was revealed in court that many of the leadership of the NDP were either planted in the organisation by the German secret services or state informants. The infiltrators included a former NDP deputy chairman who had written an anti-semitic tract that formed a central part of the government's case. The case collapsed. Various attempts have been made to ban the NDP since then but all have failed.

In an episode that proves that truth is always stranger than fiction, during the 2006 World Cup qualifiers the NDP planned a march through Leipzig to coincide with the Iran vs Angola match being played in the city. The NDP wanted to demonstrate their approval of the then Iranian president Ahmadinejad's anti-semitic and anti-Israeli rants.

The NDP leadership has sought to distance itself from its neo-Nazi and National Socialist roots and to follow the Front National 'detoxification' strategy and enter parliamentary politics. However, scratch below the surface and its ugly politics reveal themselves. The NDP is obsessed by miscegenation and 'non-Aryans' representing Germany at international sports. When asked of his feelings about the success of Marcel Nguyen, a half-Vietnamese gymnast who won two silver medals for Germany at the 2012 Olympics, Party leader Holger Apfel said: 'I can freely say it's not something that causes me euphoria', before adding hastily, 'but you won't see us calling for the deportation of half-breed children'. Charming.

Violence is never far away. In 2011 it was revealed that a Nazi terrorist cell had carried out a seven-year killing spree which left nine immigrants and a policewoman dead. Amazingly the killers managed to avoid detection and arrest, despite being on the run for other crimes. Three of them were found to have links high up in the NDP.

Although they have no seats in the central German parliament, the Bundestag, their presence in regional state assemblies has allowed them to access millions of Euros of state funds.

6. Finns or True Finns as they are often called (Finland)

The True Finns party, a right-wing populist party rooted in ethno-nationalism, is so confident of speaking on behalf of the Nordic nation that it has renamed itself simply as 'Finns'.

True Finns is the third largest group in the Finnish parliament, making it the largest opposition party. It has been described as 'a non-socialist workers party' because of its redistributive tax policies and opposition to the EU, combined with its 'Finns first' social policies. The party has gained ground by playing the anti-immigrant card, linking immigrants with crime, particularly sexual violence. It calls for immigrants and refugees to assimilate into the cultural norms of Finnish society, combined with 'dog whistle' politics exploiting issues such as forced marriages and honour-killings. True Finns MEP Jussi Halla-aho was briefly suspended from the party after comparing Islam to paedophilia and proposing a 'solution' to the economic crisis in Greece: 'right now what is needed is a military junta that could use tanks to force the strikers and rioters into submission'.

Another True Finns MEP hit the headlines after suggesting gay people and Somalis should be exiled to an island in the Baltic. The True Finns are partners in the European Parliament with Britain's UKIP.

7. Danish People's Party

The far-right populist Danish People's Party (DPP) which builds its base on opposition to immigration and multiculturalism and a Eurosceptic stance – is the third largest party in Denmark, and in the 2014 Euro elections came first after polling 26.6 per cent of the votes cast.

Since 2001, Denmark has had a decade of right-wing governments which relied on the DPP to push forward legislation. The price was the integration of far-right politics into the political mainstream – echoed on both sides of the traditional political spectrum, left and right. Immigration became a recurring theme, with the DPP presenting itself as the protector of Danish and Christian values. Tightening of immigration controls, laws restricting family reunion and forced marriages followed.

The DPP has steadily kept Denmark's Danish population within its sights – using every opportunity to 'prove' the undesirability of Islam as an influence on Danish society. Muslims make up 3-5 per cent of the country's population. The controversy that erupted after a Danish newspaper, *Jyllands-Posten* printed twelve caricatures of the Prophet Muhammad in September 2005 fed into support for the DPP.

For years the political establishment blocked the building of Copenhagen's first major purpose-built mosque (an Ahmadiyya mosque was built in a suburb of the capital in 1967). When a mosque was finally completed with Qatari money in May 2014, its opening was boycotted by city and national politicians. The DPP deputy mayor said it was wrong to allow the building of a 'symbol of a religion that doesn't recognise democracy and women's right to freedom'. Another DPP spokesperson called the mosque 'a bridgehead for an extreme version of Islam. I do not like the risk of rabid imams preaching on Danish soil.'

8. Lega Nord (Italy)

Where does one start with Northern League – Lega Nord – whose long-time leader Umberto Bossi infamously called Africans 'Bingo-Bongos', advocated that illegal immigrants attempting to reach Italy's shores should be 'shot out of the water', warned the Vatican that he would 'push it down the toilet of history' and invented a fictional kingdom 'Padania' to rule over? The Northern League was founded in 1991, and quickly established itself as a political force in the general elections of the following year. In 1994, Bossi's party joined the coalition government under that other Italian right-wing maverick, Silvio Berlusconi, allowing it to launch its campaign for separation of the prosperous north, the mythical Padania, from the rest of the country. Padania is based on the territory defined by the valley of the River Po, including the prosperous cities of Milan, Turin and Venice.

The League claims that it represents the hard-working Celtic race (as opposed to the lazy southern Romans) and its supporters are known to turn up to party rallies wearing Celtic-inspired costumes replete with broadswords and horned helmets. It could be argued that the Northern League promotes equal opportunity bigotry, in that they seem to despise everybody who is not from the north. Rome, the Catholic Church, immigrants, Muslims, poor people from the south – all stoke the rage of the League. But Muslims have come under special attention. League mayors in northern towns have passed local laws banning the use of veils or other garb that conceal people's faces. In one town the League went as far as banning the *burkini* – a bathing costume favoured by some Muslim women (we are told).

9. Attack (Bulgaria)

One in eight MPs in the Bulgarian parliament is a fascist. Bulgaria, the poorest country in the EU, presently has two rival fascist groupings – the Patriotic Front and Attack (Ataka). Ataka takes its name from *Der Agriff*

(German for 'the attack'), the paper run by Hitler's propaganda henchman Joseph Goebbels. Its symbol is a swastika-style trident, superimposed on a Celtic cross design in the colours of the Bulgarian flag. The party's ideology is based on racism, ethnic nationalism and violence. It wants 'Bulgaria for the Bulgarians'. Ataka's main victims are the Roma, but Ataka hates Bulgaria's Turkish and Muslim population too. When he is not ranting about 'Gypsy criminality', party leader Volen Siderov is denouncing the Turkish minority and 'Ottoman domination'.

The Roma people make up around 10 per cent of the population and suffer severe discrimination in housing, health, education and employment. Many live in neighbourhoods without electricity or sewage services. In 2011, anti-Roma pogroms broke out in towns and villages across Bulgaria, after a young ethnic Bulgarian was killed by a minibus driven by a Roma man. Huge armed gangs stormed into Roma areas destroying homes and attacking residents indiscriminately. The wave of violence was described as the worst since World War II.

Ataka suffered in general elections in 2014 because of its association with the outgoing administration. Ataka had propped up a government made up of the Bulgarian Socialist Party – a centre-left formation that emerged from the old Stalinist Communist Party – and the Movement for Rights and Freedoms, a centre party based on Bulgaria's ethnic Turkish minority. The rival fascist coalition Patriotic Front was able to take votes from Ataka in the general election by accusing them of selling out.

10. Austrian Freedom Party (Austria)

The Austrian Freedom Party (Freiheitliche Partei Österreichs – FPÖ) is a far-right racist populist party. It was formed in 1956 as the successor of the Verband der Unabhängigen, a group of so-called 'de-Nazified' fascists and liberal republicans. It had close links with Hitleralism, with its first two leaders being former members of the Waffen SS. The party's political breakthrough came in 1983 when it entered into a coalition government with the Social Democratic SPO party. Jörg Haider was selected as the party leader in 1986. Under his leadership the party took a sharp turn towards right-wing racist populism. Haider himself was notorious for speaking out in defence of the SS and praising Hitler's 'full employment' policies.

In 1999, FPO won 26.9 per cent of the vote in national elections, its best ever result, and entered into a coalition government with the centre right. Following a series of poor election results the FPO split in 2005. Haider and the parliamentary wing of the party left, forming the Alliance for the Future of Austria (BZO), but Haider was killed, three years later, in a car crash.

The leadership of FPO passed to Haider's long-term disciple, Heinz-Christian Strache in 2005. Since then the party has regained much of its electoral strength. It opposes European integration, is rabid in its opposition to Turkey entering Europe, portrays itself as an anti-establishment party, and pushes a racist agenda aimed against migrants and asylum seekers. Strache was widely condemned in 2012 after he posted a caricature on his Facebook page of a banker with a hooked nose, wearing Star of David cufflinks. Latterly the FPO has targeted the country's Muslim population raising the bogey of 'Islamisation' of Austria. In the run up to the European elections in 2014, Andreas Moelzer, a leading FPO candidate, declared that the EU was in danger of becoming a 'conglomerate of negroes'. The FPO subsequently polled a fifth of all votes in the election.

So where would you like to live in Europe – the cradle of civilisation? We choose United Kingdom, still (just) united, still an (overburdened) welfare state with a good (although creaking) National Health Service, still (quite successfully) holding out against the far-right; and thank the bloggers at *dreamdeferred.org.uk* for suggesting this top ten.

CITATIONS

The Colour Line by Hassan Mahamdallie

The W.E.B. Du Bois quotations are from *The Souls of Black Folk*, first published in 1903 but republished in several editions since, the latest one comes from Dover: New York, 2000. Ian Davidson's *Voltaire in Exile: The Last Years, 1753-1778* is published by Atlantic Books: London, 2005. Paul Foot's *Rise of Enoch Powell: Examination of Enoch Powell's Attitude to Immigration and Race* was published by Penguin, 1969. Gilbert Achcar, *The Arabs and the Holocaust: The Arab-Israeli War of Narratives* is published by Saqi books, London, 2011. Ziauddin Sardar's comments are from his essay 'The Excluded Minority: British Muslim Identity After 11 September', which appeared in *Reclaiming Britishness* edited by Phoebe Griffith and Mark Leonard (Development Education Association and the British Council, 2002), and can be accessed at http://fpc.org.uk/fsblob/42.pdf

See also: A review of *Troublesome Inheritance: Genes, Race and Human History* by Nicholas Wade www.nybooks.com/ 'The Sun's 'Unite against Isis' campaign is a proxy for anti-Muslim bigotry' by Nesrine Malik *The Guardian*, 8 October 2014, http://www.theguardian.com/ commentisfree/2014/oct/08/sun-unite-against-isis-muslim-bigotry; report of the Zahid Mubarek Inquiry (2006) https://www.gov.uk/ government/publications/report-of-the-zahid-mubarek-inquiry; and 'Dieudonné's war on France: the Holocaust comedian who isn't funny' by Andrew Hussey in *New Statesman*, 30 January 2014.

Is Islam a Race? By Shanon Shah

Abdullah first came to life in a paper I presented at the conference entitled 'Islamic Perspectives on the State, Society and Governance in Southeast Asia' in Canberra, 2004, organised by the Australian National University. I am indebted to Sumit Mandal for invaluable, critical comments on the original presentation.

The commentaries by Nesrine Malik and Tom Chivers on Richard Dawkins can be found at 'Message to Richard Dawkins: "Islam Is Not a Race" Is a Cop out', *The Guardian,* 20 September 2013, http://www.theguardian.com/commentisfree/2013/sep/20/islam-race-richard-dawkins; and 'Please Be Quiet, Richard Dawkins, I'm Begging, as a Fan'; *Telegraph Blogs,* 8 August, 2013, http://blogs.telegraph.co.uk/news/tomchiversscience/100230250/please-be-quiet-richard-dawkins-im-begging-as-a-fan/.

On ISMA, hudud and Malays as the 'chosen race', I referred to Sean Augustin. 2012. 'Reezal (chosen One) Gets a Roasting'. *Fz.* http://www.fz.com/content/reezal-chosen-one-gets-roasting, Rahmah Ghazali. 2014. 'PAS Targets June Submission for Private Members' Bill on Hudud in Kelantan'. *The Star Online.* http://www.thestar.com.my/News/Nation/2014/04/09/PAS-private-members-bill-hudud-laws/, Awang Selamat. 2014. 'Bisik-bisik Awang Selamat (Awang Selamat's Whisperings)'. *Utusan Malaysia Online.* http://www.utusan.com.my/utusan/Rencana/20140525/re_04/BISIK-BISIK-AWANG-SELAMAT, and Syed Jaymal Zahiid. 2014. 'Hudud Will Seal Political Position of Malays, Thwart Non-Muslim Ambitions, Says Isma'. News. *The Malay Mail Online.* http://www.themalaymailonline.com/malaysia/article/hudud-will-seal-political-position-of-malays-thwart-non-muslim-ambitions.

On the colonial construction of 'Malay', I referred to Anthony Reid. 2004. 'Understanding Melayu (Malay) as a Source of Diverse Modern Identities'. In *Contesting Malayness: Malay Identity Across Boundaries*, edited by Timothy P Barnard, 1–24. Singapore: Singapore University Press. On Muslims in Britain, I referred to Sophie Gilliat-Ray. 2012. 'Judaism, Sikhism, Islam, Hinduism and Buddhism: Post-War Settlements - Islam'. In *Religion and Change in Modern Britain*, edited by Linda Woodhead and Rebecca Catto, 110–20. Oxon: Routledge, and Nasar Meer. 2008. 'The Politics of Voluntary and Involuntary Identities: Are Muslims in Britain an Ethnic, Racial or Religious Minority?'. *Patterns of Prejudice* 42 (1): 61–81. On sociological treatments of 'ethnicity' and 'race', I referred to *Sociology: The Key Concepts* (2006) edited by John Scott. Oxon: Routledge.

The Dark Side of *The Arabian Nights* by Robert Irwin

The quotation from Stevenson's essay is from *Memories and Portraits* (Thomas Nelson &Sons, London, 1887), pp.217-8. 'The story of the fisherman and *'ifrit'* and 'The semi-petrified prince' can be found in *The Arabian Nights:Tales of 1001 Nights*, Malcolm Lyons tr. (Penguin, London, 2008), vol.1, pp.19-50 and the black slave's speech is on p.43. The quotation from Daniel Beaumont is found in *Slave of Desire: Sex, Love, and Death in* The Thousand and One Nights, (Associated University Presses, Cranbury, NJ, 2002) p.50. 'The story of Ashraf and Anjab' appears in *Tales of the Marvellous and News of the Strange*, Malcolm Lyons tr. (Penguin, London, 2014), pp.351-71. The quotation from Margaret Mitchell appears in *Gone With the* Wind, 9 Macmillan, London, 1936) p.656. 'The pious black slave' appears in the Penguin *Arabian Nights*, vol.2, pp.332-5 and 'The story of al-Ma'mun, the Yemeni and the six slave girls' appears in vol. 2, pp. 82-96. The quotation from Jahiz is from *The Life and Works of Jahiz* ed. and tr. Charles Pellat (University of California Press, Berkeley and Los Angeles, 1969) p.195. Alexander Murray discusses anti-Semitism in *Reason and Society in the Middle Ages* (Clarendon Press, Oxford, 1978) p.68. Richard Burton's version of blackamoor speech is in *The Book of the Thousand and a Night* (Kamashastra Society, Benares=Basingstoke, 1885-8) vol. 1, p.79. Burton's observation regarding debauched white women is vol.1, p.6n. The quotation from Gobineau on blacks appears in *Comte de Gobineau and orientalism, selected eastern writings*, Daniel O'Donoghue tr., Geoffrey Nash ed. (Routledge, Abingdon, 2009) p.100.

The Revolt of the Zanj by Hugh Kennedy

Alexandre Popovic's *The Revolt of the African Slaves in the 3rd/9th Century* , with an introduction by Henry Louis Gates Jr, is published by Markus Wiener Publishing, London, 1998. For the pattern of parallel lines, see H. S. Nelson, 'Abandoned irrigation system in southern Iraq" *Sumer* 18 (1962), 67-72.

The Master Race by Ziauddin Sardar

There are numerous reports on the exploitation of migrant works in Qatar, see, for example, Robert Booth, 'Qatar World Cup construction "will leave 4,000 migrant workers dead"', *The Guardian* 26 September 2013. The Quraysh hadith can be found in al-Hâkim's *Mustadrak*; 'people follow Quraysh' hadith is reported both in *Sahîh al-Bukhârî* and *Sahîh Muslim*. On Saudi labour law, see Q Javed Mian and Alison Lerrick, *Saudi Business and Labour Law: Its Interpretation and Application* (Graham & Trotman, London, 1982). On anti-black racism in the region, see the Al-Jazerra report at: http://www.aljazeera.com/indepth/opinion/2013/06/201362472519107286.html

The Human Rights Watch report on Saudi Arabia can be downloaded from: World Report 2012: Saudi Arabia; http://www.hrw.org/world-report-2012/world-report-2012-saudi-arabia

On Nawal al-Husawi see the *Al-Arabiya* report of 6 February 2014 at: http://english.alarabiya.net/en/News/2014/02/06/-Rosa-Parks-of-Saudi-Arabia-drops-racism-case-against-three-women.html; And on Imam Al Sudais' visit to India, marvel at the Bismillah News report on YouTube: http://www.youtube.com/watch?v=WFc7hzwo9EQ

On exploitation of pilgrims and racism in Mecca see Ziauddin Sardar, *Mecca: The Sacred City* (Bloomsbury, 2014).

The Republic of Islamophobia by Jim Wolfreys

For more detailed analysis of Islomophobia and racism in France, see Peter Fysh, Anne Curry and Jim Wolfreys, *The Politics of Racism in France* (Palgrave, London, 2003), second edition; Joan Wallach Scott, *The Politics of the Veil* (Princeton University Press, 2007); and Liz Fekete, *A Suitable Enemy: Racism, Migration and Islamophobia in Europe* (Pluto Press, London, 2009).

John Brown Revisited by Gary McFarlane

All quotations from Du Bois from *John Brown* by W.E.B. Du Bois, edited by Henry Louis Gates Jr. with an introduction by Paul Finkelman (Oxford University Press, Oxford, 2007). Malcolm X speech at The Second

Organisation of Afro-American Unity Rally (July 5, 1964) can be read at: http://www.blackpast.org/1964-malcolm-x-s-speech-founding-rally-organization-afro-american-unity. See also: *America's Revolutionary Heritage* by George Novack (Pathfinder, Washington DC, 1976)

Ibn Arabi and How to be Human by Sa'diyya Shaikh

For a more detailed discussion and analysis of Ibn Arabi's approach to gender and the human condition, see Sa'diyya Shaikh, *Sufi Narratives of Intimacy: Ibn Arabi, Gender and Sexuality* (Chapel Hill, The University of North Carolina Press, 2012). An earlier pioneering study of gender in Ibn Arabi's thought is Sachiko Murata's *The Tao of Islam: A Sourcebook on Gender Relationships in Islamic Thought* (Albany, State University of New York Press, 1992).

The quotation from Alexander Knysh is from *Ibn 'Arabi in the Later Islamic Tradition: The Making of a Polemical Image in Medieval Islam* (Albany, State University of New York Press, 1999), p 11. The quotations from Attar, Farid al-Din are from *Muslim Saints and Mystics: Episodes from the Tadhkhirat al-Auliya* (*Memorial of the Saints*), translated by A. J. Arberry (London, Routledge and Kegan Paul, 1966), pp 66 and 45 respectively; and the quotation from Eric Winkel is from *Islam and the Living Law: The Ibn Al-Arabi Approach* (New York, Oxford University Press, 1997) pp vii and 23-24 respectively.

The quotations from Muhyi al-Din Ibn Arabi are from *Sufis of Andalusia: The Ruh al-Quds and al-Durrat al-Fakhira*, translated by R.W.J. (Roxburgh, Beshara, 1988) pp 142; 154; and 155 respectively; and *Al-Futūhāt al-makkiyya* (Cairo, Np, 1911) Vol 3, p 89; and Vol 1, p 447 respectively. The other works of Ibn Arabi referred to in this essay are *Dīwān Ibn 'Arabi* (Cairo, Buluq, 1855); and his *Fusus al-Hikam* which goes by the English title *Bezels of Wisdom*, translated by R.W.J. (New York, Paulist Press, 1980).

Samia Rahman's, 'The Race of Women' was published in *Critical Muslim 2: The Idea of Islam* (Hurst, London, 2012) p57-74. Other works mentioned in this essay include Seyyed Hossein Nasr, *Three Muslim Sages: Avicenna, Suhrawardi, Ibn 'Arabi* (Delmar, NY, Caravan, 1976); and Homerin, Th. Emil. 'Ibn Arabi in the People's Assembly: Religion, Press, and Politics in Sadat's Egypt,' *Middle East Journal* 40:3 (1986): 462–77. See also Abdennur Prado, 'Muslim masculinities' in *Critical Muslim 8: Men in Islam* (Hurst, London, 2013), p31-46

A wonderfully insightful, inviting and nuanced introduction to the life and ideas of Ibn Arabi is Stephen Hirtenstein's, *The Unlimited Mercifier: The Spiritual Life and Thought of*

Ibn 'Arabi (Oxford, Anqa and Ashland, OR, White Cloud, 1999). Clause Addas' *Quest for the Red Sulphur: The Life of Ibn 'Arabi* (Cambridge, Islamic Texts Society, 1993) is the most thorough and detailed current biography of Ibn Arabi; William Chittick is one of the foremost and pioneering mediators of Ibn 'Arabi to Western audiences having translated and analysed significant aspects of Ibn Arabi's works. His ground-breaking detailed scholarly studies of Ibn Arabi include *The Sufi Path of Knowledge: Ibn Al-'Arabī's Metaphysics of Imagination* (Albany, State University of New York Press, 1989); and *The Self-Disclosure of God: Principles of Ibn al-'Arabi's Cosmology* (Albany, State University of New York Press, 1997). His equally nuanced but more accessible works include *Ibn 'Arabī: Heir to the Prophets* (Oxford, Oneworld, 2007); and *Imaginal Worlds: Ibn 'Arabī and the Problem of Religious Diversity* (Albany, State University of New York Press, 1994). Finally the "The Muhyiddin Ibn 'Arabi Society" has an excellent set of resources on Ibn Arabi at http://www.ibnarabisociety.org

J'accuse: South Asian Privilege by Naima Khan

Noel Ignatiev's *How The Irish Became White* (Routledge Classics, Abingdon, 1995)

See also: Noel Ignatiev's interview with Danny Postel in *Race Traitor: Journal of the New Abolitionism*: http://racetraitor.org/zmagazineinterview.pdf

Yasmin Alibhai-Brown's comments can be heard on the BBC's special report: *Uganda 40 Years On* http://www.bbc.co.uk/programmes/b01lpm1w

Background on Ugandan expulsion of Asians can be found in *Why Idi Amin Expelled The Asians* in New African Magazine: http://newafricanmagazine.com/why-idi-amin-expelled-the-asians/3/

Quotes on Asians in Uganda are from Noel O'Cleirigh's *Recollections of Uganda under Milton Obote and Idi Amin* (Trafford Publishing, Victoria, 2004)

Quotes from the BBC's 1968 news broadcast title *More Asian Kenyans Flee to Britain* are archived at: http://news.bbc.co.uk/onthisday/hi/dates/stories/february/4/newsid_2738000/2738629.stm

Quotes from BBC News Broadcast 7 September 1973 can be viewed online here: http://www.bbc.co.uk/learningzone/clips/ugandan-asians-arrive-in-britain/7699.html

Sarfraz Manzoor's article 'Black Britain's Darkest Hour' (*The Guardian* 2008) can be read online at:http://www.theguardian.com/politics/2008/feb/24/race

Last Word: On Trinidad by Hassan Mahamdallie

A recent edition of Eric Williams's *Capitalism and Slavery* has been published by University of North Carolina Press, 1984 (original, 1994). There are several edition of CLR James' *Beyond A Boundary*, the most recent of which is from Serpent's Tail, London, 2000. On Muhammad Sisei see 'Mohammedu Sisei of Gambia and Trinidad c. 1788-1838' in *Bulletin of the African Studies Association of the West Indies,* No. 7 by Carl Campbell; it also quoted in *The Muslim Standard* (Trinidad) April 1977 issue, that can be retrieved from: http://www.caribbeanmuslims.com/articles/1226/1/The-Mandingo-Muslims-Of-Trinidad/Page1.html

For the news report 'Afro-Trini Muslims are zealots', see Trinidad and Tobago Guardian: http://www.guardian.co.tt/news/2011/12/04/afro-trini-muslims-are-zealots; and 'Caribbean Muslims New Converts Bring New Challenges' see http://www.allvoices.com/contributed-news/490 3235-for-caribbean-muslims-new-converts-bring-new-challenges.

CONTRIBUTORS

Elmi Ali, a poet, writer and facilitator based in Manchester, is part of the Inna Voice Ensemble and Associate Editor at *Scarf* Magazine ● **Tasnim Baghdadi** is a multimedia artist ●**Abdelwahab El-Affendi** is co-ordinator of the Democracy and Islam Programme at the Centre for the Study of Democracy, University of Westminster ● **Robert Irwin** has written an extensive introduction to *Tales of the Marvellous and News of the Strange*, just published in Penguin Classics ● **Aiysha Jahan** is a PhD student at the University of Southampton who grew up in Dubai and has lived, studied and worked in the UAE, Pakistan, South Africa and the UK ● **Hugh Kennedy**, Professor of Arabic, Department of the Languages and Cultures of the Near and Middle East, SOAS, University of London, is author of *The Great Arab Conquests, The Courts of the Caliphs* and other books ● **Naima Khan** is a freelance writer and broadcaster; she currently produces and presents 'Shamaj', a weekly panel discussion show for Betar Bangla Radio ● **Hassan Mahamdallie**, co-director of the Muslim Institute, is the author of *Defending Multiculturalism* and *Crossing the 'River of Fire': The Socialism of William Morris* ● **Gary McFarlane** is a journalist, political activist and the developer of iGaza app ● **Avaes Mohammed** is a poet, playwright and a chemist ● **Samia Rahman** is still the Deputy Director of the Muslim Institute ● **Barnaby Rogerson**, writer and publisher, spends much of his time compiling lists ● **Declan Ryan** co-edits the *Days of Roses* anthology series and is poetry editor at *Ambit*; his debut collection of poems has just been published as part of the Faber New Poets series ● **Ziauddin Sardar's** *Mecca: The Sacred City* has just been published by Bloomsbury ● **Shanon Shah** has finally obtained his doctorate from the Department of Theology and Religious Studies, King's College, London ● **Sa'diyya Shaikh** is Associate Professor of Islamic Studies, Department of Religious Studies, University of Cape Town, South Africa ● **Dorothea Smartt**, born and raised in London and of Barbadian heritage, is a literary activist and respected poet ● **Ruth Waterman,** violinist and conductor, is the author of *When Swan Lake Comes to Sarajevo;* she is now creating a theatre-piece about war and music ● **Jim Wolfreys** lectures in French and European Politics at King's College London; he is co-author of *The Politics of Racism in France*.